£12.50

4.20

D1418623

MEGALITHIC SITES
IN BRITAIN

AVEBURY

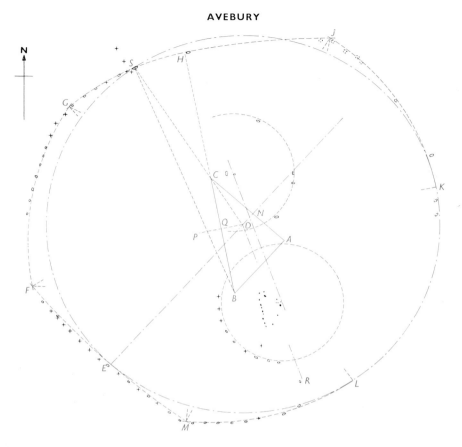

N

AB = 75 My   AC = 100 My
CB = 125   BS = 260   CS = 140
CD = 60   DE = DS = DK = DL = 200
ED is parallel to BA and H is on BC produced
Arc MEF has centre on ED and radius 750
Arc FG   ''   ''   at A   ''   ''   260
Arc GSH   ''   ''   B   ''   ''   260
Arc LM   ''   ''   C   ''   ''   260
Arc HJ   ''   ''   on CB   ''   ''   750
Arc JK   ''   ''   at P   ''   ''   PK
LCQD is 90° and PQ = DQ

Scale of feet

100   0   100   200   300   400
Scale of megalithic yards
0   50   100   150   200

In main ring concrete markers are shown by a cross +
Burning pits are shown by a dotted ring ⊙

Diameter of inner circles = 125 My = 340·0 ft
Distance between centres = 145 My

Geometrical construction superimposed in red on an accurate survey of the site
(see pages 89–91)

MEGALITHIC SITES
IN BRITAIN

BY

A. THOM

OXFORD
AT THE CLARENDON PRESS

Oxford University Press, Walton Street, Oxford OX2 6DP

OXFORD LONDON GLASGOW
NEW YORK TORONTO MELBOURNE WELLINGTON
KUALA LUMPUR SINGAPORE JAKARTA HONG KONG TOKYO
DELHI BOMBAY CALCUTTA MADRAS KARACHI
NAIROBI DAR ES SALAAM CAPE TOWN

ISBN 0 19 813148 8

© *Oxford University Press 1967*

First published 1967
Reprinted from corrected sheets of the First Edition
1972, 1974, 1976, 1979

Printed in Great Britain
at the University Press, Oxford
by Eric Buckley
Printer to the University

PREFACE

THIS work is restricted to a study of Megalithic circles, alignments, and isolated standing stones; it does not contain any systematic investigation into chambered tombs, tumuli, barps, or other similar structures. The information on which it is based was obtained almost exclusively by an examination of some 600 sites in Britain.

While I am fully capable of making surveys of any required accuracy, I do not consider myself qualified to dig an archaeological site. I restricted the measurements to what shows on the surface, augmented occasionally by prodding with a bayonet. Where trained archaeologists had already cleared the site of vegetation and loose surface accretion much information was available that would otherwise have remained hidden. It must, however, be remarked that where 're-erection' has been done by unqualified people the result is a lowering of the value of the site. I must make a plea for every stone to be left where it lies until a survey has been completed—and by 'survey' I do not mean the kind of plan that appears in many reports.

As long walks, sometimes unaccompanied, were often necessary I reduced by about one-half the weight of the theodolite that was normally used. The accuracy obtained was sufficient for most purposes, but, as the investigation proceeded, it became apparent that the precision with which some of the larger monuments had been set out demanded surveys of a high accuracy such as could be obtained only by a qualified team using high-class equipment. It is to be hoped that this will soon be appreciated and large-scale precise surveys made of all sites. One of the objects of this book is to show that many sites are worthy of the greatest care in their excavation and survey.

All the surveys except two were made by me, but some have been published before, and thanks are due to the Pergamon Press for permission to use those which appeared in *Vistas in Astronomy*, vol. 7. Acknowledgement is also made to the *Mathematical Gazette*, *Antiquity*, and the Royal Statistical Society.

It is hoped that the very many friends who assisted with the surveys will accept an over-all acknowledgement. But in this connexion I must mention specifically my wife and other members of my family. I also wish to thank the many farmers, crofters, shepherds, and foresters who helped to find many of the out-of-the-way sites.

My thanks are also due to Dr. A. E. Roy of the Department of Astronomy, University of Glasgow, for much helpful criticism and advice when the astronomical chapters were being prepared.

I am particularly indebted to the staff of the Map Room of the Bodleian Library for the tireless manner in which over the years they helped me by making available hundreds of surveys of various kinds. Thanks are also due to the Ordnance Survey for their courteous assistance in various ways.

A. T.

NOTE TO THE 1971 REPRINT

SINCE this book originally appeared much further work has been done in Britain and in Brittany, some of which is described in my book *Megalithic lunar observatories* (Clarendon Press, 1971).

A. T.

Dunlop, Ayrshire
June 1971

CONTENTS

1

INTRODUCTION

SCATTERED throughout Britain there are thousands of Megalithic sites. A few of these are well known but the great majority lie off the beaten track in the fields and on the moors. Many are not even recognized (or obviously recognizable) as being Megalithic at all. Circles seem to attract most attention, but of many circles little or nothing now remains. The destruction is mostly of recent years and is still proceeding apace. Nevertheless many hundreds are still in such a condition that much can be learned from a careful examination and analysis of accurately made surveys. Sketch plans such as many journals carry are, for the purposes we have in view here, of little use. The surveys must be made with the same accuracy as was used in the original setting out and it will be shown that some sites, for example Avebury, were set out with an accuracy approaching 1 in 1000. Only an experienced surveyor with good equipment is likely to attain this kind of accuracy. The differences in tension applied to an ordinary measuring tape by different individuals can produce variations in length of this amount or even more. The necessity for this kind of accuracy has not in the past been appreciated and has in fact only become apparent as the work recorded here progressed.

In this monograph will be found small-scale copies of a number of surveys selected from hundreds made by the author in the past thirty years. The examples have been chosen to illustrate some of the conclusions which can be drawn regarding the knowledge possessed by the Megalithic builders. Attention has been concentrated almost entirely on circles, rings, outliers, and alignments. The geometrical patterns to which the builders worked were outlined on the ground by stones of all shapes varying in size from 1 to 500 cubic feet. The features studied fall under two headings, geometrical and astronomical, but information of a wider scope can obviously be inferred.

Under the first heading we make a study of the units of measurement employed by the builders and of the geometrical shapes used for the rings, i.e. circles, flattened circles, egg shapes, ellipses, and other more complicated designs. Astronomically it has long been recognized that many of the sites contain indicators showing rising or setting points of the sun at the solstices. But the present work shows that there is a probability amounting to a certainty that other equally-spaced dates throughout the year are indicated. It also shows that the moon was carefully observed and that the first-magnitude stars may also come into the picture. An argument which has been raised against the use of the stars is that there are so many stars that almost any line is certain to show the rising or setting point of one or another. But this argument is quite untenable because we can in general only speak of the rising points of first-magnitude stars. We cannot see, for example, a third-magnitude star rise—except on an elevated horizon. This is because such a star does not become visible even in clear weather until it has attained an altitude of some three degrees. Restricting ourselves to first-magnitude stars, i.e. stars brighter than magnitude 1·5, we find that in Britain at the period in which we are interested, say 2000 to 1600 B.C., only some ten or twelve stars, depending on the latitude, etc., could rise or set. The others were either circumpolar or were too far south to be seen in these latitudes.

If we think of the long winter nights, if anything longer then than now, it is evident that throughout the greater part of the twenty-four hours the stars were the only indicators of time available. The hour would be indicated by the rising or setting of certain stars or by their transit over the meridian. There are many indications that both these methods were in use, or, to be more exact, there remain many indicators of rising and setting points of first-magnitude stars and many slabs and alignments still standing accurately in the meridian.

We can, I think, assume that in highly organized communities such as must have existed it would often be necessary to know the time of night. Much speculation has been directed to the necessity of accurate time-keeping for ritualistic purposes but certainly more practical reasons also existed. A civilization which could carry a unit of length from one end of Britain to the other, and perhaps much further afield, with an accuracy of 0·1 per cent and could call for the erection of 5000 to 10 000 megaliths must have made demands on its engineers. It is difficult to think of these responding without making use of time-keeping. One has only to think of the tremendous organizing effort which would be necessary to transport and erect numbers of stones some weighing up to 30 tons. Swampy ground might make it necessary to operate in winter when the ground was frozen. Think of feeding hundreds of men and the necessity of starting before dawn in the short winter day. The hour was important. Thus methods of obtaining time from the stars must have been well understood. To obtain time from the stars the date must be known and this as we shall see came from the sun at the calendar sites. Initially the necessary indicators would almost certainly have been of wood but it appears that in many places stone was substituted.

It is fortunate for us that Megalithic man liked, for some reason or another, to get as many as possible of the dimensions of his constructions to be multiples of his basic unit. We are thereby enabled to determine unequivocally the exact size of this unit. In fact probably no linear unit of antiquity is at present known with a precision approaching our knowledge of the Megalithic yard. The reason for his obsession with integers is not entirely clear, but undoubtedly the unit was universally used, perhaps universally sacred. It may have been that in the absence of paper and pen he found it necessary to record in stone his geometrical and perhaps also his arithmetical discoveries. Such of these as are known to us are of no mean order and there is no reason to suppose that our knowledge of what he knew is by any means complete. When it is recalled that our knowledge of his achievements in this field is only a decade or so old it is obvious that we have no right to imagine that it is complete. This mistake has indeed been made too often.

It is remarkable that 1000 years before the earliest mathematicians of classical Greece, people in these islands not only had a practical knowledge of geometry and were capable of setting out elaborate geometrical designs but could also set out ellipses based on Pythagorean triangles. We need not be surprised to find that their calendar was a highly developed arrangement involving an exact knowledge of the length of the year or that they had set up many stations for observing the eighteen-year cycle of the revolution of the lunar nodes.

It is important to do everything we can to protect the fast-vanishing sites until we are sure that we really understand them all. Places like Stonehenge and Avebury are presumably for the time being fairly safe but it should be noted how much of our knowledge has come from the humble circle on the hillside. We cannot judge by an inspection on the ground what secrets a site may yield. It must be accurately surveyed, prodded, and eventually excavated before we can assess its value. The clues which eventually led the author to the unravelling of the geometry of Avebury did not come from Stonehenge or Stanton Drew but from small unimpressive circles on the Scottish moors and the hills of Wales.

The surveys

In all some 450 sites have been visited and about 300 surveyed. A sufficient number of these surveys are reproduced here on a small scale to give an idea of what exists throughout the country.

The surveys were made usually by theodolite and tape, the orientation being determined by at least two time/azimuth observations of the sun. In overcast weather angles were measured to one or more distant points, for example mountain peaks, which could be identified on the Ordnance Survey. The azimuths of these marks were afterwards determined by a geodetic type of calculation from their geographical coordinates. If the weather or the type of country made it necessary to use marks near at hand then the azimuths might be determined by a large protractor. An accuracy of $0°·1$ is usually sufficient but for some important sites single minutes of arc were wanted.

At one or two sites the inaccessibility and the long distance to be walked precluded the use of the theodolite and the surveys were made by prismatic compass. In some places the local attraction is severe but this need not affect the accuracy provided that at every compass station a distant mark is included in the round of angles, the azimuth of the mark being computed later from the O.S. An error of $0°·2$ will produce an error of only about $0°·1$ in the declination. Orientation of the survey by compass alone is not reliable but if there is no alternative the variation appropriate to the place and date must be applied and checks made to detect local anomalies.

Ideally at every site of any importance the horizon altitudes ought to be measured round the whole horizon. Time after time sites have had to be revisited to measure the horizon altitude on a line which only became apparent when the survey was plotted. Many of the lines tabulated are uncertain because a second visit was impossible and the ground was such that estimates made from the O.S. contours were unsatisfactory. Photography can be a help here. If the coordinates, azimuth and altitude, of two points included in a picture have been measured then the whole horizon shown can be measured with sufficient accuracy from an enlargement.

During the surveys a bayonet was often used to prod the ground. In this way many buried stones were discovered and many broken stumps found. For example, at Strathaird in Skye (H 7/9) only three stones were upright but five more were felt below the peat. No attempt has been made to contour the surveys simply because this could not be done properly in the time available.

The azimuth of anything which looked like a sight line was noted together with the horizon altitude. The latter quantity is designated by h, but no symbol is used in the surveys for the azimuths. Thus where an angle is shown numerically without designation it is either the azimuth of a line drawn on the plan or of some point or object shown. In some cases the derived declination (δ) is added but it does not follow that the line was considered worthy of being included in the tables.

In recording a stone measurements were made to its base and the shaded, hatched, or blackened part on the surveys shows the plan section at or near ground level. A great many stones originally vertical are now leaning at all sorts of angles and in all directions making it impossible to be sure as to where the bases had been. A line of small v's across the plan of a stone shows where a sloping surface, for example the upper side of an inclined stone, runs into the ground. The remainder of the stone below ground may have been estimated by prodding, in which case it will be shown dotted with the other end, the top, shown in full line. One is thereby able to make a guess as to how much the shaded area has to be displaced in estimating afterwards the original position.

Much use was made of the Ordnance Survey, especially the 6-in, both the 1st and 2nd editions being sometimes consulted. Unfortunately the $2\frac{1}{2}$-in which has contours at 25-ft intervals does not cover the whole country. The

6-in has contours at this interval for the island of Lewis but most sheets are not contoured. Information regarding the orientation of the sheet edges for the 25-in can be obtained so that sometimes a reliable estimate of an azimuth can be obtained from this survey. Unfortunately many sites lie in districts which are not covered on this scale.

2

STATISTICAL IDEAS

I T will be necessary to make extensive use of statistical theory if any reliable conclusions are to be drawn from the mass of material presented in later chapters. Consequently it seems desirable to devote a chapter to some of the ideas and formulae of which extensive use will be made. This is the more necessary since some of the theory used has so far appeared only in scientific journals.

Throughout we shall use the quantity 'standard deviation' (σ) as an indication of the precision of a measurement or of a derived constant. The older method and that still used in some branches of science is to give the 'probable error', which is related to the standard deviation by the formula

$$\text{probable error} = 0.67 \times \text{standard deviation.}$$

When we write a length as $L \pm \sigma$ then we understand that the chance of an error of 2σ or more in L is about 1 in 20 or 5 per cent.

The simplest case is where we have found the arithmetic mean of a number of measurements of a single quantity. The deviation of each measurement from the mean may be called ϵ and the 'variance' is the mean of the squares of all values of ϵ. The square root of the variance is then σ, the standard deviation, so we have

$$\sigma^2 = \Sigma\epsilon^2/n,$$

where n is the number of measurements.

So long as we go on taking measurements of the same quantity by the same method we should expect to get approximately the same value for σ. It is a measure of the kind of deviation we should expect to get in any future measurement of the same kind. But when we form the mean of a group of our measurements we have a quantity of a much more precise nature and this is expressed by the formula

$$\sigma_{\text{mean}} = \sigma/\sqrt{n}.$$

This is sometimes called the 'standard error of the mean' or sometimes the 'standard deviation of the mean'.

When we write 6.23 ± 0.02 it is understood that 6.23 has been determined as the best or most likely value from the observations considered. If 6.23 has been found by taking an arithmetic mean as above then 0.02 is understood to be the standard error of the mean, but if it has been determined indirectly by a more complicated method such as a 'least squares' solution of equations based on other related measured quantities, then 0·02 still refers to the final result (6·23) and not to any individual measurement.

In many statistical investigations it is necessary to attach a 'probability level' to a quantity. This has a different meaning and refers to the probability that the quantity is real and is not a spurious result obtained by accident. The probability level is in fact the probability (usually expressed as a percentage) of the result occurring by accident.

As an illustration consider a simple application of Bernoulli's theorem. Suppose we have three dice and suspect that they have been loaded to make them tend to show VI on being thrown. We throw them once and obtain one VI. There would be nothing suspicious in this. By elementary algebra we find the probability of at least one VI to be 91/216 or 0·42. But suppose that at the first throw we get three VI's, then there is some ground for suspicion because with perfect dice the probability of three VI's in the first throw is $(1/6)^3$ or 0·5 per cent. This is not proof that the dice are loaded but we might say that we can accept the hypothesis that they are loaded at a probability level of 0·5 per cent. The natural thing to do is to throw again. If we again get three VI's we feel that our suspicion is justified because theory indicates that the probability is 1 in 46 656. In other words the probability level is about 0·002 per cent.

The value of the probability level at which we accept the hypothesis we are examining (in the above example that the dice were loaded) is a matter which depends on circumstances and in fact on the individual or group of individuals concerned. Where one man will accept a risk another will not. If the probability of a flying accident were 5 per cent very few people would fly, but for many purposes the 5 per cent level may be accepted.

In the simple example given above, elementary algebra gives a definite method of calculating the probability level, but in many cases the analysis is much more complicated. As an example, of which much use will be made later, consider the proof of the existence of a 'quantum' in a set of measurements. Suppose we have made a note of the times of the occurrence of a recurring event and we think there is a periodicity so that the event tends to happen at more or less regular intervals. How is a probability level to be assigned to our hypothesis? This is a most important type of problem which crops up in many branches of science but it is only in recent years that a solution (albeit empirical) has been available.

We shall set out the problem or rather problems in mathematical form and later, to simplify matters, give a full example.

In general we have a set of measurements $y_1, y_2, y_3, ..., y_n$. We suggest that these can be represented by a 'quantum hypothesis' of the form

$$y_i = \beta + 2m_i\delta + \epsilon_i,$$

where i takes the values 1, 2, 3, ..., n.

m is zero or an integer. The values of y are grouped round regularly spaced nodes, the groups being numbered $m = 0$, $m = 1$, etc.; 2δ and β are constants, 2δ being the quantum or uniform spacing between the groups whose existence we seek to prove or disprove. β allows for the possibility that the zero of our measurements may not agree with a node. If it does then β is zero. ϵ_i is the inevitable error or discrepancy of the ith measurement. If ϵ is everywhere zero then all the measurements fall exactly at nodes and it will be obvious without calculation that the hypothesis is true.

It is essential to recognize two distinct classes of problem.

Case I. In the first case we have come to the problem with an *a priori* knowledge that a quantum may exist. We have an idea of its magnitude and we wish to test the hypothesis that its existence is demonstrated by the measurements y_1, y_2, etc.

Case II. In the second and much more difficult case the quantum has come from the data themselves. We had in fact no idea beforehand that such a quantum existed nor with hindsight can we say, 'Ah, but we ought to have expected such a quantum because . . . .'

The logical approach to the two cases is quite different. Both have been dealt with by Broadbent, who has given in a first paper (1955) a rigid method of handling the first case and in a subsequent paper (1956) a Monte Carlo solution leading to a method of handling the second case.

There are two subdivisions of each case:

(*a*) when we know definitely from the nature of the problem that β is zero;
(*b*) when β may not be zero but must be determined from the data.

A further subdivision may be necessary. The standard deviation (σ) of the measurements may be the same for all the groups, that is for all values of m, or alternatively σ may increase with increasing m. To illustrate this point suppose that y_1, y_2, etc. have been measured with an accurate tape but suppose that the tape could not be brought into close contact with the objects being measured, then σ would be of the same order for all the groups and so the larger measures would not necessarily be less accurate than the smaller. If, on the other hand, the measuring appliance were in itself crude, then σ might be proportional to m or would at least increase with m. This would happen if distances were obtained by pacing. It will be shown that in the applications of the theory used in this monograph we need only consider the formula for constant σ. Reference to Broadbent's first paper may be made if the formulae for σ proportional to m are required.

We shall now consider the two subdivisions of Case I.

Case I (*a*). We have obtained an approximate value of the quantum and we know that the constant β must be zero. The formula for estimating the revised value of the quantum is

$$2\delta = \Sigma my / \Sigma m^2.$$

The variance of the quantum may be estimated according to Broadbent by

$$\sigma^2 = s_1^2/(n-1)\Sigma m^2,$$

where $s_1^2 = \Sigma y^2 - (\Sigma my)^2/\Sigma m^2$ and n is the total number of observations.

This formula is not always suitable for desk computation as it depends on the (small) difference of two large numbers but it can easily be modified.

Case I(b). We have obtained an approximate value of the quantum but the constant β is not necessarily zero. The formulae for obtaining the revised values of 2δ and β are

$$2\delta = (n\Sigma my - \Sigma m\Sigma y)/\Delta,$$

$$\beta = (\Sigma m^2\Sigma y - \Sigma m\Sigma my)/\Delta,$$

where $$\Delta = n\Sigma m^2 - (\Sigma m)^2.$$

The variance of the quantum may be estimated according to Broadbent by

$$\sigma^2 = s_2^2/\Delta,$$

where s_2^2 is obtained from

$$n(n-2)s_2^2 = \Delta' - (2\delta)^2\Delta \text{ and } \Delta' = n\Sigma y^2 - (\Sigma y)^2.$$

Similarly the variance of β is estimated by

$$n\sigma^2 = s_2^2[1 + (\Sigma m)^2/n\Delta].$$

It will be noticed that in applying the above formulae it is necessary to have an approximate value of 2δ initially in order to decide on the value of m to associate with each value of y or, in other words, to decide to which group each y is to be assigned. If the calculated quantum turns out to be much different from the assumed value it may be necessary to repeat the calculation.

The above expressions give a value for the quantum 2δ but we must now obtain the probability level at which we can accept the result. This is done by finding for each measurement, i.e. for each y, its deviation from the nearest node, i.e.
$$\epsilon = y - \beta - 2m\delta.$$

Values of ϵ may already have been formed for the calculation of the variance of 2δ. Having found ϵ for each observation we calculate what Broadbent calls the 'lumped variance' (s^2) from

$$ns^2 = \Sigma\epsilon^2.$$

We already have 2δ and so we can find s^2/δ^2 with which to enter Fig. 2.1. This figure shows at the top the required value of the probability level for any pair of the values of n and s^2/δ^2. The probability level so obtained is, it must be remembered, only valid if we had, before we began the investigation, an idea that a quantum existed with a value close to that obtained in the end.

Case II. We have now to consider the case where there is no *a priori* reason for expecting or adopting a particular quantum. We have merely inspected the data and have noticed that the measurements seem to group themselves round more or less evenly spaced nodes. We first determine the values of 2δ and β by using the formulae given for Case I, but when we come to consider

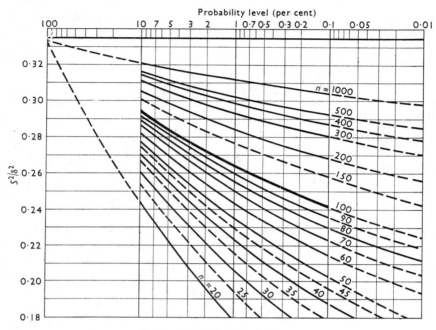

FIG. 2.1. Probability level.

the probability level the greatest care is necessary because experience has shown that almost any set of random numbers scattered between, say, 0 and 200 will show a rough periodicity of some sort and we may have by accident obtained a particularly 'good' set.

There is at present no rigid mathematical approach to the problem of assigning a probability level but Broadbent (1956), by a Monte Carlo method, has produced a criterion which is easy to apply. A reading of his paper shows that we have here a reliable method of detecting a spurious quantum. There will of course be borderline cases and for these we must either bring other considerations into the argument or obtain further measurements.

Suppose that we have a large number n of observations with no periodicity, scattered more or less uniformly but randomly along the range. If we test these by the method given for Case I for some suspected quantum (which is of course non-existent) then we ought to find s^2/δ^2 very close to 1/3. Since we are in effect finding the second moment of a rectangle this is fairly clear and in fact Broadbent calls this a rectangular distribution, each rectangle having a width equal to the quantum. The more the measurements, in an actual case, cluster round the nodes the further is the distribution from rectangular, the further the calculated value of s^2/δ^2 will fall below 1/3, and the greater becomes the likelihood that the quantum is real.

This is qualitatively obvious but it is possible to be more definite. Broadbent's criterion is

$$C = \sqrt{n}(\tfrac{1}{3} - s^2/\delta^2).$$

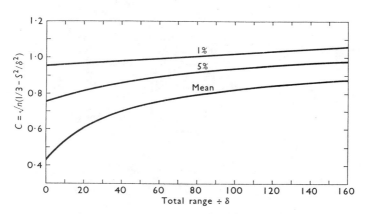

FIG. 2.2. Test of a quantum hypothesis (after Broadbent).

Roughly it may be said that C should be greater than unity. If it falls much below unity then the data lend no support to the idea that a quantum exists. A slightly more accurate idea may be obtained from Fig. 2.2, which is taken from Broadbent's second paper and shows approximate values for the probability level. For values of C definitely above unity we can accept the hypothesis with confidence. For values near the line marked 'mean' the data do not support the hypothesis, neither do they indicate that the hypothesis is definitely wrong.

Example

To illustrate the use of the above methods we shall apply them to examine the entirely imaginary data presented in the first column of Table 2.1. Here we have a set of twenty measurements (y) which we wish to examine to see if they support a quantum of about $1\frac{1}{2}$. We might, for example, think of these figures as being the measured lengths of the sides of bricks taken from an old building. The bricks were perhaps damaged or broken and had to be repaired before being measured. We might further assume that other similar buildings some distance away contained bricks having sides which were definitely multiples of $1\frac{1}{2}$. Our immediate problem is then to decide if the measurements in Table 2.1 show that our bricks belong to the same culture.

Table 2.1

y	m	ϵ	y	m	ϵ
1·4	1	−0·1	7·6	5	+0·1
1·5	1	0·0	8·0	5	+0·5
1·7	1	+0·2	8·6	6	−0·4
2·8	2	−0·2	9·0	6	0·0
4·5	3	0·0	9·1	6	+0·1
4·7	3	+0·2	9·5	6	+0·5
5·9	4	−0·1	9·9	7	−0·6
6·1	4	+0·1	10·4	7	−0·1
6·4	4	+0·4	11·8	8	−0·2
7·4	5	−0·1	12·3	8	+0·3

$$n = 20 \qquad \Sigma y = 138 \cdot 6 \qquad \Sigma \epsilon = +0 \cdot 6$$
$$\Sigma m = 92 \qquad \Sigma y^2 = 1171 \cdot 5 \qquad \Sigma \epsilon^2 = +1 \cdot 50$$
$$\Sigma m^2 = 518 \qquad \Sigma my = 778 \cdot 5 \qquad \Sigma m\epsilon = +1 \cdot 50$$

From which

$$\Delta = n\Sigma m^2 - (\Sigma m)^2 \qquad = 1896$$
$$2\delta = (n\Sigma my - \Sigma m\Sigma y)/\Delta \qquad = 1 \cdot 487, \quad \sigma = 0 \cdot 007$$
$$\beta = (\Sigma m^2 \Sigma y - \Sigma m\Sigma my)/\Delta \quad = +0 \cdot 091$$

or with $\beta = 0$ $\qquad 2\delta = \Sigma my/\Sigma m^2 \qquad = 1 \cdot 503, \quad \sigma = 0 \cdot 012.$

First we find the multiple of the assumed quantum ($1\frac{1}{2}$) which is nearest to each y. The necessary multipliers are m and we enter these in column 2. Then we find the deviations (ϵ) from the multiples, namely

$$\epsilon = y - m \times 1\tfrac{1}{2}.$$

The mean of the squares of ϵ is

$$s^2 = \Sigma \epsilon^2/n \text{ or } 0 \cdot 075,$$

where n is the number of observations, namely 20, so

$$s^2/\delta^2 \text{ is } 0 \cdot 133 \text{ where } \delta = \text{half quantum} = 0 \cdot 75.$$

Figure 2.1 does not extend as low as $s^2/\delta^2 = 0 \cdot 133$ but we see that with $n = 20$ the probability level is less than 1 per cent, being perhaps about 0·2 per cent. So the hypothesis that there is a quantum of $1\frac{1}{2}$ can be accepted at a probability level of this amount. In fact we can be reasonably certain that the bricks belong to the same culture as those of the other buildings.

We have in the above assumed that there is no constant β. Such a constant could only arise if somehow a constant amount had been added to or taken from each dimension. A shrinkage of the brick, say on firing, would not produce such a constant since the amount of shrinkage would be proportional to the size of the brick and so would affect the quantum 2δ but not β.

Let us now take the analysis further by finding the values of 2δ (the quantum) and β which fit the measurements best.

The values of the various sums Σy, Σy^2, etc., are shown and from these we find as shown $2\delta = 1\cdot487$ and $\beta = +0\cdot091$. We can find the standard deviation of 2δ and β. So we obtain

$$2\delta = 1\cdot487 \pm 0\cdot007,$$

$$\beta = +0\cdot09 \pm 0\cdot07.$$

Thus the measurements are represented by

$$y = 1\cdot487m + 0\cdot09,$$

but since the standard deviation of β is practically as large as β itself we have no real justification for assuming β to be anything else than zero.

We have assumed above that we had reason to expect a quantum of $1\frac{1}{2}$ before we began the investigation. Now suppose we had no such prior information. Can we say from the twenty measurements that a quantum exists? We find Broadbent's criterion C from

$$C = \sqrt{n}(\tfrac{1}{3} - s^2/\delta^2)$$

to be about $0\cdot89$; and so Fig. 2.2 shows that the hypothesis may be accepted at a probability level of about 2 per cent.

If we care to take the trouble we can form a new set of residuals from

$$\epsilon = y - \beta - 2m\delta.$$

Using the values of 2δ and β found above leads to $\Sigma\epsilon^2 = 1\cdot457$, from which $C = 0\cdot91$, a value which is only marginally different from that found above.

ASTRONOMICAL BACKGROUND

OMAR KHAYYAM spoke of 'that inverted bowl we call the sky' and thereby suggested the best method of thinking of the over-all appearance of the heavens —stars painted on the inside of a transparent bowl. But we cannot draw on paper a representation of the inside of a bowl or hemisphere as seen from its centre. Accordingly astronomers prefer to draw the sphere from the outside and then to apply the trigonometry of the sphere to the necessary calculations of the positions of the stars relative to one another or to the horizon. This approach will be found fully discussed in text-books on spherical astronomy.

To understand what might be called descriptive spherical astronomy it is necessary to have a grasp of the astronomers' approach and also to study the actual appearance of the night sky and its movements.

Before going further it is necessary to clear up our ideas about what is meant by terms like declination, azimuth, altitude, etc.

The *declination* of a star can be thought of as the latitude of a point on the Earth immediately under the star, i.e. it is the latitude of an observer who finds the star once a night passing through his zenith. In Fig. 3.1 let S be the star in the zenith of the observer at A_1. Then the star's declination is δ. Twelve hours later the observer is at A_2 and the star (for the values depicted) is below the observer's horizon because the line joining the observer and the star passes through the Earth. For another observer at B with a latitude of $(90° - \delta)$ the star would be on the horizon. For an observer still further north the star would never set at all. It would be circumpolar.

The *altitude* of a star or of a terrestrial object is the angle of elevation to the star or object measured from the horizontal. The true altitude is the altitude of the straight line joining the observer and the star. But the light ray from the star is bent as it passes into and through the atmosphere and so the star appears higher than it really is. The amount of the bending is known as *refraction*, so that

true altitude = apparent altitude−refraction.

The angle of refraction to a star is a function of its altitude and is at a maximum of about 0°·6 when the altitude is zero. The ray of light from a distant terrestrial point is also subject to refraction, known as terrestrial refraction, so if we wish to calculate the apparent altitude of an object such as a mountain top we must not only know its height above us and its distance but we must allow for the curvature of the Earth and for terrestrial refraction (see p. 25).

The lowest position which the apparent horizon, as viewed from a given place, can occupy is that of the apparent sea horizon. The amount by which the sea horizon appears below the horizontal is called the *dip* and is given by

$$\text{dip of sea horizon} = 0 \cdot 98 \sqrt{H},$$

where the dip is in minutes of arc and H is the observer's height in feet above sea level. It follows that if the altitude of any land horizon is calculated, or

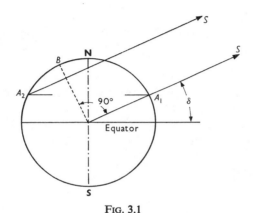

FIG. 3.1

measured in poor visibility, and is found to have a maximum value which is lower than the dip the latter must be substituted with the sign changed and used in any calculation of, say, the moon's declination setting over the point concerned. In other words, in clear weather the sea would appear above the land.

The *extinction angle* of a star is the smallest apparent altitude at which, in perfectly clear weather, it can be seen. Below this altitude its light is always absorbed by the atmosphere, however clear. The value of the extinction angle in degrees is roughly equal to the magnitude of the star, so that a third-magnitude star cannot be seen below 3° altitude. Only two stars, Sirius and Canopus, are bright enough to be seen down to zero altitude and of these only Sirius is visible in Britain.

The coordinates of a celestial body are normally referred to the Earth's centre. Looking at Fig. 3.1 it is evident that unless the body S is infinitely distant the direction in which it is seen will only be correct if the body is in the observer's zenith, that is if it appears directly overhead and its altitude is 90°. The error called *parallax* makes the altitude appear too small and is a maximum when the observer is at B. The body is then on the observer's horizon and the error is known as the *horizontal parallax*. For purposes of this book parallax can always be neglected except in the case of the moon, when it becomes very important.

The *azimuth* of a star or terrestrial object defines the direction in the horizontal plane in which we have to look to see the star or object. It is measured in the convention used in this book in degrees from north through east up to 360°.

Thus

east becomes 90°,
south   „   180°,
and   west   „   270°.

It is important to remember that azimuth is measured clockwise from the true geographical north and not from magnetic north. The latter is quite useless for our present purpose as it changes from year to year, but often surveys of archaeological sites show a north point which is really magnetic without any indication that it is not the true north and without a date from which the variation or difference between the two can be deduced.

There is a definite trigonometrical relation between the four angles—azimuth, declination, latitude, and altitude. So knowing any three the other can be found. In this way the declination of a star seen to rise at a given point can be calculated provided we can find the azimuth and altitude of the point (see p. 17). The azimuth of a point is best found by observing by theodolite the difference in azimuth between the point and the sun at a noted time. Later the azimuth of the sun at the noted time can be calculated, again by the spherical triangle, and so the azimuth of the point can be found. Once the azimuth of one point is obtained that of any other observed from the same position is easily determined.

For anyone who does not want to follow through the foregoing in detail it is perhaps easier to look at Fig. 3.2. This is an imaginary picture of the western horizon as seen from these latitudes. An attempt has been made to show the apparent movements of the stars as the night progresses. Each star will be seen to move along one of the lines according to its declination. A vertical erected in the north (N) on the inside of the bowl will pass through the pole to the zenith and so to the south point at S. This line or rather great circle is the meridian and shows the position where each star reaches its greatest altitude if it is in the south or its least altitude if it is a circumpolar star crossing the meridian in the north below the pole. A star of zero declination will be seen to travel down the thick line to set in the west and it will set in the west in any latitude. Stars with negative declinations will set between west and south and stars with positive declinations will set, if they set at all, between west and north. Since the diagram is prepared for latitude 55° N. a star with a declination greater than (90°−55°) or 35° will be circumpolar and will never set.

At midsummer the sun has its maximum declination and will appear to move along the upper dotted line at declination +24° to set in the north-west. Similarly at midwinter it moves along the lower dotted line at declination −24° to set in the south-west.

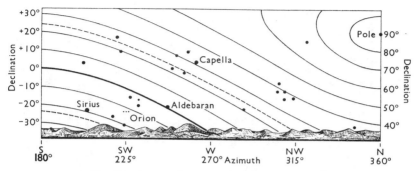

FIG. 3.2. Aspect of western sky—2000 B.C.—lat. 55° N.

Looking at the apparent movements of a close circumpolar star we see that once a day it reaches a position when its azimuth is a minimum. It is then said to be at its *western elongation*. Roughly twelve hours later it is on the other side of the pole and when its azimuth is a maximum it is said to be at *eastern elongation*. An azimuth midway between these positions is of course due north.

The figure is drawn to represent roughly the state of affairs at 2000 B.C. Orion, seen setting, was further south than it is now and consequently it was a shorter time above the horizon. The same remark applies to Sirius but the change in declination for Sirius has not been so great. These changes are not primarily due to movements of the stars themselves but are due to the *precession of the equinoxes*, a phenomenon which will be discussed later. The drawing shows that when the declination of a star is known its setting point can be found. Conversely, if the setting point is known the declination can be found. The setting point is defined by azimuth and altitude. The star Aldebaran with declination almost exactly zero sets in the west at azimuth 270° on a low horizon, but had the mountain shown been a little further to the right the setting point might have been as low as 265°.

The relation between declination, azimuth, and altitude which we require in this book is

$$\sin \delta = \sin \lambda \sin h + \cos \lambda \cos h \cos A,$$

where δ = declination, h = horizon altitude (true),

λ = latitude, A = azimuth.

Since in most cases an accuracy of $\pm 0°\cdot 1$ is sufficient, values of the declination can be taken from Table 3.1 by interpolation in the section for the latitude

Table 3.1. *Declination in terms of azimuth, altitude, and latitude*

Latitude = 50°				Latitude = 55°				Latitude = 60°			
Amp.	Decl.	Add for +1° Lat.	Add for +1° Alt.	Amp.	Decl.	Add for +1° Lat.	Add for +1° Alt.	Amp.	Decl.	Add for +1° Lat.	Add for +1° Alt.
0°	0·00°	0·00°	+0·77°	0°	0·00°	0·00°	+0·82°	0°	0·00°	0·00°	+0·87°
5	3·21	−0·07	0·77	5	2·87	−0·07	0·82	5	2·50	−0·08	0·87
10	6·41	−0·14	0·77	10	5·72	−0·14	0·82	10	4·98	−0·15	0·87
15	9·58	−0·20	0·78	15	8·54	−0·22	0·83	15	7·44	−0·23	0·87
20	12·70	−0·27	0·78	20	11·31	−0·29	0·84	20	9·85	−0·30	0·88
25	15·76	−0·34	0·79	25	14·03	−0·36	0·84	25	12·20	−0·38	0·89
30	18·75	−0·41	0·81	30	16·67	−0·43	0·85	30	14·48	−0·45	0·89
35	21·63	−0·48	0·82	35	19·21	−0·50	0·87	35	16·67	−0·52	0·90
40	24·40	−0·55	0·84	40	21·63	−0·57	0·88	40	18·75	−0·59	0·91
45	27·03	−0·61	0·86	45	23·93	−0·64	0·89	45	20·70	−0·66	0·92
50	29·50	−0·68	0·88	50	26·06	−0·70	0·91	50	22·52	−0·72	0·94
55	31·77	−0·74	0·90	55	28·02	−0·76	0·93	55	24·18	−0·78	0·95
60	33·83	−0·80	0·92	60	29·78	−0·82	0·94	60	25·66	−0·83	0·96
65	35·63	−0·86	0·94	65	31·32	−0·87	0·96	65	26·95	−0·88	0·97
70	37·16	−0·91	0·96	70	32·61	−0·92	0·97	70	28·02	−0·92	0·98
75	38·38	−0·95	0·98	75	33·64	−0·95	0·98	75	28·88	−0·96	0·99
80	39·27	−0·98	0·99	80	34·39	−0·98	0·99	80	29·50	−0·98	0·99
85	39·82	−0·99	1·00	85	34·85	−0·99	1·00	85	29·87	−1·00	1·00
90	40·00	−1·00	1·00	90	35·00	−1·00	1·00	90	30·00	−1·00	1·00

To use the tables

Correct the apparent altitude for refraction and call this true altitude. Find the amplitude from the rule:

$0° < Az < 180°$ $Amp = 90° - Az$

$180° < Az < 360°$ $Amp = Az - 270°$.

For positive amp. interpolate the decl. from the table for the nearest of the three latitudes given and then apply the correction for latitude shown, i.e. when the lat. is greater, the decl. is greater, the decl. is less and when the lat. is less, the decl. is greater.

For negative amp. the decl. is negative and the correction for latitude is reversed.

The correction for altitude is always positive if the true altitude is positive.

nearest to that of the site. The value must then be corrected for the latitude difference and for the true altitude according to the rules given on the table.

The position of the Earth's orbit

The orbit which the Earth describes about the sun is an ellipse with the sun in one of the foci but as far as appearances go we can say that it is the sun which describes an elliptical orbit about us. In this section we shall look at the changes which take place in the position of the plane which contains the orbit. Later it will be necessary to consider the changes which take place in the ellipse itself and in its position in the plane.

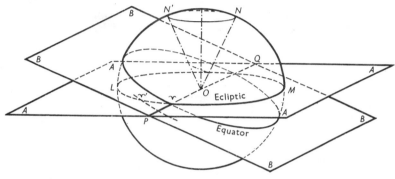

FIG. 3.3

Let $AAAA$ (Fig. 3.3) be the plane of the Earth's orbit. It is thus the plane in which the sun and the Earth lie throughout the year and so when we look at the sun our line of sight lies in this plane, which is called the *ecliptic*. The plane of the equator is $BBBB$ intersecting the ecliptic in the line PQ, which consequently lies in both planes. It is much easier to draw these planes on a sphere—the celestial sphere. This sphere is centred at O, the observer's position on the line PQ. The ecliptic and the equator then become great circles on the sphere, these circles being the circles in which the planes cut the sphere. The sun at the vernal equinox will be seen along the line OP, which is simply designated by ♈, the first point of Aries. As the spring advances the sun appears to move along the ecliptic in an anticlockwise direction till at mid-summer it is at M. Its declination is then a maximum and equal to the angle between the planes—the so-called *obliquity of the ecliptic* (ϵ).

The Earth turns on its axis ON, which is at right angles to the equator. N is the north pole of the celestial sphere, near to the present-day position of the pole-star. The axis ON precesses like the axis of a spinning top and so describes a cone. Thus N moves clockwise round the small circle NN' taking about 25 000 years to go round once. Since N is the pole of the equator the equator moves with it causing ♈ to move slowly along the ecliptic. After a few

centuries ♈ will have moved to ♈′ and the equator will have moved into the
dotted position. Since the ecliptic remains fixed in space the equator is con-
tinuously changing its position relative to the stars. But we measure declination from the equator so the declinations of the stars are steadily changing.
We have seen that a star's rising point is fixed by its declination. This means
that the rising point of a given star slowly moves along the horizon through
the ages. The change at a given time is more rapid for some stars than for
others depending as it does on the star's position on the celestial sphere. It
will be evident that for a star near *M* the change will be slower than for a star
near ♈.

The obliquity of the ecliptic has been decreasing slowly for a very long time.
The decrease is so slow that in 10 000 years it only amounts to about a degree.
Probably the best modern determination of the obliquity is by de Sitter
(1938) and his formula yields

2000 B.C.	23°·9292
1700 B.C.	23·8969
1000 B.C.	23·8175
A.D. 1900	23·4523

The moon's orbit

The moon describes an orbit round the Earth inclined to the ecliptic at an
angle which varies periodically by a small amount (about 0°·15) from the
mean value of $i = 5°·15$. Astronomers believe that this mean value has
remained constant for many thousands of years. If we substitute 'moon's
orbit' for 'equator' in Fig. 3.3 it can be used to explain the terms. The line
PQ is now called the *line of nodes*. This line, like the equinoctial line, is also
moving round in the ecliptic but much more rapidly. It completes a circuit
in 18·6 years. This rotation of the line of nodes has an important effect on
the position of the full moon in the sky. When we face the full moon the sun
is at our back below the horizon, lighting the side of the moon at which we
are looking. So the full moon is always diametrically opposite the sun. It
follows that if the inclination of the moon's orbit to the ecliptic were zero
the full moon would always be eclipsed since the Earth would be directly
between the sun and the moon. As things are, the moon can only be eclipsed
when it is near the ecliptic, i.e. when it is near the line of nodes. It also follows
that at midwinter when the sun is at its lowest declination the full moon is
at its highest declination and so is giving us the greatest and longest illumination. Just how high it then is depends on the position of the line of nodes.
We shall consider only the extreme conditions which occur at the solstices
when the line of nodes is along the equinoctial line, i.e. when one end or the
other is at the first point of Aries. The two cases are shown in Fig. 3.4, where
we are supposed to be looking along the line of intersection of the three planes

—the ecliptic, the equator, and the moon's orbit. Each plane then becomes a line. The lunar orbit can be either at *LL* or at *KK*, 5°·15 on either side of the ecliptic. When the orbit is at *LL* the moon as it goes round in this plane can attain a maximum declination of ∠*COL*, i.e. the sum of the obliquity of the ecliptic and the inclination of the lunar orbit, or about 29°. On the other hand

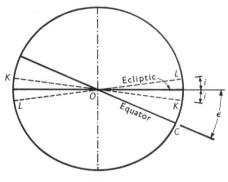

FIG. 3.4

9·3 years later the orbit is at *KK* and the maximum declination is the difference of the two angles, about 19°. So, for a midwinter full moon, the extremes of declination are +19° and +29°. Similarly at a midsummer full moon the declination lies between −19° and −29°.

One may ask in what way these changes in the position of the moon's orbit throughout the nineteen-year cycle would make themselves apparent. For a community whose only effective illumination during the long winter nights was the moon perhaps the most important apparent change would be that the midwinter full moon's altitude on the meridian varied from about 57° to 67° (latitude 52°) with a lengthening of the time the full moon was above the horizon of some 2½ hours. A difference which is evident to all but the most unobservant is that of the maximum altitude of the midsummer full moon, which in latitude 55° N. varies from 16° to 6°. Even in the south of England the change from 20° to 10° is very obvious.

But transcending these phenomena in importance lay the challenge of the eclipse. To early man the eclipse of the sun or of the moon must have been an impressive spectacle and a desire to master eclipse prediction probably motivated Megalithic man's preoccupation with lunar phenomena. Since eclipses happen only when the moon is at a node it would soon have become apparent that no eclipse occurred near the solstices when the full moon was in either of its extreme positions but only in the years which lay midway between these.

To understand some of the lunar sites dealt with in Chapters 11 and 12 it is necessary to examine the moon's motion in greater detail and to illustrate it by showing the actual changes of declination near the maximum. In

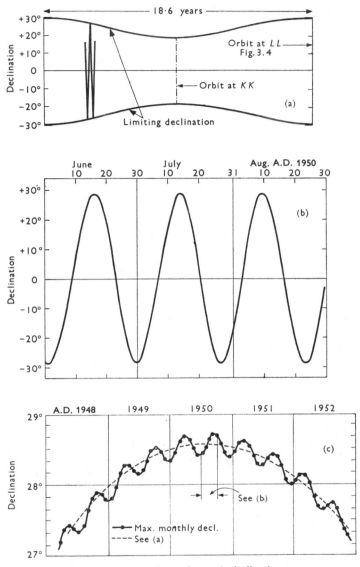

FIG. 3.5. Behaviour of moon's declination.

Fig. 3.5 (*a*) the limiting values of the declination are shown throughout one revolution of the nodes. The declination rises every lunar month to the upper line and falls to the lower. This is illustrated by plotting the actual declination during the summer of A.D. 1950, for which of course full particulars were available (Fig. 3.5 (*b*)). In Fig. 3.5(*a*) these oscillations are crowded so closely together that they could not be plotted. But neither Fig. 3.5 (*a*) nor Fig. 3.5 (*b*) could show the small oscillation of ±9′ which is brought out in Fig. 3.5 (*c*) by greatly increasing the declination scale and using a time scale which allows several years to be included. In this figure each dot represents one of the upper peaks of Fig. 3.5 (*b*). The mean dotted line is a small portion of the top of the upper line in Fig. 3.5 (*a*) and so has a period of 18·6 years. Superimposed on this we see the small ±9′ oscillation already mentioned.

Every 346·62 days the sun comes round to the ascending node of the lunar orbit. This is consequently known as the length of the 'eclipse year' because eclipses can only happen when the sun is near one of the nodes. But there are two nodes, the ascending and the descending, and so the time taken from one to the other is half an eclipse year or 173·31 days. This is the period of the small oscillation seen in Fig. 3.5 (*c*).

The lunar declination reached one of its maxima in 1950 but for several months the mean value shown by the dotted line changed very little. Consequently two or three waves of the small oscillation would be clearly observable. These would show up in the movement of the setting moon along the horizon, especially in northern latitudes, where the path of the setting moon at its lowest declination makes a very small angle with the horizon (e.g. see Fig. 11.4). We shall see that Megalithic man understood very clearly the advantage in sensitivity of observing a glancing phenomenon of this kind and so it was quite possible for him to have observed these two or three oscillations around the maximum or minimum positions of the moon. Evidence will be given that he did observe this phenomenon, but to be able to assess this evidence it is necessary to understand clearly what happens when the moon is in one of the limiting positions. This is the reason why we have gone into the matter in some detail.

Earth's orbit

Just as on the Earth's surface a point can be located by giving its latitude and longitude so a point in the heavens can be specified by two coordinates called by the same names. But when an astronomer speaks of (celestial) latitude and longitude he is thinking of coordinates which while similar in conception to terrestrial latitude and longitude refer to entirely different planes or axes. Celestial *longitude* is measured along the ecliptic anticlockwise from the first point of Aries (γ) and *latitude* is measured from the ecliptic towards its poles.

When the Earth is at the point in its elliptic orbit nearest to the sun it is said to be at *perihelion*. Today the longitude of perihelion is about 102°·3. So the sun's longitude at perigee (i.e. when it is nearest the Earth) is this increased by 180°, or 282°·3. This occurs in the first week in January so that the Earth's speed in its orbit, obviously a maximum at perihelion, is greater in the winter months than in the summer. It follows that the interval between the autumnal equinox ($l = 180°$) and the vernal equinox ($l = 0°$) is shorter by some $7\frac{1}{2}$ days than the summer half of the year. This has not always been so. In 4040 B.C. perihelion occurred at the autumnal equinox so that the winter and summer halves of the year were equal.

Astronomers speak of the *longitude of the dynamic mean sun,* meaning thereby the longitude of an imaginary body which moves round the ecliptic with a speed uniform and equal to the mean speed of the actual sun in a year. Due to the varying speed of the Earth in its orbit the sun is sometimes ahead and sometimes behind the mean sun. This is expressed mathematically by

$$\odot = l + 2e\sin(l-\pi),$$

where

$\odot =$ longitude of sun,

$l =$ longitude of the dynamic mean sun,

$\pi =$ longitude of sun at perigee,

$e =$ eccentricity.

Knowing the longitude of the sun we can calculate its declination from

$$\sin\delta = \sin\odot\sin\epsilon,$$

where $\epsilon =$ obliquity of ecliptic.

Azimuth and altitude from Ordnance Survey maps

When an Ordnance Survey map has the national grid superimposed it shows in the margin the angle between grid north and true north for definite positions on the sheet. Hence if the azimuth of a line is calculated, or measured, with respect to the grid it can be reduced to true north by applying the correction obtaining at the observer's end of the line. Alternatively one can obtain formulae and tables for finding the azimuth of a line joining two points when the grid coordinates of the points are known.

The seventh series of the 1-in O.S. maps have, in addition to the national grid, the intersection points of latitude and longitude marked by a cross at $5'$ intervals. Using these or otherwise it is possible to obtain the latitude and longitude to about one second of arc. Using the $2\frac{1}{2}$-in or the 6-in maps the coordinates can be obtained to a fraction of a second. Given then two points probably on different sheets the following formulae will give the required azimuth and distance. The distance will be necessary in the calculation of angles of altitude.

Let λ_c, L_c be the latitude and longitude of the observer at C and λ_d, L_d be the same coordinates for the observed point D.

$\Delta\lambda = \lambda_d - \lambda_c$,

$\Delta L = L_d - L_c$ (east longitude reckoned positive),

$\lambda_m = \frac{1}{2}(\lambda_d + \lambda_c) =$ mean latitude,

$A =$ required azimuth measured clockwise from north.

Then find tan B from

$$\tan B = K \cos \lambda_m \Delta L / \Delta \lambda,$$

which gives B. Find ΔA from $\qquad \Delta A = \Delta L \sin \lambda_m$

and the required azimuth of D from C is $A = B - \frac{1}{2}\Delta A$.

If the Earth were a sphere K would be unity. To allow for the fact that the Earth is not a sphere but approximately an oblate spheroid K can be taken as varying from $1 \cdot 0028$ in latitude $50°$ to $1 \cdot 0017$ in latitude $60°$.

The distance CD in statute miles is obtained with sufficient accuracy from

$$c = CD = 0 \cdot 01922 \Delta \lambda / \cos B \quad \text{or} \quad 0 \cdot 01926 \Delta L \cos \lambda_m / \sin B.$$

It is often necessary to calculate the apparent angle of altitude of one point D as seen from another point C in terms of the distance c between the points and the amount by which the height of D exceeds that of C. It is necessary to take account of the curvature of the Earth and of the refraction which bends the ray between D and C. Both of these effects are taken into account with sufficient accuracy for most purposes in the formula

$$h = H/c - c(1 - 2k)/2R,$$

where
$$H = \text{height of } D \text{ above } C,$$

$$c = \text{distance of } D \text{ from } C,$$

$$R = \text{radius of curvature of the spheroid},$$

$$k = \text{coefficient of refraction}.$$

Commonly used values for k are $0 \cdot 075$ for rays passing over land and $0 \cdot 081$ over the sea.

If H is expressed in feet, c in statute miles, and h in minutes of arc then the above formula becomes approximately

$$h = 0 \cdot 65 H/c - 0 \cdot 37 c.$$

It must be remembered that the refraction of a ray near to a land or water surface is liable to be considerably affected by the steep temperature gradients (with height) which may exist.

It is as well to be quite clear about the difference between astronomical refraction and terrestrial refraction. The ray of light from a star is refracted along the whole length of its track through the atmosphere. The total effect on the altitude of the star is the astronomical refraction. Suppose now that the ray passes close to a mountain top before it reaches the observer, then the deflexion which it suffers after the mountain top produces terrestrial refraction. The effect is to make the mountain top appear too high by an angle of kc/R, while the curvature of the earth makes it appear too low by $c/2R$. Hence the above formula.

C

The astronomical refraction used in this work is indicated by the values:

Apparent altitude	$-\frac{1}{2}°$	0°	1°	2°	3°	5°	10°
Refraction	40′	33′	24′	18′	14′	10′	5′

Normally the apparent altitude of the mountain top would be measured and the altitude of a star on the mountain top would be found by deducting the astronomical refraction. But if the altitude of the mountain top is to be found by calculation what we require is the apparent altitude and this is found by the above formula.

4

MATHEMATICAL BACKGROUND

As we shall see later the builders of the circles, rings, alignments, etc., had a remarkable knowledge of practical geometry. In this chapter we shall set out in modern terminology some of the ideas which they developed and show how their constructions can be analysed. They were intensely interested in measurements and attained a proficiency which as we shall see is only equalled today by a trained surveyor. They concentrated on geometrical figures which had as many dimensions as possible arranged to be integral multiples of their units of length. They abhorred 'incommensurable' lengths. This is fortunate for us because once we have established their unit of length we can very often unravel designs which would otherwise be meaningless. These people also measured along curves and so it is necessary to devote some space to the methods of calculating the perimeters of the various rings which they developed.

The basic figure of their geometry, as of ours, is the triangle. Today everyone knows the Pythagorean theorem which states that the square on the hypotenuse of a right-angled triangle is equal to the sum of the squares on the other two sides. We do not know if Megalithic man knew the theorem. Perhaps not, but he was feeling his way towards it. One can almost say that he was obsessed by the desire to discover and record in stone as many triangles as possible which were right-angled and yet had all three sides integers. The most famous of the so-called Pythagorean triangles is the 3, 4, 5—right-angled because $3^2 + 4^2 = 5^2$. He used this triangle so often that he may well have noticed the relation. Limiting the hypotenuse to 40 there are six true Pythagorean triangles. These are

(1) 3, 4, 5		(4) 7, 24, 25
(2) 5, 12, 13		(5) 20, 21, 29
(3) 8, 15, 17		(6) 12, 35, 37

Megalithic man knew at least three of these. He may have known all six and we simply have not yet found the sites where they were used, but we shall see later that there were other conditions to be fulfilled and these certainly restricted the use of some of these triangles. The remarkable thing is that the largest, the 12, 35, 37, was known and exploited more than any other with the exception of the 3, 4, 5.

But Megalithic man used many close approximations to Pythagorean triangles. For example, he used the triangle 8, 9, 12, but 8^2+9^2 is 145 and 12^2 is 144. The error in the hypotenuse is only 1 in 300, which he probably accepted because the triangle as he used it gave as we shall see a suitable perimeter to the ring which he based on it. Some of his approximations were worse than this and some very much better. When he used a poor value it was not because he believed it to be perfect but because other conditions had to be fulfilled.

Flattened circles

In many places flattened circles were used of two very definite types. So far thirty or so have been found but there were probably many more, some of which may yet be located.

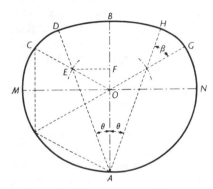

FIG. 4.1. Flattened circle. Type A.

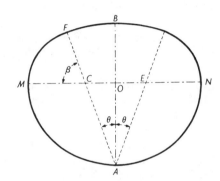

FIG. 4.2. Flattened circle. Type B.

The construction and geometry of these rings is shown in Figs. 4.1 and 4.2. To draw a Type A ring set out a circular arc of 240° $CMANG$. The angle COA is easily constructed by making two equilateral triangles as shown. This makes the required 120°. Bisect OC at E. Then E is the centre for the arc CD. The remaining flat arc DBH is drawn with centre at A. To calculate π', the ratio of the perimeter to the diameter, take, for easy calculation, the radius OC to be 4. Then $OE = 2$ and since the angle EOF is 60°, $EF = \sqrt{3}$ and $OF = 1$. Also $\tan \theta = EF/FA = (\sqrt{3})/5$ which makes θ in radians equal to 0·33347. $\beta = \pi/3-\theta$, $AE = 2\sqrt{7}$, $AB = 2+2\sqrt{7}$. From these we can deduce that

$$\text{perimeter}/MN = \pi' = \frac{5\pi}{6} + \frac{\sqrt{7}}{2} \times \theta = 3\cdot0591,$$

$$AB/MN = 0\cdot9114.$$

The construction of a Type B ring is easier. Divide the diameter MN into three equal parts at C and E. These are the centres for the small arcs. The flat closing arc is, as in Type A, struck with centre at A. Making the calculations as before leads to

$$\pi' = \text{perimeter}/MN = \frac{5\pi}{6} + \frac{\sqrt{10}}{3}\theta = 2{\cdot}9572,$$

where
$$\tan \theta = \tfrac{1}{3},$$

and
$$AB/MN = 0{\cdot}8604.$$

We find one or two sites where a slight modification to the above types has been used. At two sites a Type A construction was used but OE was made equal to one-third of OC instead of one-half. This can be called Type D. π' for Type D is $3{\cdot}0840$ and $AB/MN = 0{\cdot}9343$. At one site Type B has been modified by making $OC = CM$. This modification makes $\pi' = 2{\cdot}8746$ and reduces the diametral ratio to $0{\cdot}8091$.

Egg-shaped rings

Ten sites are known with these peculiarly shaped rings. They can be classified into two types both of which are based on a Pythagorean or near Pythagorean triangle. In Type I (Fig. 4.3) two of these triangles are used placed base to

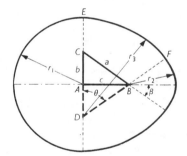

FIG. 4.3. Egg-shaped circle. Type I.

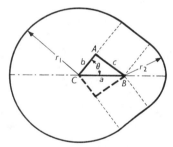

FIG. 4.4. Egg-shaped circle. Type II.

base at AB. A semicircle is drawn with centre at A, an arc EF is drawn with centre at D, and the pointed end of the egg is drawn with centre at B. The result of using triangles which have all sides integral is that, provided the semicircle has an integral radius, then all the other radii must also be integral. Any given Pythagorean triangle can be used in two ways depending on which side is chosen as the base and in fact we find the 3, 4, 5 triangle turned both ways, but once the triangles are arranged the size and shape of the egg can still be varied infinitely by choosing different integers for the radius of the semicircle.

In Type II (Fig. 4.4) the triangles are placed together with a common hypotenuse. The arcs at each end are drawn with centres at the ends of this hypotenuse and joined by straight lines parallel to the side of the triangle. As in Type I if one radius is integral so is the other.

The perimeter of a Type I egg can be found as follows. Referring to the figure, let

$$r_1 = \text{radius of the large end,}$$
$$r_2 = \quad\text{,,}\quad\text{,,}\quad\text{small end,}$$
$$r_3 = \quad\text{,,}\quad\text{,,}\quad\text{arc } EF.$$

Evidently $r_3 = r_1+b$, but it is also equal to r_2+a, from which $r_1-r_2 = a-b$. The half-perimeter can obviously be written

$$\tfrac{1}{2}P = r_1\tfrac{1}{2}\pi+r_3\theta+r_2\beta,$$

from which, with the above relations, we find

$$P = 2\pi r_1+\pi b-2a\beta,$$

β being obtained from $\qquad \tan\beta = b/c.$

Similarly we find that the perimeter of a Type II egg is given by

$$P = 2\pi r_1+2c-2\theta b,$$

θ being obtained from $\qquad \tan\theta = c/b.$

The ellipse

The earliest known study of the properties of the sections of a cone, of which the ellipse is one, seems to have been made by Menaechmus in the

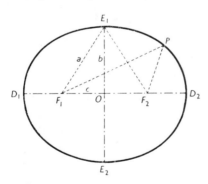

FIG. 4.5. Ellipse drawn by rope.

middle of the fourth century before Christ (Heath, 1921) but the ellipse may have been known to earlier Greeks. Our forefathers early in the second millennium B.C. were laying out ellipses but their approach was much simpler. Almost certainly their ellipses were set out either with a loop of rope round two stakes or with a rope tied to two stakes (F_1 and F_2 in Fig. 4.5). In either method a third stake round which the rope could slide would be used to scribe the curve on the ground. The fixed stakes were at the points F_1 and F_2 and the stake at P was moved round keeping the rope F_1PF_2 always tight. F_1 and F_2 are known as the foci, D_1D_2 and E_1E_2 are the *major and minor axes*. The ratio F_1F_2/D_1D_2, that is $2c/2a$, is known as the *eccentricity* (e). As the eccentricity gets smaller and smaller the ellipse gets nearer and nearer to being a circle. So we can regard an ellipse as being a circle with two centres.

A circle has a constant radius but an ellipse has the average of the two lengths $F_1 P$ and $F_2 P$ constant.

When Megalithic man set out a circle with a diameter of 8 units he found the circumference very nearly 25 units but in general he could not get nice whole numbers like these for both the diameter and the circumference simultaneously. Probably the attraction of the ellipse, and we know of over 30 set out by these people, was that it had an extra variable ($F_1 F_2$) and so it was easier to get the circumference near to some desired value. But the ellipse has, as it were, two diameters, the major and minor axes. How is it possible to get both of these and at the same time the focal distance $F_1 F_2$ all integral? Looking at Fig. 4.5 we see that $F_2 D_2$ is equal to $F_1 D_1$. When P is at D_2 the total length of the rope is $F_1 D_2 + F_2 D_2$ and so is $F_1 D_2 + F_1 D_1$ and so is $F_1 D_2 + F_1 D_1$ which is the major axis ($2a$). That is, half the length of the rope is the semi-axis major (a). So when P is at E_1 we see that $F_1 E_1$ is equal to a. Thus a, b, and c are the sides of a right-angled triangle and if the triangle is Pythagorean we can have the major axis, the minor axis, and the focal distance all integral. Just as for the egg-shaped rings so for the ellipses it was desirable to start with a Pythagorean triangle. For both eggs and ellipses Megalithic man had a further very difficult task, namely, to get the perimeter integral. To be able to examine his success we must be able to calculate accurately the perimeters of his figures. We have seen how this can be done for the flattened circles and for the eggs.

Table 4.1. *Perimeter of ellipse in terms of b/a. $2a =$ major axis, $2b =$ minor axis, $P =$ perimeter*

b/a	$P/2a$	b/a	$P/2a$	b/a	$P/2a$
0·30	2·1930	0·54	2·4733	0·78	2·8067
0·32	2·2135	0·56	2·4994	0·80	2·8361
0·34	2·2346	0·58	2·5259	0·82	2·8658
0·36	2·2563	0·60	2·5527	0·84	2·8957
0·38	2·2786	0·62	2·5798	0·86	2·9258
0·40	2·3013	0·64	2·6072	0·88	2·9561
0·42	2·3246	0·66	2·6349	0·90	2·9865
0·44	2·3483	0·68	2·6629	0·92	3·0172
0·46	2·3725	0·70	2·6912	0·94	3·0481
0·48	2·3971	0·72	2·7197	0·96	3·0790
0·50	2·4221	0·74	2·7484	0·98	3·1101
0·52	2·4475	0·76	2·7774	1·00	3·1416

For the ellipse we require special tables. In the absence of these we can use Table 4.1 which gives the ratio π' of the perimeter to the major axis for values of b/a between 0·30 and 1·00 advancing by intervals of 0·02. Simple linear interpolation will give π' for any intermediate value of b/a without any appreciable error in the fifth figure.

A piece of thread and two drawing-pins can be used on a drawing-board to construct an ellipse but this is not a very satisfactory method. One of the best methods is that shown in Fig. 4.6. Two circles are drawn, the diameters

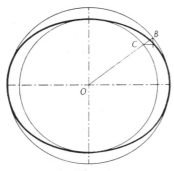

being the major and minor axes. A radial line is drawn cutting the circles at *C* and *B*. Lines parallel to the axes are drawn through *C* and *B* and where these meet is a point on the required ellipse. Thirty or forty radial lines can be drawn without any confusion and so an accurate ellipse can be completed.

The accuracy with which some of the large rings are set out shows it to be unlikely that a rope was used for the actual measurements although it must have been used in scribing the quadrants of the ellipses. The most accurate method available to these people was

FIG. 4.6. Ellipse drawn on drawing-board.

that still used today in a more sophisticated manner in measuring short base lines. This involves the use of two rods A and B each of a known length. A and B are laid down end to end and carefully levelled. Then A is lifted over B and again laid down touching B at the other end. In this way moving A and B alternately the required length is set out.

One is entitled to ask what error would be introduced where this method was used with straight rods when measuring round a curve. Each rod in fact forms the chord of a short arc and we require to know the difference in length between the arc and the chord. Approximately the difference is given by

$$\text{arc minus chord} = c^3/24R^2,$$

where c = length of the chord and R = radius of the curve. As an example consider a circle of diameter 8 units measured with a rod 1 unit long. There are roughly 25 chords in the circle and the error in each is $1/24 \times 16$. So the total accumulated error is 25/384 or 0·065 units. This error 1 in 384 ought with careful work to be just appreciable, but one would need level ground and carefully prepared supports for each rod. To detect the difference between the actual circumference of the circle, namely 8π or 25·133, and that determined by the rods, 25·065, ought to be just possible.

Number of lengths at a site which can be integral

To fix the position of n points relative to one another by linear measurements we need $2n-3$ lengths but the number of lines which can be drawn joining the points is $n(n-1)/2$. Thus we can connect four points with five lines so that all are fixed relative to one another but we can still draw another line and the length of this line can be calculated from the length of the original five. We can say that only five are disposable.

So we get

n points	Disposable lengths	Possible lengths
2	1	1
3	3	3
4	5	6
5	7	10
etc.		

It follows that at a site with five circles only seven of the ten possible distances between the circles can be expected to be integral multiples of a unit length. An exception would be if the circles were in a straight line.

5

MEGALITHIC UNIT OF LENGTH

TODAY we use the yard as a standard unit of length. The word yard meant originally a rod of wood or a stick. The French *verge* has the same meaning and the Spanish word *vara* shows that this old length unit also meant originally a rod. In all three measures the idea was the same: the unit of length was carried about as a rod of wood just as today we carry a foot-rule or a metre stick. For our present discussion the most interesting is the *vara*, which has the following values in feet.

2·766	Burgos	Szymański, 1956
2·7425	Madrid	
2·749	Mexico	
2·778	Texas and California	W. Latto and W. S. Olsen, private communication
2·75	Peru	

It is one of the objects of this chapter to demonstrate unequivocally the existence of a common unit of length throughout Megalithic Britain and to show that its value was accurately 2·72 ft. We might speculate that this unit was left in the Iberian Peninsula by Megalithic people to become the *vara* of recent times and to be taken to America by Spain.

To demonstrate the actual size of the Megalithic yard it might be logical to confine the argument to data based on what were intended to be true circles, since everyone will admit that such circles exist, and actually we obtain an identical value if we do so restrict ourselves, but in view of the fact that the existence of other definite shapes has been demonstrated in a number of papers already published it seems better in the present analysis to strengthen the case by including all the available data. That is we shall include true circles, both types of flattened circles, both types of eggs, and compound rings: but exclude ellipses and the Avebury ring. The latter will be seen to play its own part and provide a check on the whole result.

Using all the data but excluding circles where the uncertainty in the measured diameter exceeds 1 ft, we desire to find definite answers to the following questions.

1. Can it be definitely established that a universal unit of length was in use in all parts of the country?
2. If so, what was its value?

3. Was it ever subdivided, and if so, how?

4. Was a different unit, perhaps a multiple, used for the longer distances?

5. In setting out circles was the measurement made to the inner side of the stone, to the centre of the stone, or to the outside?

6. Was the same unit used for circles, for alignments, and for the distances between circles?

The difficulty we encounter at the outset is that nearly all sites are in a ruinous condition. Stones have fallen out of place or have been bodily displaced by growing trees, by earth movement, or worst of all by well-meaning persons who have re-erected fallen stones without proper excavation to determine the original position and without leaving a record of their activities. Thus a statistical approach is necessary making use of the formulae and methods given in Chapter 2. But it is first necessary to obtain estimates of the diameters, distances between circles, etc., from the sites. It is useless to attempt to measure these quantities directly on the ground. One must first have an accurate survey and for our purpose most published surveys are quite unsuitable. So practically all the data used here are from the author's surveys, except the measurements at Callanish, where Somerville has made a reliable survey perhaps only inaccurate in azimuth and then only by a few minutes of arc, and measurements from a recent survey of Stanton Drew by Prain and Prain.

To obtain the diameter of a circle from a large-scale survey one can use a statistical 'least squares' method (Thom, 1955). This was used for the earlier surveys but latterly, using fairly complete circles, a simpler and very much more rapid method was found to be sufficient. For this method a carefully drawn circle is passed through the stones. The exact size chosen is unimportant as is also the position of the centre. Divide the ring into four quadrants. Mark what appears to be the centre of the base of each stone and measure the distance of this centre from the circle; positive if the stone centre is outside the circle, negative when it is inside. Find the mean for each quadrant separately. Call these means δ_{ne}, δ_{se}, δ_{sw}, and δ_{nw}. Then the required diameter is the diameter of the superimposed circle increased by

$$\tfrac{1}{2}(\delta_{ne} + \delta_{se} + \delta_{sw} + \delta_{nw}).$$

The chosen centre of the superimposed circle should now be moved to the north-east by $\tfrac{1}{2}(\delta_{ne} - \delta_{sw})$ and to the north-west by $\tfrac{1}{2}(\delta_{nw} - \delta_{se})$. The diameter should then be corrected for tape stretch if this has been determined.

In the case of a flattened circle the same kind of procedure can be applied with slight modification provided that the geometrical construction is definitely known.

If it is necessary to use fallen stones then measure to the centre of the end which lies nearest to the superimposed circle. It is seldom possible to say on the site which way the stone has fallen. Often the original top of a fallen stone is found to be lying lower than the original base. This is because the builders sometimes packed small stones round the base of upright stones and these have prevented the lower end of the fallen stone from sinking so much as the top. Diameters obtained from fallen stones only cannot be accurate especially if all have fallen out or all in. Sometimes the stump of a broken stone can be found by prodding with a bayonet. Where only part of a circle remains it may still be possible to obtain an accurate diameter provided the remaining stones are small and upright.

Surveys of some of the circles used will be found in the figures and some have been published elsewhere. These are all on a very much reduced scale but the diameters given in Tables 5.1 and 5.2 were determined from the original surveys, which were plotted to scales which varied from 1/32 to 1/264 according to the size of the circle. The diameters tabulated for Types A, B, and D are the longest diameter of the figure and for the egg-shapes I and II the shortest.

We first demonstrate that there is a presumption amounting to a certainty that a definite unit was used in setting out these rings. It is proposed to call this the Megalithic yard (MY). Two of these might be called the Megalithic fathom. Obviously if the radius is an integral number of yards the diameter will be the same integral number of fathoms. It will appear that the Megalithic yard is 2·72 ft and so the Megalithic fathom is 5·44 ft.

Table 5.1. *Circles and rings of which the diameter is known to ± 1 foot or better*

$$y = \text{diameter (feet)}$$

$$\epsilon_1 = y - 2 \cdot 72 m_1$$

$$\epsilon_2 = y - 5 \cdot 44 m_2 \quad m_1 \text{ and } m_2 \text{ integers}$$

For flattened circles the diameter given is the longest and for eggs the shortest.

Site	Diameter, y (ft)	m_1	ϵ_1	m_2	ϵ_2
Scotland, circles					
B 7/4	10·8	4	−0·08	2	−0·08
A 2/8	11·2	4	+0·32	2	+0·32
P 2/14	12·7	5	−0·90	2	+1·82
P 1/13	16·4	6	+0·08	3	+0·08
B 1/10	16·9	6	+0·58	3	+0·58
N 2/3	20·5	8	−1·26	4	−1·26
B 2/4	20·6	8	−1·16	4	−1·16
G 4/9	20·9	8	−0·86	4	−0·86
A 2/12	21·0	8	−0·76	4	−0·76
P 2/6	21·0	8	−0·76	4	−0·76
B 4/2	21·3	8	−0·46	4	−0·46
A 2/5	21·4	8	−0·36	4	−0·36
M 2/14	21·8	8	+0·04	4	+0·04
B 7/2	22·0	8	+0·24	4	+0·24

Table 5.1 (*cont.*)

Site	Diameter, y (ft)	m_1	ϵ_1	m_2	ϵ_2
G 8/2	23·2	9	−1·28	4	+1·44
H 1/1	24·0	9	−0·48	4	+2·24
N 2/2	24·0	9	−0·48	4	+2·24
P 2/8₁	27·5	10	+0·30	5	+0·30
P 2/8₂	27·5	10	+0·30	5	+0·30
P 2/3	28·0	10	+0·80	5	+0·80
B 7/19	30·1	11	+0·18	6	−2·54
B 7/17	32·0	12	−0·64	6	−0·64
B 3/4	32·5	12	−0·14	6	−0·14
B 2/7	33·4	12	+0·76	6	+0·76
B 6/1	35·6	13	+0·24	7	−2·48
B 1/18	37·6	14	−0·48	7	−0·48
B 7/6	39·2	14	+1·12	7	+1·12
B 2/5	43·6	16	+0·08	8	+0·08
M 2/14	44·1	16	+0·58	8	+0·58
A 2/8	44·2	16	+0·68	8	+0·68
B 1/5	45·0	17	−1·24	8	+1·48
B 2/16	46·8	17	+0·56	9	−2·16
P 2/1	48·5	18	−0·46	9	−0·46
B 1/16	49·0	18	+0·04	9	+0·04
B 3/1	49·7	18	+0·74	9	+0·74
A 8/6	54·9	20	+0·50	10	+0·50
B 3/7	56·4	21	−0·72	10	+2·00
B 2/17	56·9	21	−0·22	10	+2·50
B 1/23	57·0	21	−0·12	10	+2·60
B 7/2	59·1	22	−0·74	11	−0·74
B 2/4	59·2	22	−0·64	11	−0·64
B 2/1	59·3	22	−0·54	11	−0·54
B 6/2	63·0	23	+0·44	12	−2·28
B 1/6	64·0	24	−1·28	12	−1·28
A 1/2	65·1	24	−0·18	12	−0·18
B 2/3	66·9	25	−1·10	12	+1·62
B 1/26	67·2	25	−0·80	12	+1·92
B 6/1	68·4	25	+0·40	13	−2·32
B 7/19	69·1	25	+1·10	13	−1·62
B 2/16	73·3	27	−0·14	13	+2·58
B 2/8	74·1	27	+0·66	14	−2·06
B 7/18	74·3	27	+0·86	14	−1·86
B 3/1	75·1	28	−1·06	14	−1·06
B 7/12	76·0	28	−0·16	14	−0·16
G 4/14	82·1	30	+0·50	15	+0·50
B 7/15	82·9	30	+1·30	15	+1·30
B 2/2	83·2	31	−1·12	15	+1·60
G 4/3	89·1	33	−0·46	16	+2·26
B 4/4	92·0	34	−0·48	17	−0·48
B 7/1₁	103·9	38	+0·34	19	+0·34
B 7/1₂	104·2	38	+0·84	19	+0·84
B 1/8	108·4	40	−0·40	20	−0·40
B 5/1	110·0	40	+1·20	20	+1·20
B 7/16	113·2	42	−1·04	21	−1·04
B 7/15	119·9	44	+0·22	22	+0·22
N 1/13	188·3	69	+0·62	35	−2·10

Table 5.1 (*cont.*)

Site	Diameter, y (ft)	m_1	ϵ_1	m_2	ϵ_2
Scotland, Type A					
G 7/4	37·7	14	−0·38	7	−0·38
B 7/12	43·0	16	−0·52	8	−0·52
H 1/1	43·3	16	−0·22	8	−0·22
G 4/12	54·5	20	+0·10	10	+0·10
G 7/2	65·5	24	+0·22	12	+0·22
B 7/16	66·8	25	−1·20	12	+1·52
G 3/7	69·3	25	+1·30	13	−1·42
Scotland, Type B					
A 1/2	16·0	6	−0·32	3	−0·32
B 1/9	28·0	10	+0·80	5	+0·80
B 2/6	58·9	22	−0·94	11	−0·94
Scotland, egg-shaped rings					
B 7/18	38·3	14	+0·22	7	+0·22
G 9/15	43·9	16	+0·38	8	+0·38
B 2/4	76·1	28	−0·06	14	−0·06
B 7/1	103·6	38	+0·24	19	−0·24
G 9/10	136·0	50	+0·00	25	+0·00
Scotland, compound rings					
B 7/10	60·0	22	+0·16	11	+0·16
England and Wales, circles					
S 2/4	11·9	4	+1·02	2	+1·02
S 5/2	12·0	4	+1·12	2	+1·12
W 2/1	13·2	5	−0·40	2	+2·32
S 5/2	13·6	5	0·00	2	+2·72
W 8/3	17·2	6	+0·88	3	+0·88
S 5/2	19·3	7	+0·26	4	−2·46
S 2/5	22·3	8	+0·54	4	+0·54
L 2/13	24·0	9	−0·48	4	+2·24
W 11/2	24·3	9	−0·18	4	+2·54
L 5/1	27·7	10	+0·50	5	+0·50
S 5/2	30·9	11	+0·98	6	−1·74
L 3/1	31·5	12	−1·14	6	−1·14
W 13/1	32·7	12	+0·06	6	+0·06
S 5/2	34·3	13	−1·06	6	+1·66
D 1/3	35·5	13	+0·14	7	−2·58
S 2/4	41·2	15	+0·40	8	−2·32
W 6/2	42·0	15	+1·20	8	−1·52
W 11/2	43·7	16	+0·18	8	+0·18
W 9/4	43·7	16	+0·18	8	+0·18
S 5/2	46·8	17	+0·56	9	−2·16
S 1/2	49·6	18	+0·64	9	+0·64
L 1/6B	49·7	18	+0·74	9	+0·74
L 1/13	49·7	18	+0·74	9	+0·74
L 1/6D	52·0	19	+0·32	10	−2·40
S 1/10	53·6	20	−0·80	10	−0·80

Table 5.1 (*cont.*)

Site	Diameter, y (ft)	m_1	ϵ_1	m_2	ϵ_2
L 1/6C	54·6	20	+0·20	10	+0·20
W 5/2	55·5	20	+1·10	10	+1·10
W 11/5	58·6	22	−1·24	11	−1·24
S 5/2	64·8	24	−0·48	12	−0·48
W 11/4	68·2	25	+0·20	13	−2·52
S 1/11	71·6	26	+0·88	13	+0·88
W 9/2	73·2	27	−0·24	13	+2·48
W 11/2	76·3	28	+0·14	14	+0·14
S 1/14	77·8	29	−1·08	14	+1·64
S 2/3	81·4	30	−0·20	15	−0·20
S 1/6	81·5	30	−0·10	15	−0·10
L 2/13	86·0	32	−1·04	16	−1·04
L 1/3	93·7	34	+1·22	17	+1·22
S 6/1	103·6	38	+0·24	19	+0·24
S 2/1	104·5	38	+1·14	19	+1·14
S 1/1	107·6	40	−1·20	20	−1·20
S 1/5	108·3	40	−0·50	20	−0·50
S 2/1	108·5	40	−0·30	20	−0·30
S 1/1	113·7	42	−0·54	21	−0·54
S 5/2	129·7	48	−0·86	24	−0·86
S 1/4	147·0	54	+0·12	27	+0·12

England and Wales, Type A

Site	Diameter, y (ft)	m_1	ϵ_1	m_2	ϵ_2
S 1/3	38·6	14	+0·52	7	+0·52
D 1/9	54·2	20	−0·20	10	−0·20
S 1/16	71·6	26	+0·88	13	+0·88
D 2/2	76·0	28	−0·16	14	−0·16
D 2/1	93·3	34	+0·82	17	+0·82
L 1/1	107·8	40	−1·00	20	−1·00
S 1/8	139·7	51	+0·98	26	−1·74

England and Wales, Type B

Site	Diameter, y (ft)	m_1	ϵ_1	m_2	ϵ_2
D 1/7	47·7	18	−1·26	9	−1·26
S 2/2	67·4	25	−0·60	12	+2·12
S 1/13	82·6	30	+1·00	15	+1·00
D 1/8	86·6	32	−0·44	16	−0·44

England and Wales, Type D

Site	Diameter, y (ft)	m_1	ϵ_1	m_2	ϵ_2
L 1/10	88·9	33	−0·86	16	+1·86
S 1/7	150·7	55	+1·10	28	−1·62

England and Wales, egg-shaped rings

Site	Diameter, y (ft)	m_1	ϵ_1	m_2	ϵ_2
W 11/3	59·8	22	−0·04	11	−0·04
S 1/1	136·7	50	+0·70	25	+0·70

England and Wales, compound rings

Site	Diameter, y (ft)	m_1	ϵ_1	m_2	ϵ_2
W 5/1	38·2	14	+0·12	7	+0·12
W 6/1	86·9	32	−0·14	16	−0·14

Table 5.2. *Diameters known with less accuracy*

Site		Diameter (ft)	Site		Diameter (ft)
Scotland					
N 2/3	Shin River	13·6	B 3/3	Raedykes	60±
M 1/9	Ardnacross	12	P 1/19	Croftmoraig	60
"	"	15	M 4/2	Balemartin	65±
P 1/4	Weem	15·4	B 1/11	Balquhain	67·4
P 1/10	Fowlis Wester	15	B 1/7	Kirtkown of Bourtie	71
G 8/7	Dere Street	19	B 2/18	Tillyfourie Hill	72±
P 1/7	Aberfeldy	19	B 2/11	Cairnfauld	75±
H 7/9	Strathaird	21±	P 1/5	Weem	76
G 9/11	Ninestone Rig	21	B 1/23	Yonder Bognie	80±
P 2/4	Courthill	22·8	B 4/1	Carnoussie House	84
P 1/14	Tullybeagles Lodge	23	B 1/13	Old Rayne	86±
B 7/10	Easter Delfour	23·6	H 4/2	Gramisdale (S)	88
B 4/1	Carnoussie House	27	H 4/1	" (N)	87±
P 1/14	Tullybeagles Lodge	31·4±	B 2/14	Leylodge	97
H 6/5	Bernera (Barra)	32±	B 6/2	Moyness	98·5
G 7/3	Wamphrey	38	G 6/2	Auldgirth	100·0
P 1/19	Croftmoraig	41	H 3/17	*Pobull Fhinn*	124±
G 7/4	*Loupin Stanes* (W)	44±	G 7/5	*Girdle Stanes*	131±
B 1/1	Strichen	44	H 3/18	*Sornach Coir Fhinn*	139
B 3/4	Raedykes	47	N 1/5	Forse, Latheron	157·5
P 3/2	Blackgate	55	G 6/1	*Twelve Apostles*	
B 1/26	Loanhead	54		Type B	288·4
B 2/14	Leylodge	54 (?)	G 7/6	*Whitcastles*	
				Special Type	184·8
England					
L 2/11	Castlehowe Scar	21±	Type A		
L 6/2	Staintondale	32	L 1/6	Burnmoor E	104
S 4/3	Hampton Down	35·6	L 2/14	Orton	146
D 1/4	*Ninestone Close*	42·5			
W 9/5	St. Nicholas	43±	Type B		
L 1/9	Glassonby	46·5	L 2/12	Harberwain	49
L 2/10	Gunnerkeld	48±	S 4/2	Kingston Russell	91
L 1/12	Lacre	53	L 3/4	Lilburn	100±
L 1/6	Burnmoor A	71	S 1/12	Porthmeor	113
L 2/10	Gunnerkeld	100±	L 1/7	*Long Meg, etc.*	358·8
L 1/14	Dean Moor	110			
L 1/2	Elva Plain	113·4			
W 4/1	Penbedw Hall	116±			
S 3/1	Stanton Drew	372·4			

Let us take, in the notation of Chapter 2, $2\delta = 5\cdot44$, and examine the residuals (ϵ_2) of the diameters from integral fathoms. That is, we put

$$\epsilon_2 = |y - 5\cdot44m_2|$$

where y is the diameter in feet and m_2 is the integer which gives the smallest ϵ_2. For all the 145 diameters in Table 5.1 we find $\Sigma\epsilon_2^2 = 238\cdot68$, so

$$s^2 = \Sigma\,\epsilon_2^2/n = 1\cdot646 \quad \text{and} \quad s^2/\delta^2 = 0\cdot222.$$

If there were an *a priori* reason for expecting that the diameters were set out in units of 5·44 ft then we might enter Fig. 2.1 with $n = 145$ and $s^2/\delta^2 = 0.222$. We should find that the probability that the hypothesis is correct is so high that the point is off the figure to the right showing a probability level of about 10^{-5} or 0·001 per cent. If we deny that there is an *a priori* reason for the hypothesis then we calculate

$$C = \sqrt{n}(\tfrac{1}{3}-s^2/\delta^2)$$

and find $C = 1.33$, thus showing that we can accept the existence of the fathom for the diameter and so of the yard for the radius with complete confidence.

From a common-sense point of view we do not need to depend on this last step. We can say that the Megalithic fathom was first demonstrated in 1955. So from that date we expect all future work to show the same unit. Thus the many surveys made subsequent to 1955 can be analysed by the method used on p. 40 and will show such a probability level as to remove all doubt.

In setting out a circle one uses the radius and so it is probable that it was the half-fathom or yard of 2·72 ft which was the unit. It will, however, be shown later that the yard was sometimes halved when used for alignments and ellipses. Accordingly we shall analyse the diameters in terms of the yard to determine the exact value of the latter and of the additive constant β; thus we allow for the possibility of half-yards happening sometimes in the radius.

We write $$\epsilon_1 = y - 2.72m_1.$$

The values of m_1 and ϵ_1 are given in columns 3 and 4 (Table 5.1). We first show that the residuals do not increase seriously with increasing size of circle. To do this the data are divided into four groups according to the size of the diameter and the variance is found for each group. The results are shown in Table 5.3.

Table 5.3

Group	Diameters between	n	$\Sigma\epsilon_1^2$	$s^2 = (\Sigma\epsilon_1^2)/n$	$\sigma = \sqrt{s^2}$
1	0 and 31 ft	35	15·27	0·436	0·66
2	31 ,, 54 ,,	35	14·53	0·416	0·65
3	54 ,, 76 ,,	37	19·31	0·522	0·72
4	76 ,, 189 ,,	38	21·91	0·577	0·76

It will be seen how far wrong it would be to take σ proportional to the diameter. In fact it appears that σ changes so little that the formulae for constant σ are appropriate. Making the rather long calculations indicated we find from the figures in Table 5.1 the values in Table 5.4.

Table 5.4

	n	Σy	Σm_1	Σm_1^2	$\Sigma m_1 y$
England and Wales, circles only	46	2688·5	987	28391	77189·3
Scotland ,, ,,	66	3540·1	1304	35346	96094·0
Britain ,, ,,	112	6228·6	2291	63737	173283·3
England and Wales, all types	63	4115·2	1511	46995	127893·4
Scotland ,, ,,	82	4481·0	1650	44564	121165·1
Britain ,, ,,	145	8596·2	3161	91559	249058·5

Using the formulae of p. 9 the values in Table 5.5 immediately follow.

Table 5.5

	β	2δ	$\Sigma m_1 y/\Sigma m_1^2$
England, circles only	+0·23 ft	2·704 ft	2·719 ft
Scotland ,, ,,	−0·28	2·729	2·719
Britain ,, ,,	0·00	2·719	2·719
England, all types	+0·22	2·714	2·721
Scotland ,, ,,	−0·25	2·728	2·719
Britain ,, ,,	−0·07	2·722	2·720

The range of the values obtained for β is merely a reflection of the essential difficulty of determining this quantity. One or two poorly determined diameters, especially at the lower end of the scale, can have a large effect. A reasonably accurate value can only be expected if we have a large number of measurements well spread through the scale. For this reason we must give a high weight to the result for Britain as a whole, namely −0·07 ft. But the standard error of this quantity as determined by the formula of p. 9 is ±0·06 ft. So we have no reason for believing β to be significantly different from zero. Suppose that the stones in the circles have an average thickness of b ft, measured radially, and suppose that the erectors measured the diameters to the inner side of the stones. If we now come along and measure to the centres of the stones then all our deduced diameters will be too large by roughly b and will be represented by

$$2·72m_1+b.$$

The thickness of the stones actually ranges from under a foot to several feet. So the supposition that the erectors measured to the inside of the stones must be wrong. The explanation of β being zero is of course that the erectors measured to the stone centres. Perhaps where the stones formed a retaining wall the measurement may have been taken to the outside of the wall, i.e. the outside relative to the rubble filling behind the wall.

Taking then $\beta = 0$ we are entitled to use the simpler formulae of Case 1 (*a*) and to deduce the value of the yard from $\Sigma m_1 y/\Sigma m_1^2$. These values are given in the last column (Table 5.5). An estimate of the standard error can be made by the formulae given and so the data of the main table (Table 5.1) give finally

$$1 \text{ MY} = 2 \cdot 720 \pm 0 \cdot 003 \text{ ft.}$$

A further conclusion is that this unit was in use from one end of Britain to the other. It is evident from Table 5.5 that it is not possible to detect by statistical examination any difference between the values determined from the English and Scottish circles. There must have been a headquarters from which standard rods were sent out but whether this was in these islands or on the Continent the present investigation cannot determine. The length of the rods in Scotland cannot have differed from that in England by more than 0·03 in or the difference would have shown up in Table 5.5. If each small community had obtained the length by copying the rod of its neighbour to the south the accumulated error would have been much greater than this.

Circles of which the diameters are known with less accuracy

A list of these circles with their estimated diameters is given in Table 5.2. The uncertainty may be because of an indifferent survey but in most cases it lies in the ruinous condition of the site. An example is the circle in Strathaird, Skye. Here only three upright stones remain, unfortunately adjacent. The others were never seen, being buried in peat, but prodding revealed their position roughly. The circle almost certainly belongs to the 8-MY diameter group but of course no accuracy is possible.

Circles from other sources

There are many circles in Britain which the author has not yet surveyed. The number is certainly fifty but it may well be 100. Published plans of a number of these will be found scattered in books and journals and many more circles are mentioned as being in existence or as having vanished. Even when the published plans are based on accurate surveys the scales are usually too small to permit the diameters to be estimated nearer than ±1 per cent. The surveys by R. H. Worth (1953) seem to be reliable, but when he states a diameter there is a suspicion that he refers to the inside measurement.

A list of circles from various sources is given in Table 5.6. Circles surveyed by the author are excluded. An attempt was made to survey the Fedw Circle but it was found to be in such a ruinous condition that without clearing and excavation nothing could be done. Apparently in 1861 it was still complete. Many other recorded sites were visited only to find the ground cleared. Of the great circle, the Gray Yauds, only one stone remained. In several places the local people admitted that there had been stones there and in others the near-by walls built with large stones showed where the circle had gone.

The diameters given in the table for the various rings at Stonehenge were scaled from the published Ministry of Works survey. This survey carries two scales, one in metres and one in feet, but unfortunately these scales differ by about 1¼ per cent. All that one can do is to take a mean.

Table 5.6. *Circles from other sources*

Site	Diameter (ft)	Source	Remarks
Langston Moor	58·0	Worth	Ref. 33
Cordon Whitemoor	67·0	,,	
Down Ridge	82·0	,,	
Buttern Hill	82·0	,,	
Scorhill	89·0	,,	
Sherberton	97·0	,,	
Image Wood	11·3	Keiller	Ref. 13
Cairnwell	28·0	,,	
Binghill	33·6	,,	
Raes of Cluny	54·2	,,	
Auld Kirk o' Tough	102·7	,,	
Egryn Abbey	111·0	Hawkes	
,, ,,	159·0	,,	
Crick Barrow	92·0	North	
Rempston	76	Piggott	
The Fedw Circle	77·6	*Arch. Camb.* 1861	
Zadlee	27·2	St. Act. East Lothian	
East Lothian 240	40·5	,, ,, ,, ,,	Type A
Cerrig Pryfaid	71·5	*R. Com. on An. Mon.*, Vol. 1	
The Druids' Circle	83	,, ,, ,, ,, ,, ,,	
Isle of Purbeck	76	Antiquity	
Barpa Langass	82·6	St. Act. 137 N. Uist	Type A
Brogar	340·5		
Stonehenge			
Aubrey Holes	285		
Y Holes	177		
Z Holes	128		

In spite of these difficulties and uncertainties the mean value of the yard as deduced by the usual statistical method from the values in Table 5.6, with or without Stonehenge, is again 2·72 ft.

The sizes of the circles

The erectors of Megalithic monuments were evidently interested in getting the dimensions of their structures to be multiples of certain units of length. Since they were capable of measuring to a high degree of accuracy how does it come about that many circles which seem to have been undisturbed have mean diameters which differ by appreciable amounts from what were presumably their nominal diameters? It will be shown that in a significant number of cases the discrepancy is produced by a small adjustment made by the erectors to the diameter, to bring the circumference nearer to an integer. This desire to have both dimensions integral has a further consequence in that at many sites it affects the integer chosen for the diameter.

The distribution of known circle diameters is shown in Fig. 5.1. Here each circle is represented by a small gaussian area placed at the appropriate diameter. The ordinates of the gaussians are added so that we get a kind of histogram showing the favoured diameters. The true circles are shown above the base line and the flattened circles below. The circles listed in the main table (Table 5.1) have diameters known with an uncertainty between ± 0.3 and ± 1.0 ft. These are shown by hatched areas. The circle diameters listed in Table 5.6 have been collected from various published sources and are considered to have an uncertainty of about 1 ft. Accordingly the same gaussian area has been used but unshaded. The diameters in Table 5.2 are uncertain but those which are considered to be known to about ± 1.5 ft are shown with a wider and flatter area unshaded. A key to the areas used is given in the figure.

Three scales are shown. Below the base the diameter is given in feet and immediately above the histogram in Megalithic yards. Above this again the corresponding circumference is given in Megalithic yards. In examining the figure bear in mind that some of the diameters may be in error by 1 ft or more, although the half-width of the shaded gaussians is only about half this.

The figure is in itself a pictorial proof of the existence of the Megalithic yard, but it contains much more information. Most of the diameters are seen to lie near to an even number of yards. In other words the radii are integers. But there are also concentrations at odd numbers, so the designers frequently used half-yards for the radius. We shall see that in the alignments also the yard was sometimes divided in two and even in four.

In the histogram there are concentrations at diameters 10, 20, 30, and 40 MY but only a few at 15, 25, and 35. The concentrations at 4, 8, 12, 16, 20, 24, and 28 are obvious. The reason for this last sequence becomes evident when we consider the circumferences.

The circumferences

Perhaps the most striking feature of the circumferences shown in Fig. 5.1 is that large concentrations occur at $12\frac{1}{2}$, 25, $37\frac{1}{2}$, 50, $62\frac{1}{2}$, 75, and $87\frac{1}{2}$, all multiples of $12\frac{1}{2}$. If we accept the approximation $\pi = 3\frac{1}{8}$ then a circle with diameter 4 has a circumference of $12\frac{1}{2}$. So the above sequence of circumferences follows from a diameter sequence of 4, 8, 12, etc. This immediately explains why there are so many circles with a diameter of 8 or 16, since these have circumferences very close to 25 and 50 MY.

For the larger circles the error in taking $\pi = 3\frac{1}{8}$ would begin to show up seriously. In fact with a diameter of 28 the approximation $\pi = 3\frac{1}{7}$ gives $P = 88$ and we may suppose that this rather than the poorer value of $3\frac{1}{8} \times 28$ or 87·5 was the reason for the four circles having this diameter. The reader may also have noticed the small groups at diameters 7, 14, and 21.

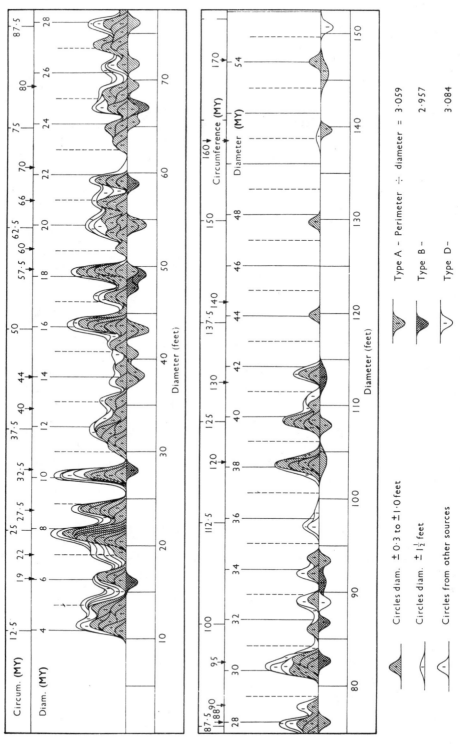

Fig. 5.1. Histogram of observed diameters.

Turning to the large circles beyond the range of Fig. 5.1 we find

Aubrey Holes, Stonehenge $D \doteqdot 105$ MY giving $P = 329 \cdot 87$
Avebury (inner ring)   125 $392 \cdot 70$
Brogar   125 $392 \cdot 70$
Stanton Drew   137 $430 \cdot 39$

If these circumferences are all intended to be multiples of $2\frac{1}{2}$ we can write them 330, 392·5, and 430 giving the interesting approximations for π: $3\frac{1}{7}$, 3·1400, and 3·139.

Looking again at the histogram it is seen that many of the peaks do not lie at what might be called the nominal diameters. Consider, for example, the concentrations at or near to 10, 18, 30, and 38 MY. Multiplying by π we find 31·4, 56·5, 94·2, and 119·4. Assuming that a multiple of $2\frac{1}{2}$ was required these circles were perhaps enlarged slightly to bring the circumferences nearer to 32·5, 57·5, 95, and 120. It will be seen that the peak in all four concentrations lies a little to the right of the nominal diameter but falls just short of the circumference which is a multiple of $2\frac{1}{2}$. There is ample evidence that, when they wanted, these people could measure with an accuracy better than 1 in 500, so it is certain that they knew what they were doing when they made adjustments of this kind. Since we do not know the reason for their preoccupation with integers we cannot tell how worried the designer would be when other considerations forced him to use a diameter which had to be adjusted to make the circumference fit. Had he to demonstrate his solution to a visiting inspector?

In the next section a statistical examination will be made of the above idea that when the diameter and the circumference were irreconcilable an adjustment was made to the diameter so that the circumference fitted a little better.

The adjustment of the diameter

The examination of the diameter distribution (Fig. 5.1) has given the definite impression that it was more important to have the perimeter a multiple of $2\frac{1}{2}$ than to have it an integer. Further evidence comes from the eggs and ellipses. At Woodhenge, for example, the perimeters are all multiples of 10 and to attain this the integral condition for practically all the radii was sacrificed although the basic 12, 35, 37 triangle was retained. At Moel ty Uche (W 5/1) the enclosing circle has a diameter of 14 so its circumference is $3\frac{1}{7} \times 14$ or 44. But this was not enough and an elaborate geometrical construction was used to obtain a perimeter of 42·8 as an approximation to $42\frac{1}{2}$.

Accordingly, in the examination to be made we assume that the target for the circumferences of circles (P) was a multiple of $2\frac{1}{2}$. Further we shall assume arbitrarily that the condition was satisfied if P was within one quarter of $2\frac{1}{2}$ (i.e. 0·625) of being a multiple. So we find that the following diameters satisfy

4	16	28	39	51
7	19	31	42	54
8	20	32	43	etc.
11	23	35	46	
12	24	36	47	
15	27	38	50	

each of these when multiplied by π being within 0·625 of a multiple of $2\frac{1}{2}$.

We now proceed to examine what the designer did when he used a diameter which did not satisfy. All such circles are listed in Table 5.7, with the actual measured diameters in feet designated by y and in Megalithic yards by d. The actual circumferences are designated $P_a \; (= \pi d)$ and the amount by which this exceeds a multiple of $2\frac{1}{2}$ is given under ϵ_{pa}. The nominal diameters appear under D (MY) and the corresponding circumferences under $P_n \; (= \pi D)$. The excess of P_n over a multiple of $2\frac{1}{2}$ is called ϵ_{pn}. These values of ϵ_{pn} are, of course, all greater than 0·625.

We see that of the five circles having a nominal diameter D of 9 all are set out with an actual diameter d slightly smaller than 9. Had the diameter been 9 the circumference would have been $P_n = 28\cdot27$. By reducing the diameter slightly the circumference was brought nearer to $27\frac{1}{2}$, a multiple of $2\frac{1}{2}$.

Table 5.7. *Circles for which* $\pi \times$ *(nominal diameter) is not near a multiple of* $2\frac{1}{2}$ *MY, i.e. where* $|\pi D - 2\frac{1}{2}m| > 0\cdot625$

Material from Table 5.1 only

$$y = \text{actual diam. (ft)} \qquad D = \text{nominal diameter (MY)}$$
$$d = \quad \text{,,} \quad \text{,,} \quad \text{(MY)} \qquad P_n = \pi D$$
$$P_a = \pi d \; (= 1\cdot155y)$$
$$\epsilon_d = (d - D) \qquad \epsilon_{pa} = (P_a - 2\frac{1}{2}m) \qquad \epsilon_{pn} = (P_n - 2\frac{1}{2}m)$$
$$m = \text{appropriate whole number}$$

Site	y (ft)	d (MY)	ϵ_d	P_a (MY)	ϵ_{pa}	D (MY)	P_n (MY)	ϵ_{pn}
P 2/14	12·7	4·67	−0·33	14·67	−0·33	5	15·71	+0·71
W 2/1	13·2	4·85	−0·15	15·24	+0·24	,,	,,	,,
S 5/2	13·6	5·00	0	15·71	+0·71	,,	,,	,,
P 1/13	16·4	6·03	+0·03	18·94	−1·06	6	18·85	−1·15
B 1/10	16·9	6·21	+0·21	19·52	−0·48	,,	,,	,,
W 8/3	17·2	6·32	+0·32	19·87	−0·13	,,	,,	,,
G 8/2	23·2	8·53	−0·47	26·80	−0·70	9	28·27	+0·77
H 1/1	24·0	8·82	−0·18	27·72	+0·22	,,	,,	,,
N 2/2	24·0	8·82	−0·18	27·72	+0·22	,,	,,	,,
L 2/13	24·0	8·82	−0·18	27·72	+0·22	,,	,,	,,
W 11/2	24·3	8·93	−0·07	28·07	+0·57	,,	,,	,,
P 2/8	27·5	10·11	+0·11	31·76	−0·74	10	31·42	−1·08
P 2/8	,,	,,	,,	,,	,,	,,	,,	,,

Table 5.7 (*cont.*)

Site	y (ft)	d (MY)	ϵ_d	P_a (MY)	ϵ_{pa}	D (MY)	P_n (MY)	ϵ_{pn}
L 5/1	27·7	10·18	+0·18	31·99	−0·51	10	31·42	−1·08
P 2/3	28·0	10·29	+0·29	32·34	−0·16	,,	,,	,,
S 5/2	34·3	12·61	−0·39	39·62	−0·38	13	40·84	+0·84
D 1/3	35·5	13·05	+0·05	41·00	+1·00	,,	,,	,,
B 6/1	35·6	13·09	+0·09	41·11	+1·11	,,	,,	,,
B 1/18	37·6	13·82	−0·18	43·43	+0·93	14	43·98	−1·02
B 7/6	39·2	14·41	+0·41	45·28	+0·28	,,	,,	,,
B 1/5	45·0	16·54	−0·46	51·97	−0·53	17	53·41	+0·91
B 2/16	46·8	17·21	+0·21	54·05	−0·95	,,	,,	,,
S 5/2	46·8	17·21	+0·21	54·05	−0·95	,,	,,	,,
P 2/1	48·5	17·83	−0·17	56·02	+1·02	18	56·55	−0·95
B 1/16	49·0	18·01	+0·01	56·60	−0·90	,,	,,	,,
S 1/2	49·6	18·24	+0·24	57·29	−0·21	,,	,,	,,
B 3/1	49·7	18·27	+0·27	57·40	−0·10	,,	,,	,,
L 1/4	,,	,,	,,	,,	,,	,,	,,	,,
L 1/13	,,	,,	,,	,,	,,	,,	,,	,,
B 3/7	56·4	20·74	−0·26	65·14	+0·14	21	65·97	+0·97
B 2/17	56·9	20·92	−0·08	65·72	+0·72	,,	,,	,,
B 1/23	57·0	20·96	−0·04	65·83	+0·83	,,	,,	,,
W 11/5	58·6	21·54	−0·46	67·67	+0·17	22	69·12	−0·88
B 7/2	59·1	21·73	−0·27	68·26	+0·76	,,	,,	,,
B 2/4	59·2	21·76	−0·24	68·38	+0·88	,,	,,	,,
B 2/1	59·3	21·80	−0·20	68·49	+0·99	,,	,,	,,
B 2/3	66·9	24·60	−0·40	77·27	−0·23	25	78·54	+1·04
B 1/26	67·2	24·71	−0·29	77·62	+0·12	,,	,,	,,
W 11/4	68·2	25·07	+0·07	78·77	−1·23	,,	,,	,,
B 6/1	68·4	25·15	+0·15	79·00	−1·00	,,	,,	,,
B 7/19	69·1	25·40	+0·40	79·81	−0·19	,,	,,	,,
S 1/11	71·6	26·32	+0·32	82·70	+0·20	26	81·68	−0·82
S 1/14	77·8	28·60	−0·40	89·86	−0·14	29	91·11	+1·11
S 2/3	81·4	29·93	−0·07	94·02	−0·98	30	94·25	−0·75
S 1/6	81·5	29·96	−0·04	94·13	−0·87	,,	,,	,,
G 4/14	82·1	30·18	+0·18	94·83	−0·17	,,	,,	,,
B 7/15	82·9	30·48	+0·48	95·75	+0·75	,,	,,	,,
G 4/3	89·3	32·83	−0·17	103·14	+0·64	· 33	103·67	+1·17
B 4/4	92·0	33·82	−0·18	106·26	−1·24	34	106·81	+0·69
L 1/3	93·7	34·45	+0·45	108·22	+0·72	,,	,,	,,
S 1/1	107·6	39·56	−0·44	124·28	−0·72	40	125·66	−0·66
S 1/5	108·3	39·82	−0·18	125·09	+0·09	,,	,,	,,
B 1/8	108·4	39·85	−0·15	125·20	+0·20	,,	,,	,,
S 2/1	108·5	39·89	−0·11	125·32	+0·32	,,	,,	,,
B 5/1	110·0	40·44	+0·44	127·05	−0·45	,,	,,	,,
B 7/15	119·9	44·08	+0·08	138·48	+0·98	44	138·23	+0·73
S 5/2	129·7	47·68	−0·32	149·80	−0·20	48	150·80	+0·80
N 1/13	188·3	69·23	+0·23	217·49	−0·01	69	216·77	−0·73

$\Sigma\epsilon^2$		4·0114		24·6227		46·8803		
n		58		58		58		
$s^2 = (\Sigma\epsilon^2)/n$		0·0691		0·425		0·808		
Quantum $= 2\delta$		1·00		2·5		2·5		
s^2/δ^2		0·276		0·272		0·517		
Probability level		8%		6%		—		

We see that in the same way and for the same reason the four circles with a nominal diameter of 10 were increased and of the six with $D = 18$ five were increased, thus in both sets improving the circumference. An examination of the whole table shows, however, that not all have suitable adjustments. This may be due to errors or uncertainties in the determination of the diameters. So we must apply a statistical method to see if the improvements are significant.

The 'lumped variance' of the actual circumference P_a is

$$s^2 = (\Sigma \epsilon_{pa}^2) \div n = 0\cdot425 \quad \text{(see Table 5.7).}$$

The quantum 2δ is $2\frac{1}{2}$. This makes $s^2/\delta^2 = 0\cdot272$ and so from Fig. 2.1 we see that the probability level is about 6 per cent. In the ordinary way this is not low enough for acceptance of the hypothesis, but in the context it is definitely significant. We are dealing with a set of data chosen so that with no adjustments to the diameters we ought to get something very far from significant. To show this, suppose that these circles had been set out with their exact nominal diameters. The residuals would then have been those in the last column, which is seen to give $s^2 = 0\cdot808$ or $s^2/\delta^2 = 0\cdot517$. As explained on p. 11, a random distribution would give s^2/δ^2 very near to $\frac{1}{3}$. This has become $0\cdot517$ because we are dealing with nominal diameters chosen because they do not fit. The improvement shown by the actual diameters over the nominal (from $0\cdot517$ to $0\cdot277$) is so great that adjustments in the right direction must have been made by the builders in a significant number of cases. Uncertainties in the surveys would act in a random manner and could produce no improvement of this magnitude.

Full adjustment of the diameters would, in most cases, make the diameter too far from the integral value and so has not in general been made. To look into this the actual diameters in the table have been analysed to see if they have remained near enough to integers to continue to show significance. It will be seen from the figures below the first four columns that the probability level is also about 8 per cent. Thus the adjustments made have left the diameters near enough to integers to show some significance (8 per cent probability level) while making the circumferences significantly multiples of $2\frac{1}{2}$.

The statistical examination just made thus bears out the impression formed from a visual examination of the histogram in showing that when the diametral and circumferential conditions were irreconcilable a compromise was effected.

Possible effect of the above adjustments to diameters on the derived value of the yard

In the investigation into the value of the Megalithic yard made on p. 42 all diameters of reasonable accuracy were used. We have just seen that when the circumference did not measure up to a multiple of $2\frac{1}{2}$ the erectors usually changed the diameter slightly from its integral value. Since this adjustment may have had an effect on the derived value of the yard, the calculation has been repeated retaining only those circles where little or no adjustment was necessary, i.e. where πD was within 0·625 of a multiple of $2\frac{1}{2}$, thus excluding the circles in Table 5.7.

There is some evidence that the non-circular rings were also adjusted, so it would be safer to exclude those with nominal diameters giving perimeters which do not satisfy. The ratios of the perimeter to the main diameter for flattened circles are

Type A—3·0591   Type B—2·9572
Type D—3·0840

With this information we can calculate the perimeters from the nominal diameters and discard those outside the range. From the remainder we find the values in Table 5.8 below.

Table 5.8

	n	Σy	Σm	Σm^2	Σmy
Circles	55	2866·0	1054	27536	74863·2
Non-circular rings	16	1119·4	411	13665	37232·5
All	71	3985·4	1465	41201	112095·7

From these we can deduce that both for the circles alone and for all, β is small (+0·03 and −0·02). So we put $\beta = 0$ and find $2\delta = 2·719$ for the circles and 2·721 for circles and rings together. Thus we obtain a complete check on the previously deduced value.

A possible criticism of these methods of deducing the value of the yard is that we must start off the calculation by using an initial value. Since we used 2·72 as initial value and end up with 2·720 one might wonder if the calculation means anything. In fact, the process is one of successive approximation and what we are seeing here is the result of many years of preliminary work. Some confirmation of the yard can also be obtained from the consideration of the distances between circles given in the next section.

Distances between circles

The distance between circle centres is a satisfactory length to examine for investigating the use of the yard in longer distances. If an accurate survey of a circle exists the centre can be found with a precision equal to or greater than that of the diameter. The distance between two such centres is then an unambiguous length unaffected by any additive constant. There are many places where there are two, three, or more circles in a group. Details from those so far surveyed will be found in Tables 5.9 and 5.10. It will be seen that four of the sites used have three circles in each. If the directions (azimuths) of the sides of the triangle formed by the circle centres are controlled by other considerations (perhaps astronomical) then the length of only one side is

Table 5.9. *Distances between circles*

l = distance between circle centres (feet)

Site		l	Site		l
L 1/6	Burnmoor	122·3	W 2/1	Penmaen-Mawr	829·0
,,	,,	150·4	W 11/2	Trecastle	144·2
,,	,,	340	W 11/4	Usk River	365·8
,,	,,	420	B 7/1	Clava	189·2
,,	,,	1568	,,	,,	232·7
,,	,,	1307	,,	,,	413·7
,,	,,	1297	B 1/26	Loanhead	65·3
,,	,,	1238	B 1/27	Sands of Forvie	132·8±
,,	,,	1375	,,	,, ,, ,,	144·0±
,,	,,	1515	,,	,, ,, ,,	246·8±
S 1/1	Hurlers	419·1	B 3/3	Raedykes	315·5
,,	,,	204·0	B 4/1	Carnoussie	163·1
,,	,,	215·9	G 7/4	Loupin Stanes	65·5
S 2/1	Grey Wethers	128·1	N 2/3	Shin River	119·8
S 3/1	Stanton Drew	381·0	P 1/14	Tullybeagles	54·0
,,	,, ,,	711·5	P 2/8	Shianbank	70·5
,,	,, ,,	1054·0			

Table 5.10. *Distances between circles—Megalithic yards*

Site	L	Site	L	Site	L
P 1/14	19·9	B 4/1	60·0	L 1/6	154·4
B 1/26	24·0	B 7/1	69·6	S 1/1	154·1
G 7/4	24·1	S 1/1	75·0	S 3/1	261·6
P 2/8	25·9	S 1/1	79·4	W 2/1	304·8
N 2/3	44·0	B 7/1	85·6	S 3/1	387·5
L 1/6	44·9	B 1/27	90·7	L 1/6	455·1
S 2/1	47·1	B 3/3	116·0	L 1/6	476·8
B 1/27	48·8	L 1/6	125·0	L 1/6	480·5
B 1/27	52·9	W 11/4	134·5	L 1/6	505·5
W 11/2	53·0	S 3/1	140·1	L 1/6	557·0
L 1/6	55·3	B 7/1	152·1	L 1/6	576·5

disposable; once one side is fixed in length the lengths of the other two follow. At one site there are five circles and so even if there is no restriction on the azimuths out of the ten sides only seven are disposable (p. 33). So to construct such a figure with all ten sides integral multiples of a unit is in general impossible. A great deal of trial and error might result in an approximate solution. Perhaps such an approximation was attempted at Burnmoor (L 1/6), where out of ten lengths eight seem to lie within $\frac{1}{2}$ MY of being multiples of $2\frac{1}{2}$ MY, but this site needs to be resurveyed before we can be certain of the longer lengths. The points just mentioned should be remembered in examining the material presented in Tables 5.9 and 5.10.

In the first table all the distances between circles are collected and given in feet. In the second (Table 5.10) the distances have been converted to

Megalithic yards and arranged in order of size. It may be noticed that the first ten items, i.e. up to a distance of 53 yds, all lie very close to a whole number. These are swamped by the larger values further down the table, as is evident in the analysis given in Table 5.11, but they do contribute to the favourable s^2/δ^2 shown by the half-yard. The use of $2\frac{1}{2}$ MY and 5 MY as units for measuring the longer distances is brought out. The importance of the former measure will become apparent in the study to be made later of the perimeters of ellipses and egg-shaped rings. We have already seen how it affected the diameters of circular rings.

Table 5.11. *Probability levels*

Assumed quantum 2δ (MY)	$\Sigma\epsilon^2$	$s^2 = \dfrac{\Sigma\epsilon^2}{n}$	s^2/δ^2	Probability level (Fig. 2.1)
0·5	0·34	0·0103	0·165	0·06%
1·0	2·44	0·074	0·296	30
2·5	12·79	0·39	0·25	5
5·0	45·04	1·36	0·22	2
10·0	395·04	12·0	0·48	—

To appreciate fully the arrangement of the Burnmoor circles let us anticipate the astronomical results for this site. In Table 8.1 it will be seen that at least six of the lines joining the circles give important declinations, one of the lines in both directions. So the azimuths were controlled astronomically, and yet looking at Table 5.10 it appears that of the ten lengths seven are within one unit of being a multiple of 5 and several are much closer. The surrounding mountains helped with the astronomical part of the problem, but to solve this and at the same time satisfy the length requirement seems almost impossible. We shall see at Castle Rigg in the same district another perhaps more striking but not more remarkable example of the combination of geometrical design with astronomical requirements. We begin to see why these people went to such trouble to mark permanently the five points they had established after presumably years of experiment.

The residuals

It is of interest to examine the data in Tables 5.1 and 5.9 by making a histogram of their residuals from the Megalithic yard. For the circles and rings we take

$$\epsilon = |R - 2\cdot72m|, \quad \text{where } R \text{ is the radius,}$$

and for the distances between circles we take

$$\epsilon = |l - 2\cdot72m|.$$

As indicated we do not distinguish between positive and negative values.

A histogram for both lots combined is shown in Fig. 5.2 (*a*). The evidence for the Megalithic yard is of course the high pile at the left, which simply shows the tendency for the various measurements to cluster together round multiples of 2·72 ft. There is also a cluster at the right indicating that some

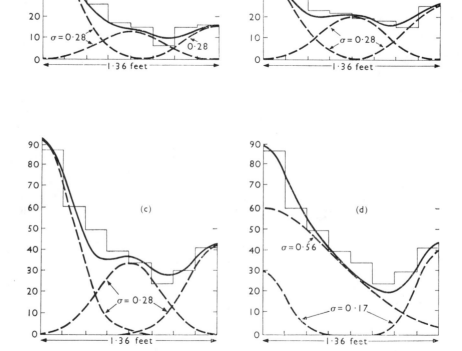

FIG. 5.2. Histograms of deviations, $\epsilon = |l - 2.72\,m|$, compared with some suggested gaussians. In each case the full line shows the sum of the gaussians. (*a*) Radii and distance between circles. (*b*) Distance between stones. (*c*) and (*d*) Radii and distance between circles and distance between stones.

30 per cent of the measures contain a half-yard. There is a suspicion of a concentration in the middle. If real, this indicates the occasional use of the quarter-yard. Three gaussian distributions have been drawn in, each having the same standard deviation (0·28). Summing these gives the full line, which is seen to approximate to the actual histogram, but we are on insecure ground here because there seems to be no rigid mathematical method of investigating this arbitrary subdivision and in fact other gaussians can be drawn to represent the data.

The distances between stones

In view of the difficulty of assigning a probability level to the idea that the yard was subdivided into halves and quarters it was decided to seek other evidence. This is to be found in the distances between stone centres where the stones obviously belong to the same line. We exclude the distances between stones in circles. A histogram of these separately showed nothing. The diverging stone rows in Caithness were also excluded. An analysis of these has already been published (Thom, 1964) and this shows that the spacing in these rows was controlled by other considerations.

A list was made of the distances between the centres of the stones in all the other alignments and stone rows in the author's surveys. Where there is an obvious gap in the row the distance between the stones on either side of the gap was used. Even if a stone is really missing this procedure cannot affect the issue, because if each of the original intervals was an integer then the sum (i.e. the distance measured) is also an integer. All distances over 30 ft were arbitrarily neglected.

It should be said that no two individuals will make the same selection. The reason becomes obvious if Figs. 12.9 and 12.13 are examined. Where one man would include a given stone as being in the line another would pass it over. A first survey of the material was published in 1961. A re-measurement of all the surveys in 1964 (with of course much new material) showed many differences in selection. But the over-all picture remains the same. The up-to-date histogram will be found in Fig. 5.2 (*b*). This shows the deviations from the integral yard. Here again we have concentrations at the ends (yard and half-yard) and the possibility of the quarter-yard. The combination of all the data in Fig. 5.2 (*a*) and (*b*) is shown in Fig. 5.2 (*c*). An attempt has again been made to explain the observed distribution by three gaussians of the same standard deviation. This would seem to be the best explanation, but the kind of thing suggested in Fig. 5.2 (*d*) cannot be entirely ruled out. Here we assume that the majority of the circles set out to the full yard were carelessly done (s.d = 0·56) but that a few and also those using the half-yard were more carefully laid out (s.d. = 0·17). The fit is seen to be reasonable, but the idea of two distinct groups is less attractive.

One fact emerges very clearly and that is that there is no evidence whatsoever of the yard being subdivided into three. This would have shown up by the appearance of a lump in the histograms two-thirds along from the left, i.e. at 0·91 ft. This is just where all three histograms are low; in fact where the combined histogram is at its lowest.

6

CIRCLES AND RINGS

THE stones used for setting out the circles and rings vary greatly in size and shape. Sometimes small boulders of two or three cubic feet were used, sometimes small slabs set on edge along the periphery, but, for the casual visitor, the most impressive circles are those consisting of tall pillars five, ten, or more feet high. Examples of many types will be found in the plans given here and in the references. In most of these surveys the bases of the upright stones are shown cross-hatched or in black. Fallen stones are shown in outline only. A dotted outline usually means that the stone is below ground and its position estimated by prodding with a bayonet. From our present point of view the circle of small slabs is not to be despised. The small stones define the outline with greater accuracy and are very unlikely to have been disturbed. Undoubtedly many such circles have vanished completely. Particularly good examples are seen in Figs. 6.1 and 6.2, where, largely due to the small size of the stones, the geometrical design can be exactly determined. The slabs of the circle at Cauldside (Fig. 6.3) are of such a soft stone that several have weathered away above ground leaving only a crumbling sandy stump below the turf.

There is very little relation between the size of the circle and the size of the stones. Some small circles are built of very large stones. The example mentioned above at Dinnever Hill (S 1/8) is 130 ft across and yet the stones hardly show in the long grass. But the largest circles, Avebury, Stanton Drew, Long Meg and her Daughters, and the Twelve Apostles, are mostly of large stones. It is exceptional to find the stones in a circle of a uniform size or uniformly spaced and only in a few circles are the stones placed on opposite ends of a diameter. There is a suspicion that diametrically opposite stones may define a sight line so this arrangement would only be used where it was desired to define an azimuth. The largest stone in the Castle Rigg circle was certainly used in this way as will be seen later. Cauldside circle (above) uses at least two diameters as indicators of other marks.

The 'recumbent stone circles' of north-east Scotland belong to a class by themselves and will be discussed later. They often had an outer ring of very large uprights with a particularly big slab in the south-west quadrant. These slabs are too large to define of themselves an azimuth as seen from the centre, but they may have supported or located other structures or sighting devices long since rotted away.

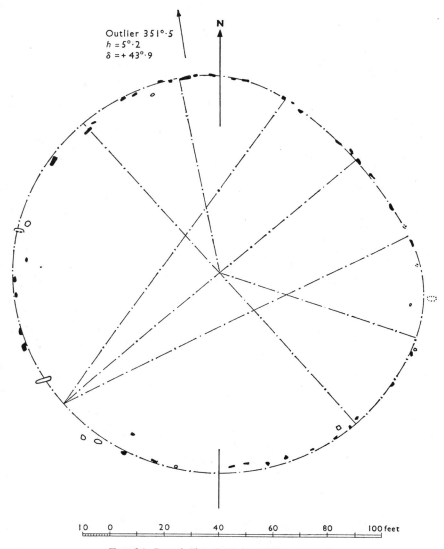

Outlier 351°·5
$h = 5°·2$
$\delta = + 43°·9$

N

10   0   20   40   60   80   100 feet

FIG. 6.1. Rough Tor, S 1/7 (50° 35'·4, 4° 37'·4).

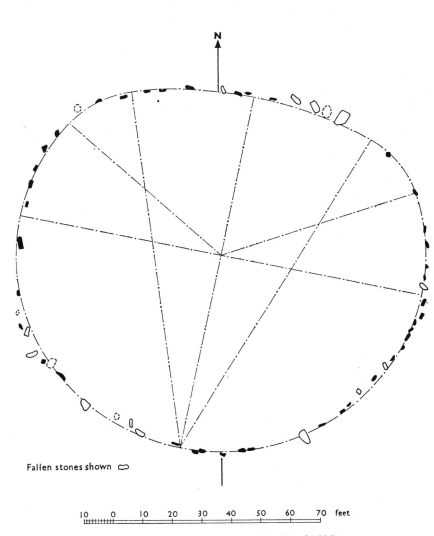

Fallen stones shown ⌒

FIG. 6.2. Dinnever Hill, S 1/8 (50° 35′·4, 4° 38′·8).

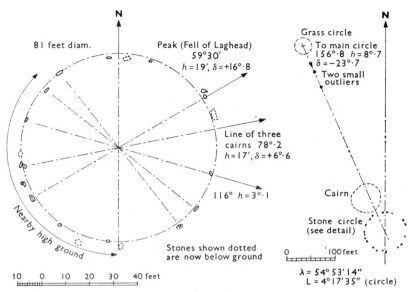

FIG. 6.3. Cauldside, G 4/14.

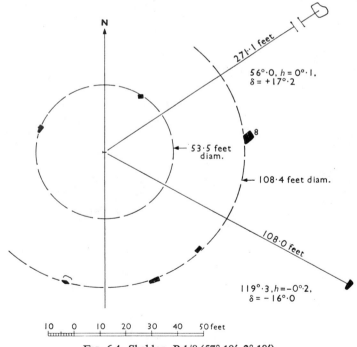

FIG. 6.4. Sheldon, B 1/8 (57° 19′, 2° 18′).

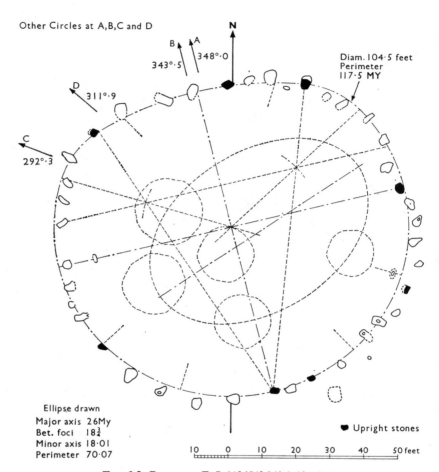

Other Circles at A,B,C and D

N

B   A

343°·5   348°·0

D
311°·9

Diam. 104·5 feet
Perimeter
117·5 MY

C
292°·3

Ellipse drawn
Major axis 26My
Bet. foci 18¾
Minor axis 18·01
Perimeter 70·07

● Upright stones

10   0   10   20   30   40   50 feet

FIG. 6.5. Burnmoor E, L 1/6 (54° 24′·6, 3° 16′·5).

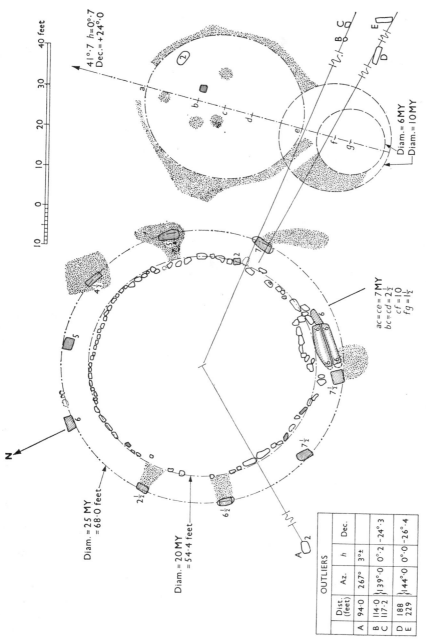

Fig. 6.6. Loanhead, B 1/26 (57° 21′, 2° 25′).

OUTLIERS	Dist. (feet)	Az.	h	Dec.
A	94·0	267°	3°±	
B	114·0	}139°·0	0°·2	-24°·3
C	117·2			
D	188	}144°·0	0°·0	-26°·4
E	229			

41°·7 h=0°·7
Dec.=+24°·0

Diam.= 6 MY
Diam.=10 MY

$ac=ce=7$ MY
$bc=cd=2\frac{1}{2}$
$cf=10$
$fg=\frac{1}{2}$

Diam.= 25 MY
= 68·0 feet

Diam.= 20 MY
= 54·4 feet

40 feet

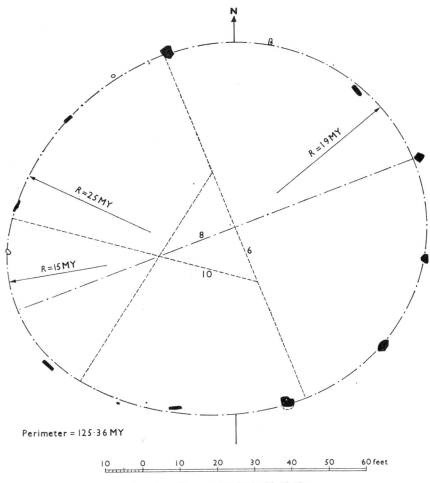

FIG. 6.7. Clava, B 7/1 (57° 29′, 4° 5′).

In looking at a stone circle we see only what remains after more than 3000 years. Much of the smaller detail has probably vanished, as certainly have all those parts of the structure originally made of perishable material. There must have been posts at the centre or centres for setting out and for sighting purposes. It is significant that none of these centres is occupied by a stone although there are several places where a stone stands against the centre of the circle or against one of the auxiliary centres. We may picture all sorts of ancillary structures of wood such as raised platforms, roofed portions, sighting posts, fences, or marked out divisions, but in our ignorance we probably fail completely to picture the complete structure. At some sites we can be

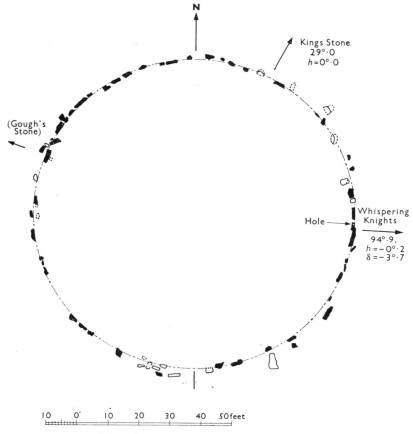

N

Kings Stone
29°·0
$h = 0°·0$

(Gough's
Stone)

Hole ——

Whispering
Knights
94°·9.
$h = -0°·2$
$\delta = -3°·7$

10   0   10   20   30   40   50 feet

FIG. 6.8. Rollright, S 6/1 (51° 58′, 1° 34′).

misled by superimposed modern work; for example, at Sheldon of Bourtie (Fig. 6.4) the walls have evidently been put there long after many of the menhirs had vanished. The walls are so placed that they show their builders to have been in complete ignorance of the original plan, which can only be deduced by making use of our recently acquired knowledge of the units of length used by the original builders. The plan in Fig. 6.4 ignores these walls. But in some places there are remains of structures which presumably belonged to the original plan. For example, in the main circle of the Burnmoor group there are five peculiar hollow cells. These are shown by dotted rings in Fig. 6.5. Perhaps by accident, but more likely by design, four of these lie on an ellipse which has the expected properties of a Megalithic ellipse. Its major and minor axes are 26 and 18 MY and the calculated perimeter is almost exactly 70 MY. The fifth cell lies on the major axis. This

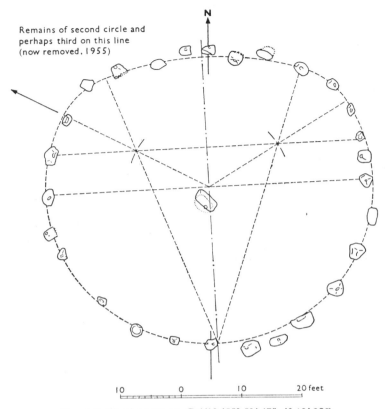

Remains of second circle and
perhaps third on this line
(now removed, 1955)

FIG. 6.9. Cambret Moor, G 4/12 (55° 53′ 47″, 4° 19′ 28″).

Type A circle is very nearly the same size as the Type A circle at Castle Rigg,
also in the Lake District. Curiously enough, in the latter circle can be seen
a grass ring in such a position that if transferred to the Burnmoor circle it
would lie on the ellipse. While this is probably accidental, it shows the
necessity for a careful excavation at both circles. Such an excavation at Loanhead of Daviot shows how much can be discovered (Kilbride-Jones, 1934 and
Fig. 6.6). There, a complex of two circles and an ellipse all aligned on the rising
solstitial sun has been revealed outlined in beds of small stones. Similarly
the clearance at Callanish I (Fig. 11.1) has revealed a peculiar design which
includes a small ellipse, again with its axis indicating the solstitial sun, the
backsight being one of the auxiliary centres of the Type A circle. The importance of these auxiliary centres will also be demonstrated when the astronomical significance of Castle Rigg is discussed. Here we should also mention
the internal structures at Clava B 7/1 (Fig. 6.7; Piggott, 1956), the cells in

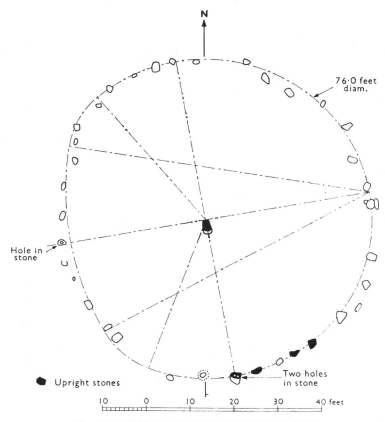

N

76·0 feet
diam.

Hole in
stone

Upright stones

Two holes
in stone

10   0   10   20   30   40 feet

FIG. 6.10. Black Marsh, D 2/2 (52° 35'·5, 2° 59'·9).

other Burnmoor circles, and the isolated stones found inside some circles, notably at the Hurlers (S 1/1) and at the south circle, Stanton Drew.

A cairn supported at its edge by large stones may be removed to provide road-making material. The ring which is left looks like a stone circle. The position becomes more complicated if the cairn was originally inside a circle of free-standing stones. One sees that if one of the Clava cairns was denuded the remains might look like three concentric circles. Traces of what may be entrances or may be sighting directions are found in several free-standing circles, e.g. Rollright S 6/1 (Fig. 6.8), Sunkenkirk L 1/3, and Pobull Fhinn H 3/17. The peculiar 'entrance' arrangement at many of the recumbent stone circles of the north-east of Scotland should also be mentioned (p. 135 and Keiller, 1934).

The layout of some of the multiple circle sites was apparently very complicated, as is shown by Borlase's plan of the Botallek circles reproduced by

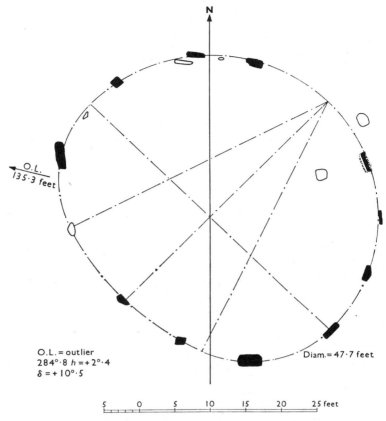

FIG. 6.11. Bar Brook, D 1/7 (53° 16'·6, 1° 34'·9).

Lockyer. One of the circles in the group is evidently of the flattened type. This group has been completely destroyed so that today we cannot determine the azimuths.

There are still remains of at least thirty-three flattened circles of Type A, B, or D. These rings differ from the egg-shaped rings and ellipses in that they all conform to definite designs: for example, all Type A circles are geometrically similar whatever the size, whereas there are very few known examples of geometrical similarity amongst the eggs and ellipses. As a result one would expect to find in the flattened circles a preference for diameters giving acceptable perimeters. But the actual sizes lend no support to this idea. There is, however, some evidence that the diameters were adjusted slightly to help the circumference to conform, just as we found with the circles. This indicates that the size and design were controlled by factors unknown to us today. The size might have been connected with the size of the local

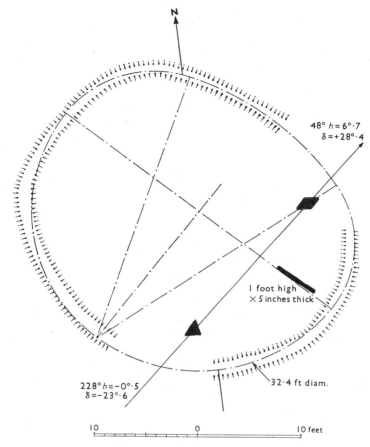

48° h = 6°·7
δ = +28°·4

I foot high
× 5 inches thick

228° h = -0°·5
δ = -23°·6

32·4 ft diam.

10   0   10 feet

FIG. 6.12. Thieves, G 4/2 (55° 01′, 4° 35′).

population, and certainly the largest circles in Britain are in districts capable of supporting a large community. But against this we find large circles and small circles in the same district. The shape is sometimes related to the orientation. For example, the very large Type B circle Long Meg and her Daughters L 1/7 (Fig. 12.11) has its axis of symmetry in the meridian and the axis of the central circle at the Hurlers lies east and west as does the axis of the Type B circle near Porthmeor S 1/12. Other orientation peculiarities will be mentioned in connexion with the astronomical uses of the rings.

A good example of a Type A circle is seen on Cambret Moor (Fig. 6.9). Here we see that six points on the geometrical construction are marked by stones. Notice also that the line through the left auxiliary centre pointed to two other similar circles in line. Remains of these were seen and surveyed in

1939 but both are now removed although they were on the Ordnance Survey. It is interesting that the north and south points are accurately marked but that the whole construction is slewed slightly to get the above-mentioned indication of the other circles. As usual the centre stone stands beside, not at, the centre.

It is interesting to see that in the Type A circle at Black Marsh (Fig. 6.10) one end of the axis of symmetry is marked by a stone with a hole cut in it, and one end of the cross axis by a stone with two cut holes. In neither case do the holes go right through.

A good example of a Type B circle is seen at Bar Brook Derbyshire, (Fig. 6.11). An interesting example is found at the Thieves in Galloway (Fig. 6.12). The Thieves are two tall menhirs but they are surrounded by a low bank of earth and small stones. Stakes were stuck in the estimated top of the bank and the position of the stakes surveyed. A Type B circle adjusted to size was later superimposed. It will be seen that it is almost exactly 12 MY in diameter and that the transverse axis lies along a long low slab set on edge. The Thieves themselves show a limiting lunar declination in one direction and the midwinter setting sun in the other.

The largest circle in the north is at Long Meg and her Daughters and is Type B, while at two of the most important sites in Britain we find Type A, namely at Castle Rigg and Callanish I.

The circle at Whitcastles is in a class by itself. It is like a Type B but the cross axis is divided into four instead of three. Since the main radius is 34 MY we get very nearly a Pythagorean triangle, because $34^2 + 17^2$ is 1445 and 38^2 is 1444. This was probably the reason for departing from the usual Type B.

All good Type A, B, and D rings will be found listed in Table 5.1.

Egg-shaped rings

Ten examples of egg-shaped rings are now known and will be found listed in Tables 6.1 and 6.2. The geometry of these rings has already been discussed

Table 6.1. *Egg-shaped rings—type I*

Site		b	c	a	r_1	P	$P-2\frac{1}{2}m$
B 2/4	Esslie Major	3	4	5	14	90·95	+0·95
B 7/1	Clava	6	8	10	19	125·36	+0·36
B 7/18	Druid Temple	4	3	5	7	47·28	−0·22
G 9/15	Allan Water	$5\frac{1}{2}$	$6\frac{1}{2}$	8·51	8	55·60	+0·60
P 7/1	Cairnpapple Hill	12	16	20	$17\frac{1}{2}$	121·91	−0·59
S 5/4	Woodhenge	$17\frac{1}{2}$	6	$18\frac{1}{2}$	Six values	40	0·00

in Chapter 4. A good example of a Type I ring will be found in the inner ring at Druid Temple near Inverness (Fig. 6.13). This ring is based on the 3, 4, 5 triangle with the 3 side along the axis of symmetry. Note how near the

Table 6.2. *Egg-shaped rings—type II*

Site	b	c	a	r_1	P	$P-2\frac{1}{2}m$
G 9/10 Borrowston Rig	$9\frac{1}{2}$	$12\frac{1}{4}$	$15\frac{1}{2}$	25	164·27	−0·73
S 1/1 The Hurlers	6	$4\frac{1}{2}$	$7\frac{1}{2}$	25	158·36	−0·86
Leacet Hill	$1\frac{1}{2}$	2	$2\frac{1}{2}$	$6\frac{1}{2}$	42·06	−0·44
W 11/3 Maen Mawr	2	$2\frac{1}{4}$	3·01	11	70·24	+0·24

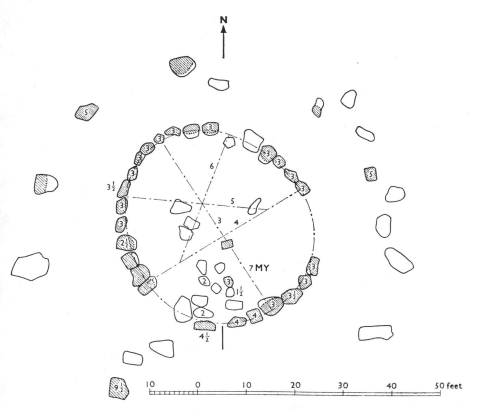

FIG. 6.13. Druid Temple, B 7/18 (57° 27′, 4° 11′·4).

perimeter 47·27 MY comes to being a multiple of $2\frac{1}{2}$. At Clava (Fig. 6.7) and at Esslie (B 2/4) the 3 side is across the axis. An interesting triangle is found in the ring high up on a hill above Allan Water (Fig. 6.14). Here we have in units of $\frac{1}{2}$ MY $11^2+13^2 = 290$ and $17^2 = 289$. The discrepancy in the hypotenuse is only 1 in 580 and would hardly be appreciable.

The best example of a Type II ring is that on Borrowston Rig (Fig. 6.15). The over-all size is exactly 56×50 MY. The hypotenuse of the basic triangle

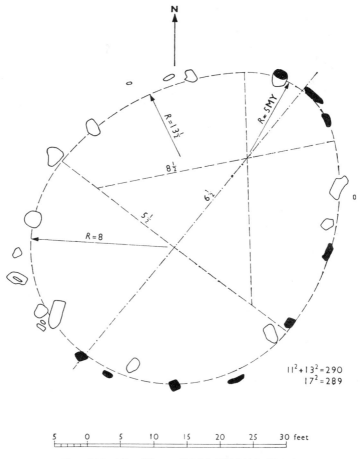

FIG. 6.14. Allan Water, G 9/15 (55° 20'·8, 2° 50'·1).

is 15½. Taking one side as 9½ the other is calculated as 12·247, which would be assumed to be 12¼ without any possibility of the discrepancy being measurable. A peculiarity of this ring is that the arc forming the sharp end, if continued, passes through the main centre. The site is so unimpressive that the stones are hardly noticeable on the rough ground. But it is possible to recognize those which are in their undisturbed position and on the plan these are blacked in. It will be seen how closely the superimposed outline fits these black stones.

In two of the Type II rings, namely The Hurlers and Maen Mawr, alternative triangles fit almost as well as those suggested (Thom, 1961 (2)), but the effect on the calculated perimeter is small.

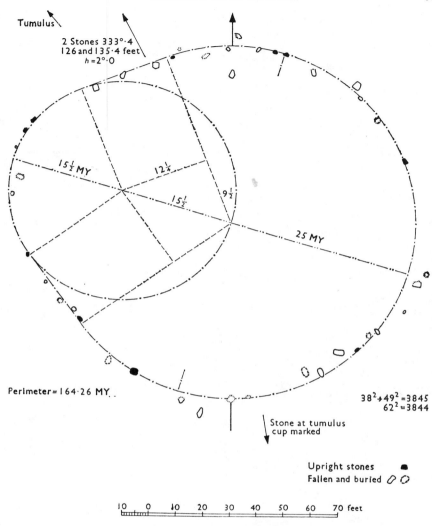

Tumulus

2 Stones 333°·4
126 and 135·4 feet
$h = 2°·0$

$15\frac{1}{2}$ MY

$12\frac{1}{2}$

$15\frac{1}{2}$

$9\frac{1}{2}$

25 MY

Perimeter = 164·26 MY

$38^2 + 49^2 = 3845$
$62^2 = 3844$

Stone at tumulus
cup marked

Upright stones
Fallen and buried

10   0   10   20   30   40   50   60   70 feet

FIG. 6.15. Borrowston Rig, G 9/10 (55° 46′, 2° 42′).

The perimeters (P) have been calculated as outlined in Chapter 4 and are tabulated together with the amount by which they differ from the nearest multiple of $2\frac{1}{2}$. The discrepancy in the actual statistical diameters, as calculated from the actual stones, from the nominal diameters will be found in the main list (Table 5.1). It is found that $(\Sigma\epsilon_1^2)/n$ for the eggs and compound rings is only 0·08 as against 0·51 for the table as a whole. This may be due to greater care, but is also probably due to the design of these shapes being

Table 6.3. *Compound rings* (see Chapter 7)

Site			r_1	P	$P-2\frac{1}{2}m$
W 5/1	Moel ty Ucha	See Fig. 7.1	14	42·85	+0·35
B 7/10	Easter Delfour	See Fig. 7.4	22	67·56	+0·06
W 6/1	Kerry Pole	See Fig. 7.5	32	97·38	−0·12

Table 6.4. *Ellipses*

Site		$2a$ (MY)	$2c$ (MY)	$2b$ (MY)	P (MY)	$\epsilon = \lvert P-2\frac{1}{2}m \rvert$
(*a*) *Definite ellipses*						
A 9/2	Ettrick Bay	18	12	13·42	49·61	0·39
B 1/24	Blackhill of Drachlaw	$10\frac{1}{4}$	$5\frac{1}{8}$	8·88	30·08	0·08
B 1/26	Loanhead of Daviot	14	5	13·08	42·54	0·04
B 1/27	Sands of Forvie	$16\frac{1}{2}$	6	15·37	50·08	0·08
B 7/4	Boat of Garten	$17\frac{1}{2}$	7	16·04	52·89	0·39
B 7/5	Daviot	$18\frac{1}{2}$	6	$17\frac{1}{2}$	56·56	0·94
P 1/3	Killin	12	$6\frac{1}{2}$	10·09	34·76	0·24
P 1/16	Mickle Findowle	$9\frac{1}{2}$	5	8·08	27·66	0·16
P 2/2	Ballinluig	$9\frac{1}{2}$	$5\frac{1}{2}$	7·75	27·16	0·34
S 2/7	Lee Moor	7	4	5·75	20·07	0·07
S 2/8	Postbridge	$10\frac{1}{2}$	3	10·06	32·30	0·20
S 4/1	Winterbourne Abbas	11	$5\frac{1}{2}$	9·53	32·28	0·22
W 2/1	Penmaen-Mawr	31	$9\frac{1}{2}$	29·51	95·06	0·06
W 11/4	Usk River	25	10	22·91	75·30	0·30
P 1/19	Croftmoraig	11	$7\frac{1}{2}$	8·05	30·10	0·10
(*b*) *Definite ellipses from other sources*						
	Tormore	18	$9\frac{1}{2}$	15·29	52·38	0·12
	Auchengallon	18	6	16·97	54·94	0·06
	Clauchreid	13	7	10·95	37·70	0·20
	Braemore	34	17	29·45	99·79	0·21
	Learable Hill	24	$12\frac{1}{2}$	20·48	69·99	0·01
(*c*) *Less-definite ellipses*						
B 7/13	Loch nan Carraigean	$22\frac{1}{2}$	5	21·93	69·79	0·21
G 4/1	Carsphairn	30	20	22·36	82·68	0·18
H 1/1	Callanish I	5	3	4	14·18	0·82
H 1/2	,, II	26	14	21·91	75·39	0·39
H 1/3	,, III	21	$12\frac{1}{4}$	17·06	59·94	0·06
,,	,, ,,	$12\frac{1}{2}$	$9\frac{1}{2}$	8·12	32·75	0·25
H 1/4	,, IV	$15\frac{1}{2}$	$10\frac{1}{2}$	11·40	42·50	0·00
H 1/10	Steinacleit	21	13	16·49	59·10	0·90
H 3/11	Leacach an Tigh Chloiche	20	15	13·23	52·74	0·24
L 1/6	Burnmoor	26	$18\frac{1}{2}$	18·27	70·07	0·07
L 2/12	Harberwain	$8\frac{1}{2}$	4	$7\frac{1}{2}$	25·16	0·16
P 2/9	Guildtown	12	$8\frac{1}{2}$	8·47	32·39	0·11
P 2/11	New Scone Wood	9	5	7·48	25·95	0·95
S 3/1	Stanton Drew	39	15	36	117·86	0·36
,,	,, ,,	52	20	48	157·14	0·36

such that adjustments to the diameter to bring the perimeter nearer the desired value were unnecessary or at least seldom made. When we remember that in each case an attempt was made, with considerable success, to fulfil two conditions, triangle and periphery, we realize how remarkable these designs are. A statistical examination will be made of the perimeters of these rings together with the ellipses in a later section. Meanwhile it is desirable to examine in detail that most remarkable set of egg rings found at Woodhenge.

Woodhenge

A very careful survey, using a steel tape and theodolite, was made of the concrete posts which the excavators placed in the post-holes in the chalk. A reproduction to a very much reduced scale is shown in Fig. 6.16. The axis drawn is chosen to be along the azimuth of the point on the horizon where the midsummer sun first appeared about 1800 B.C. Using centres on this axis we then find

(1) the arcs at the large end have a common centre at A,
(2) the arcs at the small end have a common centre at B,
(3) the distance AB between these centres is 6 MY,
(4) the arcs are equally spaced with one gap,
(5) the radius at the small end is in each ring 1 MY smaller than the radius at the large end.

These facts are indisputable but in themselves they do not explain the construction, because the radii are not integral multiples of the yard.

With the method and notation explained on p. 30 we write:

$$r_1 - r_2 = a - b = 1,$$

$$c = 6,$$

$$a^2 - b^2 = c^2.$$

The solution of these equations is $a = 18\frac{1}{2}$, $b = 17\frac{1}{2}$. The fact that these are rational numbers shows that we are dealing with a Pythagorean triangle. In units of half-yards the triangle is $12^2 + 35^2 = 37^2$. The discovery of this triangle must be considered as one of the greatest achievements of the circle builders. That they themselves considered it important is shown by the use they made of it at Woodhenge. Its use at another site will be discussed later.

But we have yet to show how the radii of the rings were chosen. The scheme used only becomes apparent when we realize that the rings were intended to have perimeters which were multiples of 20 MY. The values selected were 40, 60, 80, 100, 140, and 160 MY. Accepting these we can easily calculate the necessary radii. These can then be compared with what we find on the ground.

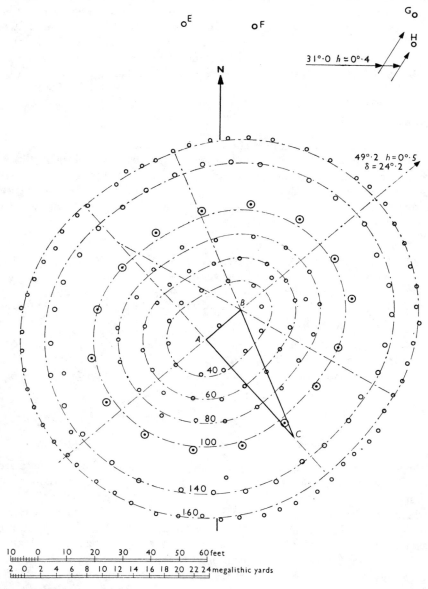

FIG. 6.16. Woodhenge, S 5/4 (51° 12', 1° 48'). Construction superimposed: $AB = 6$, $AC = 17\frac{1}{2}$, $CB = 18\frac{1}{2}$ MY; r = radii struck from $A = (P-9\cdot08)\div 2\pi$; $P = 40$, 60, 80, 100, 140, and 160 MY (P = perimeter).

We have seen on p. 30 that for a Type I ring the perimeter is

$$P = 2\pi r_1 + \pi b - 2a\beta$$

where $\tan \beta = b/c$. Substituting $a = 18\frac{1}{2}$, $b = 17\frac{1}{2}$, $c = 6$, we find

$$2\pi r_1 = P - 9 \cdot 0794.$$

Values of r_1 corresponding to the various values of P can now easily be calculated and will be found in the table below. Values of r_2 and r_3 follow from $r_2 = r_1 - 1$, $r_3 = r_1 + 17\frac{1}{2}$.

Table 6.5

Ring	P (MY)	r_1 (MY)	Major axis (MY)	π'	P_a (MY)
I	160	24·02	53·04	3·02	161·0
II	140	20·84	46·67	3·00	138·2
III	100	14·47	33·94	2·95	104·2
IV	80	11·29	27·58	2·90	79·9
V	60	8·10	21·21	2·83	61·3
VI	40	4·92	14·84	2·70	39·4

Egg-shaped rings were drawn very carefully on tracing paper to these radii and superimposed on the survey (Fig. 6.16). It was then possible, by the method of p. 35, to determine the adjustments necessary to each ring to obtain the best agreement with the concrete posts. The perimeters of the rings so found are given in the last column. It will be seen that ring III is some 4 per cent large. This ring is very nearly represented by taking $r_1 = 15$ and $r_2 = 14$, which gives a ring about 0·53 MY or 1·44 ft outside the hypothetical 100-MY ring everywhere. It thus appears that if the posts were 2·88 ft (or about 1 MY) diameter the inside of the structure would be a perfect fit. The excavators found that there were deep ramps to all the holes in this ring, indicating that very large posts had been used carrying perhaps a platform or roof.

We can, by the statistical method described and used earlier, find from P_a, neglecting ring III, the value of the Megalithic yard which best fits Woodhenge. This turns out to be about 2·718, a value so close to 2·72 (used in drawing the rings) as to show that we can be quite certain we are using the identical geometric construction to that used by the builders.

In the above table π' is the theoretical ratio of P, the nominal perimeter, to the greatest diameter $(2r_1 + 5)$. It will be seen that π' gradually increases as the rings get larger until at ring II it is 3·00. A more exact calculation gives 2·9994. No matter how carefully the builders made their measurements they could never have detected the difference between this and 3. One is tempted to surmise that the whole set of rings may be a permanent record of an

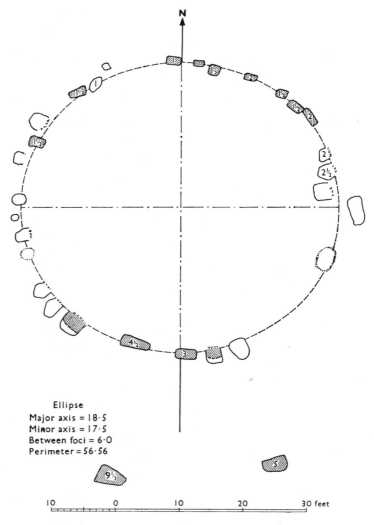

Ellipse
Major axis = 18·5
Minor axis = 17·5
Between foci = 6·0
Perimeter = 56·56

FIG. 6.17. Daviot, B 7/5 (57° 26'·4, 4° 07'·2).

elaborate empirical determination of a geometrically constructed ring which
would have as it were $\pi = 3$ and at the same time have a circumference a
multiple of 20 yds. Certainly none of our modern circle squarers have obtained
a closer approximation. It may be remarked that ring-II post-holes are better
marked than ring I which overshot the mark with $\pi' = 3·02$. Presumably the
inner ring was laid out first. One wonders how many rings were set out before
the builders discovered that every 20 yds they added to the circumference gave

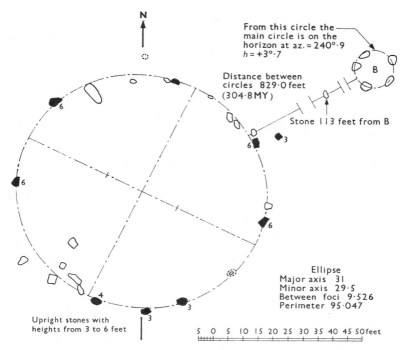

N

From this circle the
main circle is on the
horizon at az.= 240°·9
h = +3°·7

Distance between
circles 829·0 feet
(304·8 MY)

B

Stone 113 feet from B

6 3

6

6

Ellipse
Major axis 31
Minor axis 29·5
Between foci 9·526
Perimeter 95·047

4

3

3

Upright stones with
heights from 3 to 6 feet

5 0 5 10 15 20 25 30 35 40 45 50 feet

FIG. 6.18. Penmaen-Mawr, W 2/1 (53° 15', 3° 55').

them the same increment to the radius (actually $10/\pi$). Did they notice this after four rings and then attempt an extrapolation? It is much more likely that they already possessed this kind of knowledge, because this cannot have been their first attempt. They had probably experimented with many other triangles before arriving at the 12, 35, 37.

One is entitled to reject the above reason for making the structure, but everyone must be impressed by the laborious, painstaking work which preceded the discovery of the sixth member of the list of perfect Pythagorean triangles and the construction of a set of rings based on this triangle with perimeters exact multiples of 20 yds.

Ellipses

There are about twenty known stone rings in Britain which are definitely ellipses and another dozen or so less certain. In most cases the uncertainty is a result of the ruinous condition of the site making it difficult to be certain of the exact outline. There is seldom much doubt about the shapes being elliptical.

In Table 6.4, $2a$ and $2b$ are the major and minor axes, $2c$ is the distance between foci, and P is the perimeter calculated from $2a$ and $2b$. The amount

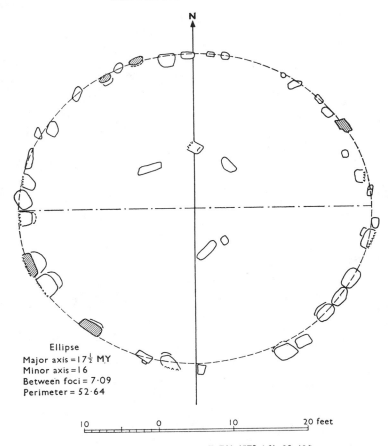

Ellipse
Major axis = 17½ MY
Minor axis = 16
Between foci = 7·09
Perimeter = 52·64

FIG. 6.19. Boat of Garten, B 7/4 (57° 16′, 3° 43′).

by which P differs from the nearest multiple of $2\frac{1}{2}$ MY is given in the last column.

We have seen that in an ellipse a, b, and c must be capable of forming the sides of a right-angled triangle and it appears that in Table 6.4 nearly all the ellipses are based on triangles which are nearly Pythagorean but in only five is the triangle exact. One is the ellipse at Daviot (Fig. 6.17) near Clava, but we see that at the same time it shows the largest ϵ in the table. The triangle used is the 12, 35, 37 which figures so prominently at Woodhenge and one is tempted to surmise that the builders knew of the perfection of the triangle they were using and were prepared to sacrifice the perimeter.

One of the almost perfect triangles is that at Penmaen-Mawr, where in half-yard units we get $19^2 + 59^2 = 3842$ against $62^2 = 3844$. It would have

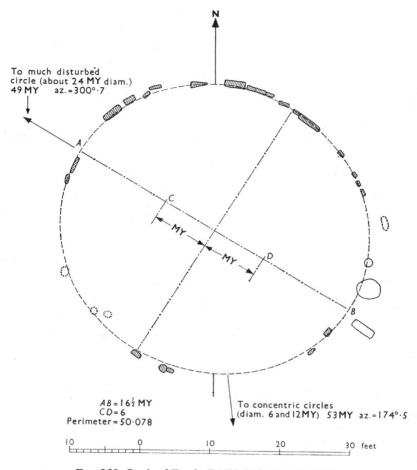

To much disturbed
circle (about 24 MY diam.)
49 MY az.=300°.7

N

A

C

MY

MY

D

B

$AB = 16\frac{1}{2}$ MY
$CD = 6$
Perimeter = 50·078

To concentric circles
(diam. 6 and 12 MY) 53 MY az.=174°·5

10   0   10   20   30 feet

FIG. 6.20. Sands of Forvie, B 1/27 (57° 19'·6, 1° 58'·8).

been quite impossible for the builders to detect the discrepancy in the hypotenuse (1 in 3800). From their point of view the perimeter was also perfect
with an error of only 1 in 1500. It will be seen in Fig. 6.18 how nearly the
ellipse drawn to the values given passes through those stones which are still
upright.

The ellipse at Boat of Garten, that at Sands of Forvie, and that near Postbridge (Figs. 6.19, 6.20, and 6.21) are also good examples.

It seems that at Blackhill of Drachlaw (B 1/24), in order to get a perimeter
of 30, the builders used a major axis of $10\frac{1}{4}$ and an eccentricity of one-half
giving $2b = 8\frac{7}{8}$ and $2c = 5\frac{1}{8}$. The triangle is $41^2+71^2 = 6722$ against
$82^2 = 6724$. They also used eighths at Sands of Forvie, the triangle being

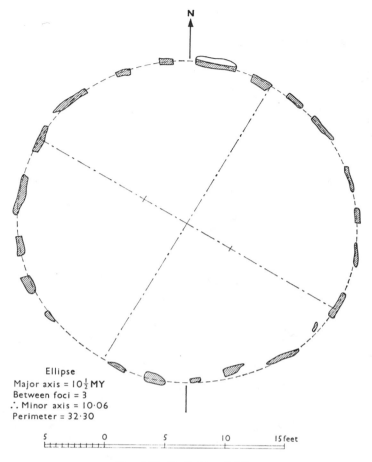

Ellipse
Major axis = $10\frac{1}{2}$ MY
Between foci = 3
∴ Minor axis = 10·06
Perimeter = 32·30

FIG. 6.21. Postbridge, S 2/8.

$48^2 + 123^2 = 17\ 433$ against $132^2 = 17\ 424$. This subdivision into eighths was done here to achieve a perimeter of 50, actually 50·08. In some places they used quarter-yards but in most ellipses they succeeded without subdividing beyond halves.

No good purpose would be achieved by discussing the sites in Table 6.4 (c) because, as already said, the dimensions are uncertain.

Major Prain, after his recent accurate survey of Stanton Drew, suggested that the north circle was an ellipse. On looking into the matter it appeared that an ellipse based on a 5, 12, 13 triangle fitted much better than a circle. When an ellipse was fitted to the third circle it proved to be again based on the 5, 12, 13 triangle but it was of a different size. Table 6.4 (c) shows that the

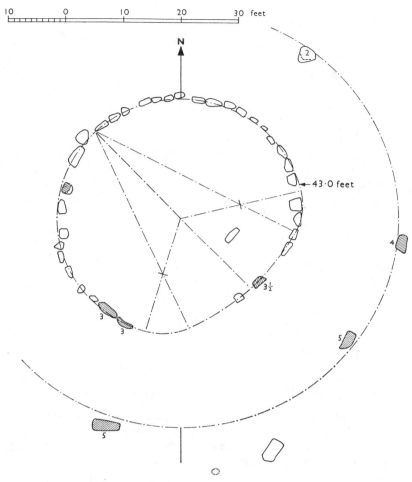

10   0   10   20   30 feet

N

43·0 feet

FIG. 6.22. Aviemore, B 7/12 (57° 12′, 3° 50′).

perimeters of both satisfy the usual requirement. The major axes of both ellipses seem to lie on the same line.

The construction near Loch nan Carraigean near Aviemore (B7/13) consists of a large ruinous hollow cairn which apparently, like the Clava cairns, was surrounded by a circle of menhirs now presumably in the foundation of the railway. It did not seem worth while to make a detailed survey but spot points were put in on the outside of the cairn wall. Curiously enough an ellipse $22\frac{1}{2} \times 22$ seems to fit these excellently, which could well be a coincidence but when one finds that the calculated perimeter is very close to 70 MY one wonders.

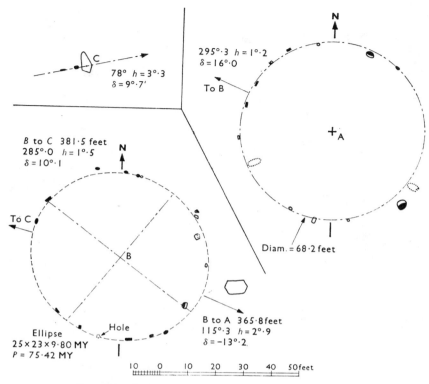

FIG. 6.23. Circles near Usk river, W 11/4 (51° 55′, 3° 43′).

In the ellipses in Table 6.4 (*b*) whole or half-yards were used except perhaps at Tormore. It was this fine ring which first suggested to Dr. Roy (Roy, 1963) that ellipses were used and his interpretation is that, as at Blackhill of Drachlaw, the eccentricity was intended to be one-half, with a slightly different major axis.

The 2½-yard unit in ellipses and eggs

A glance at the values of *P* for the ellipses in Table 6.4 shows that there is no doubt that the perimeters were intended to be multiples of 2½ yds. In fact, s^2/δ^2 is lower for this group than for any so far examined, but in view of the small number it is best to take the eggs and ellipses together.

For all eggs, compound rings, and definite ellipses, for *P* we get

$$\Sigma\epsilon^2 = 5\cdot15, \quad n = 33, \quad 2\delta = 2\tfrac{1}{2},$$

so $s^2 = (\Sigma\epsilon^2)/n = 0\cdot156$ and $s^2/\delta^2 = 0\cdot100$.

Applying this to Fig. 2.1 to obtain the probability that the unit of 2½ was real we find that s^2/δ^2 is so small as to be off the sheet but it is evident that the probability level is well below 0·1 per cent. Broadbent's criterion turns out to be 1·34 so that even with no *a priori* knowledge of the yard we must accept the reality of the $2\frac{1}{2}$ MY unit. It will be remembered that in the distances between circles units of $2\frac{1}{2}$ and 5 MY appeared, though not so conclusively as the $2\frac{1}{2}$ unit above. Five MY or 13·6 ft is about as long a rod as can conveniently be handled on the straight but it would be much too long for measuring circumferences. Perhaps for a preliminary measurement in the trial-and-error process of finding a suitable ring a $2\frac{1}{2}$-MY rod would be used, but the error *per yard* would be, as we have seen (p. 32), about $c^3/24R^2$, which works out about 0·2 yds in a circle of 16 yds diameter.

7

THE COMPOUND RINGS

WE shall discuss Avebury in this chapter, but before doing so it is advisable to look at three rings whose designs lead up to the Avebury construction. These three sites seem to the author to be amongst the most important in Britain. Their geometrical construction shows a mastery of the technique of finding designs which, while possessing an elegance of symmetry and proportion, yet incorporate a hidden significance in that integral lengths were obtained for the basic dimensions and the perimeters were multiples of $2\frac{1}{2}$ MY.

It is true that today we can be petty and apply our short-cutting knowledge of trigonometry to show that their lengths were only approximations. Their $13\frac{1}{2}$ is our 13·503, their 15 our 14·99, but this does not show that they failed. Within their limitations they succeeded. To our modern thinking they were attempting the impossible, but in more advanced spheres so are we.

In the last chapter we examined rings based on Pythagorean triangles and we saw how successfully close approximations to these triangles had been invented as required. But in Moel ty Ucha the builders were attempting something much more difficult. They started with a circle 14 yds diameter and therefore $3\frac{1}{7} \times 14$ or 44 yds in circumference. But this was not enough: they wanted also to have a multiple of $2\frac{1}{2}$ yds in the perimeter. So they proceeded to invent a method of drawing flattened portions on the ring which, with a minimum of distortion, would reduce it to $42\frac{1}{2}$. To introduce these flattened portions they had to use at least two radii and each had to be integral. Finally the finished ring had to have, like nearly all others, an axis of symmetry. Later we shall see that they had still another external condition to fulfil if possible. Deneb rose at an azimuth of 17°·3 and they wanted this angle to be shown on the construction so that when the cross axis pointed to the rising star true north would also be shown. They did not get 17°·3, they got 18°. This is the complement of 72°, which is one-fifth of 360°. The Greek geometers showed much later how to construct an angle of 72°, but it can hardly be imagined that the builders of Moel ty Ucha used anything more elaborate than trial and error. Having divided the circle into five or perhaps ten parts the construction proceeds as in Figs. 7.1 and 7.2. Draw an inner circle of radius 4 and centred on this draw the five short arcs of radius 3 touching the main circle at its subdivision points. Two of these arcs are half length, because the final ring lies on the original circle for 72° at the left. Finally the short-radius arcs are connected by flat arcs centred as in the flattened circles on the far side of the main circle at the 'corners' where this is touched by the short arcs. We wish now to calculate the radius of these closing arcs and the length of the circumference.

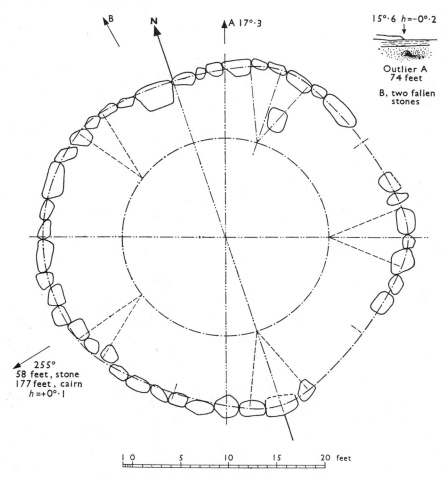

FIG. 7.1. Moel ty Ucha, W 5/1 (52° 55′·4, 3° 24′·2).

Referring to Fig. 7.3 we have $a = 4$, $b = 7$, and so $r = 3$.

$$c^2 = a^2 + b^2 + 2ab \cos \pi/5 \quad \text{and so} \quad c = 10·503.$$

The required radius is AD which is $c+r$ or 13·503. We also easily find $\angle A = 0·22\ 578$, $\angle B = 0·40\ 254$, and the perimeter P is found to be

$$P = 8 \times r \times B + 8(r+c)A + 2b \times \pi/5$$

which is 42·85.

Thus we see that the required radius exceeds $13\frac{1}{2}$ by only 0·003, an amount which could only be detected by the most advanced modern techniques, and the discrepancy in the perimeter is only 0·35, which is comparable with the discrepancies we have seen in the circles, eggs, and ellipses.

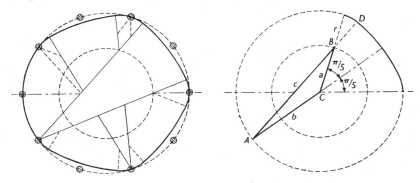

FIG. 7.2. Geometry of W 5/1.   FIG. 7.3. Geometry of W 5/1.

Fortunately this beautiful little ring has been very little disturbed and we can see how perfectly the construction fits the stones. One must of course expect frost to have moved some of the stones slightly. The gaps seem symmetrical and may have been entrances to the original structure.

Because of the importance of this site the calculations have been given in detail, but there seems to be no necessity to treat the next sites so fully.

Easter Delfour

The outer ring at this site (Fig. 7.4) is partly buried in rubble, showing that the original structure was perhaps a hollow cairn. This view is borne out by the dimension of the inner ring, which measures 8 MY diameter to its *inner* face. So the rings are retaining walls and measurements will be taken to the outside of the outer stones. This ring has much in common with Moel ty Ucha but it is divided into four instead of five. With an even number of sides the centre of any one of the flat arcs must be on the radius bisecting the opposite arc, not as at Moel ty Ucha on a 'corner'. So if the usual convention was followed of putting this centre on the circumference ambiguity would arise— is it on the arc or on the circumference of the circumscribing circle? Perhaps for this reason all eight centres lie on a much smaller circle with a diameter of $6\frac{1}{2}$ MY. We can be sure of this dimension because

(1) its use produces a figure which fits the stones perfectly,
(2) it makes the length *AB* (as calculated by the method shown for Moel ty Ucha) 6·005,
(3) it makes the minimum diameter of the ring across the flat arcs 21·010,
(4) it makes the perimeter 67·56.

These remarkable dimensions cannot be accidental. So we can be certain that we have uncovered the geometry of this site.

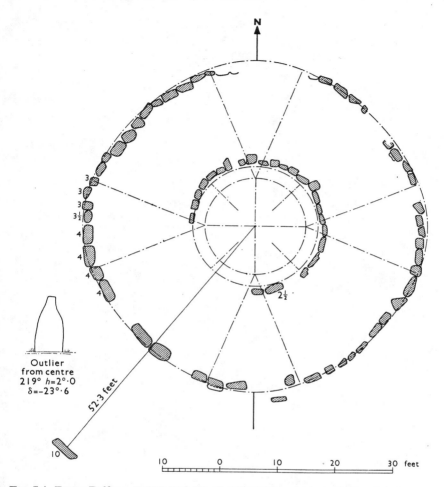

FIG. 7.4. Easter Delfour, B 7/10 (57° 09′, 3° 54′). Taking maximum outer diameter = 22 MY and diameter of small circle = 6½ MY, calculation shows minimum outside diameter = 21·01 and $P = 67·56$

Ring near Kerry Pole

On the ground this is a very unimpressive site, but when it is surveyed (Fig. 7.5) and the geometry studied it turns out to be another member of the group we are examining.

The construction is again based on two circles. Here their diameters are definite, 32 and 16 MY. Two points are then established on the outer circle,

E at 5 MY from the axis and *G* at 14. Bisect the angle *GOE* by the line *LOK*. Draw *KP₂T* and *KP₁S*. The corner arcs *ES* and *TG* are centred on *P₁* and *P₂* and the closing arc on *K*. A little trigonometry gives the radius *KS* of the closing arc and the perimeter. The remarkable thing is that these are 29·98 and 97·38 MY. Thus all the radii are integral, 16, 8, and 30 MY, and the perimeter only 0·12 different from a multiple of 2½.

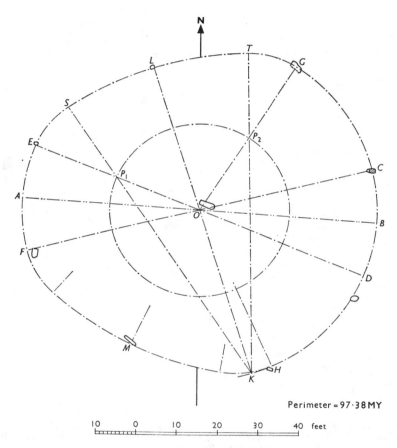

FIG. 7.5. Kerry Pole, W 6/1. (52° 28′, 3° 14′). Construction: *AB* = 32 MY; *CD* = 10 MY; *EF* = 10 MY; *GH* = 28 MY; *OP* = 8 MY; then *KS* = 29·98

It is indeed fortunate that this ring is so little disturbed. We see that the changes of radius at *G*, *H*, *F*, and *E* are still marked, as are the points at *L* and *M* bisecting the angles *GOE* and *HOF* and so fixing the centres for the long arcs. Note also that while the axis is not east and west the line *KT* is very nearly due north.

Avebury

The tragic destruction of Avebury is perhaps one of the worst acts of vandalism of recent centuries. But the present educated generation driving its tractors and bulldozers through other monuments is even more unforgivable. Today our power of destruction is greater and we remove the monuments without leaving a trace and often without allowing time for a survey. At Avebury more than a trace is left. Careful excavation made possible and controlled by Alexander Keiller has re-established the positions of many of the menhirs in the main ring and has indeed made it possible to establish the diameter and position of the older circles inside the ring. The extensive excavations are described in detail in a work prepared by I. F. Smith which also gives a full description of the site as it is today.

But the kind of survey necessary for our present purpose was lacking and so the author, assisted by Brigadier A. Prain and Miss E. M. Pickard, made an accurate survey of the upright stones and of the concrete posts which now mark the positions of many of the destroyed stones. The traverse necessary, about 3000 ft long, was checked at three points by astronomical determination of azimuth and closed to 0·6 ft. Thus the survey can be accepted as sufficiently accurate. It is shown on a reduced scale in the Frontispiece.

The geometrical design to which the stones in the outer ring are set out differs from anything so far discussed in that the arcs forming the ring meet at definite corners not appreciably rounded off. Without a knowledge of the exact length of the Megalithic yard and of the simpler designs it is doubtful if the construction could have been discovered. The basis of the design is a 3, 4, 5 triangle set out in units of exactly 25 MY so that the sides are $AB = 75$, $AC = 100$, and $BC = 125$. The main centre for the whole design is a point (D) inside this triangle exactly 60 MY from C and so placed that a perpendicular dropped from D to CA is 15 MY. The peculiarity of this position of D is that if DC is produced 140 MY to S, so that DS is 200, the distance SB is 259·97 MY, which was certainly thought to be 260. Now draw the main circle with centre D and radius 200 and draw a line parallel to AB through D to meet the circle at E.

The next stage is to draw three arcs all of radius 260, each centred on one of the corners of the basic triangle. To be specific, with centre B draw the arc HG where H is on BC produced, with centre A draw the arc GF, and with centre C draw the arc ML. This last arc will run into the main circle tangentially at L on CD produced. Now passing through E draw the arc FEM with centre 750 MY from E on ED produced. So far we can be perfectly certain of the geometry. This half of the ring has been excavated, but in the other half the suggested construction is less certain, there being only a few stones with only one now upright. But there are some depressions which probably show the positions of the burning-pits dug to assist in the destruction of some of the stones. These would be near the base of the upright stones and so offer some guidance. Nevertheless the suggestion cannot have the same weight as what has gone before. From H to J draw an arc centred on CB produced and having a radius of 750 MY. Drop a perpendicular to CB from D and produce it to P making $PQ = QD$. As in the egg-shaped constructions there may have been a mirror image of the triangle ABC mirrored about BC, in which case P would occupy the position corresponding to D. Produce PD to meet the main circle at K and from K draw the arc KJ with centre at P. Probably from K to L the stones followed the main circle.

The whole design was set out on tracing paper with the greatest possible accuracy. When this was superimposed on the large-scale survey the manner in which the outline passed through the stones and stone positions was remarkable. The yard was taken as 2·720 ft. Had, say, 2·730 ft been used, the ring would have been too large by some 5 ft and would have passed outside the stones, a striking proof of the value of the yard and of the precision with which the builders set out the ring.

When the tracing paper was adjusted to the best fit with the stones it appeared that the point S of the construction fell inside the plan of the largest stone on the site, that is the stone to the west of the road leading north from the village. The most likely position is under the overhang of the west end of the stone. It will be seen that E is also marked by a stone and that the two large stones at the south entrance are placed one on the main circle and one on the ring.

The detailed trigonometrical calculation of all the dimensions would occupy several pages and is much too long to give here, but the results throw some light on the reasons for the peculiar design. The calculated lengths of the arcs are as follows.

ME	97·23	MY perhaps accepted as		97·5
EF	117·43	„	„	117·5
FG	199·87	„	„	200
GH	129·68	„	„	130
HJ	150·09	„	„	150
JKLM	608·10	„	„	607·5
Total	1302·40	„	„	1302·5

It is seen that all arcs in the portion where we have definite evidence that the assumptions are correct are close to being multiples of $2\frac{1}{2}$, a rule which we have seen is almost universal for perimeters. Here we find it applying to the portions of the perimeters between the 'corners'. If the total perimeter was intended to be 1300 the error was only about 1 in 550, but it is unjustifiable to accept this until excavation on the east side has gone far enough to prove the assumed geometry.

The two inner circles have a diameter of 125 MY, which curiously is exactly

340 ft. Taking $\pi = 3\cdot140$ makes the circumference 392·5, again a multiple of 2½. This is one of the best rational approximations to π left us by these people. It was used in the large circle at Brogar in Orkney. Note the theme of 25 and 2·5 running through all the Avebury dimensions.

The line joining the two inner circles is 145 MY long and lies at an azimuth of about 340°·2. The meaning of this azimuth will be discussed later. The only indication of a connexion between the inner circles and the main ring comes from the fact that the line joining the stump of the ring stone R and the main centre D shows the same azimuth and so is parallel to the line of the inner circles. Keiller's excavations showed the depth of the hole under the ring stone, which had apparently been considered important.

8

MEGALITHIC ASTRONOMY

THE conclusions in previous chapters regarding Megalithic metrology rest on a sound statistical basis: the probability levels are such as to leave no doubt about the reality of the units. But it is much more difficult to deal with astronomical hypotheses in the same rigid manner. In 1955 the author published a statistical examination (Thom, 1955) which showed a high degree of probability that many of the sites contained lines with an astronomical meaning. Since then much additional information and knowledge has been obtained. The calendar hypothesis has been set up as an explanation of many previously puzzling lines. Other lines group themselves unmistakably round four lunar limiting declinations. These advances have come about by the gradual accumulation of observed declinations at certain values demanding explanations. As we saw in the chapter on astronomy there are definite limitations to the magnitude of solar and lunar declinations. So any definite group of declinations with a value beyond these limits demands a stellar explanation. Any group inside the limits may be solar, lunar, or stellar. It would be very difficult to devise a rigid statistical method of handling the material in this important part of the declination range which would be universally acceptable. Accordingly it is proposed to adopt the simple visual demonstration of plotting histograms of the observed declinations and to present these in such a manner that they can be compared with (1) calendar declinations, (2) lunar declinations, and (3) the declinations of first-magnitude stars between 2000 and 1600 B.C.

The difficulty of laying down working terms of reference to assist in the objective selection of the lines to be included makes it perhaps impossible to put the demonstration on a perfectly sound basis, but although other workers might discard this line and include that, it is considered that the material presented is sufficiently representative to give a correct over-all picture. It is hoped that in the future other workers will find many other sites here and in Ireland and will produce more accurate surveys of sites already included. Then with much new material it ought to be possible to make a complete analysis using only first-class lines, but even then a certain degree of subjectivity will remain. In the meantime it is hoped that the scheme adopted of dividing the lines into classes of different reliability will allow any serious student to decide for himself whether or not to reject the various hypotheses put forward.

The azimuths

It is desirable for the reader to be familiar with what is meant by the terms *outlier, alignment*, and *indicated foresight*. An outlier is an upright stone near a circle or other well-defined site. An alignment is a row of upright stones. Two stones can be considered as an alignment when one (or both) is an upright slab set up on the line to the next stone. In some places a row of boulders can be accepted provided the row occurs in association with other remains. A look through the figures will show examples. An *indicated foresight* is a prominent natural feature on or near the horizon indicated by a slab, an alignment, or an outlier. All these three arrangements can be used to define an azimuth.

Let us think of the possible uses of an azimuth. Apart from ritualistic purposes there are three—time indication, calendar purposes, and studying the moon's movements. To use the rising or setting of a star to show the time of night the star must be identified. To the question 'where will it rise?' the obvious answer is to point with the finger and not much greater accuracy is in general necessary. So a slab set on edge will do as a minimum requirement. But the sun controls the calendar and it is no longer a matter of identification but of indicating precisely where the sun will rise or set on the specified days of the year. The moon is most useful as a giver of light in those years when it is highest in the midnight sky (and therefore longest above the horizon), but to discover the cycles controlling the changes demands accurate definition of azimuth. Today an astronomer uses a transit circle to measure the positions of the stars as they cross the great circle of the meridian. Megalithic man had to use another great circle, namely the horizon. To obtain accuracy a slab is not enough. There must be a backsight and a foresight. The backsight might be a stone, a hole in a stone, a gap between two stones, or a staff at the centre of a circle. The foresight may be a distant stone or a pole at the centre of a circle. It can most effectively be a distant mountain peak, a distant notch in the horizon, or, when a sea horizon is involved, it can be a rock far out at sea or the fall of a steep island. If the foresight is artificial then perhaps it needs no pointer. If it is a natural feature there ought to be something to distinguish it, but the indicator need only provide enough accuracy to avoid confusion.

In these latitudes the rising point of the sun at the equinoxes moves along the horizon about 0·7 degrees per day, so a method of indicating azimuth to about ¼ degree will make possible the definition of any required day in the spring or autumn, but as we get nearer the solstices the accuracy necessary becomes progressively greater. The precision which can be obtained by a suitably chosen natural foresight is very much greater than is commonly recognized. Think of the right-hand slope of a distant mountain running down to form a notch in the horizon. Suppose that the slope is a little flatter than the apparent path of the setting sun. Then we can choose a viewpoint from which the upper edge of the sun will appear to vanish half-way down the slope. Had the viewpoint been slightly to the right the sun's edge would have reached the bottom of the slope before it vanished. In this way very small changes of declination can be detected. Vegetation such as heather will have very little effect. For example, at ten miles a foot subtends an angle of about 4 seconds of arc or about 0·001 degree.

When the sun sets behind a clean-cut horizon in a clear sky the last vestige of the disk appears momentarily as a brilliant emerald green point of light. The author has watched the phenomenon countless times. Once when we were lying anchored in the Outer Hebrides the horizon to the west consisted of low hills not very far away. It so happened that the upper edge of the setting sun did run down such a slope as has just been discussed. When it vanished it was only necessary to step along the deck a few feet to bring it again into view. By moving quickly my son and I were able to see the small emerald flash three times before the sun finally vanished. We shall see later that there are several places on the west coast where such a foresight was used. The erectors of the backsights must have been well acquainted with the phenomenon and probably made use of it at the solstices. The point is made here that the backsight had to be marked and some rough indicator used to identify the particular slope to be used.

It is evident that such foresights were only useful for the sun or moon. For a star the indicator had to be near enough to be seen in starlight. If it was, say, half a mile away it could be illuminated by a fire but it would in general be impossible to arrange for a fire ten or twenty miles away.

To summarize, we might expect to find as azimuthal indicator for a star:

(1) a slab,
(2) two or more stones not too far apart,
(3) a circle and a close outlier,
or (4) two circles.

For the sun or moon we must have as a minimum:

(1) a long alignment,
(2) two well separated stones,
(3) a circle with an outlier some hundreds of feet distant,
or (4) a natural foresight identified by some simple indicator.

It follows that when we find a circle or even an isolated stone we ought to look round the horizon. If there is a suitable natural foresight which gives a commonly found solar or lunar declination exactly then we are entitled to suspect that there had been a secondary indicator which would have identified the foresight but that it has vanished. Such a line could only be given a low classification and would not be put on a general histogram. Similarly a short alignment incapable of giving the accuracy necessary for a solar or lunar line may have had a distant extension now removed.

The problem of knowing in which direction to use an alignment is an interesting one. If local high ground blocks one view then no problem arises, but when the alignment stands in open ground then there are two possible declinations. There seem to be a number of alignments in which both the declinations are significant. This is, in general, only possible where the varying heights of the surrounding hills allowed the builders to move about on the flat until they found a position which would allow a line to be laid out having hill altitudes giving the required declinations. Obviously years of work would be necessary to find a suitable line if one or both of the declinations were solar or lunar, so it is not surprising that they were well marked when found. An outstanding example is the line *AB* across the circle at Castle Rigg where both declinations are solar, but others will be found listed. This arrangement perhaps explains why a long line is used sometimes for a star. The line may have had to be long for the solar or lunar declination given by the other direction. It is too much to expect a natural foresight to be found at both ends of such a line. This would seem to be almost impossible.

Indications of the meridian

There are a great many sites with very definite indications of a north/south line. Many circles have one of the stones in the ring placed at the north point. This happens oftener than would be expected on a random distribution. Merrivale circle (S 2/2) has a large outlier at 181°·5. The Seven Brethren circle (G 7/2) has an outlier at 358°·9 and Mitchel's Fold (D 2/1) has one at 178°·5. Remains of a north/south passage can be seen in the circles at B 7/17, B 7/18, and B 7/19. Several of the flattened circles Type B and of the egg-shaped rings have either the axis of symmetry or the transverse axis in the meridian.

Perhaps the most interesting meridional sites are the alignments listed below.

Site	Azimuth	Remarks
Tobermory	3°·5	3 stones, one fallen
Loch Stornoway	357·0	2 slabs
Laggangarn	1·8	2 slabs
Callanish I	0·1	Natural rock and alignment
Mid Clyth	358·6	Axis of alignments

It is possible today to use the first three or four as indicators of local apparent noon by watching the shadow of the south stone fall on the stone to the north. At many places throughout the country there are single flat slabs with the flat face in the meridian. A notable example is the large slab at Dalarran G 5/1, where the face is so flat that the glancing shadow can be used to obtain the time to within a few minutes.

In a few places we find two circles on a north/south line, e.g. Carnoussie House (B 4/1), the Grey Wethers (S 2/1), and Burnmoor (L 1/6).

It is not clear how these lines were determined. There was no pole-star to show the north point. The method using the shadow cast by a vertical pole on a horizontal plane surface could not be used in country where flat sand does not exist. The method of bisecting the angle between the rising and setting points of the solstitial sun is only applicable in perfectly flat country, whereas most of these sites are in hilly country. For the kind of accuracy attained at Callanish a more sophisticated method must have been used. The most likely seems to be the bisection of the angle between the east and west elongations of a circumpolar star. This would involve the use of a plumb-line hung from a high pole or frame. Stakes or smaller plumb-lines would be used to mark the two backsights from which the two elongations were observed. The point midway between the stakes and the foot of the main plumb-line would then give the required direction. This method could only be used in winter, since roughly twelve hours elapse between the elongations. It may be noted that today Polaris is about 50′ from the pole and this, if the observation were made when the star is at elongation, would produce an error of 50′/cos latitude or about $1\frac{1}{2}°$. If we observe the star on the meridian the long plumb-line is still necessary. It will be seen that the determination of the north/south line at Callanish correct to 0°·1 is no mean feat.

′The observed lines showing declinations

The most difficult part of the whole investigation is to decide when to include a line and when to exclude it. The decision must always be a matter of personal opinion and is influenced by the viewpoint and the other lines with which, at the time, it is being compared. An attempt to get some measure of objectivity, however small, in the material presented in Table 8.1 has been made by dividing the lines into three classes, A, B, and C.

Class A contains those lines which it is considered would be accepted by any unbiased observer.

Class B contains borderline cases which some people might accept and others discard.

Class C contains lines which would be excluded from a statistical analysis. For example, a line from a site to an impressive natural foresight is marked C when its only claim is that it gives one of the declinations in which we are interested. If the hypothesis on which the declination depends is later accepted then some importance attaches to the line. These lines are naturally excluded from the main declination histogram in Fig. 8.1.

Table 8.1 contains all lines which seem worthy of consideration. No line has been excluded which appeared impressive except one or two for which

Table 8.1. *List of observed lines*

Class A — Definitely indicated line
  „ B — Poorer indication
  „ C — Little or no indication

Description of lines

Type CC Site to site
  CO Site to outlier
  CS Site to stone
  OC Outlier to circle
  A Alignment
  A3 Alignment with three stones
  SSS Three stones in line

Type OS Orientated stone to stone
  SO Stone to orientated stone
  P Line along tumulus passage
  IF Indicated foresight
  COIF IF indicated by outlier
  SSIF IF indicated by two stones
  AIF IF indicated by alignment

Az—Azimuth *h*—horizon altitude h_E—extinction angle

Site			Class	Type	Az	*h*	h_E	Decl.	Star	Date	Remarks
A 1/2	Loch Nell		A	CO	147·5	6·6		−21°·8	Sun		
A 1/4	Loch Seil		A	AIF	146·8	6·9		−21·3	Sun		
„	„		A	AIF	326·1	5·3		+32·1	Capella	1870	
A 2/1	Inveraray		C	IF	23·7	11·1		+41·2	Vega	1900	Or Arcturus 1750
A 2/5	Kintraw		B	IF	223·9	0·5		−23·6	Sun		
„	„		B	IF	307·5	2·7		+21·9	Sun		
A 2/8	Temple Wood		A	SSS	206·1	0·3		−30·3	Moon		$S_3 S_1 S_4$
„	„	„	A	SSS	26·1	2·6		+32·3	Capella	1830	$S_4 S_1 S_3$
„	„	„	A	SSS	21·0	1·8		+32·7	„	1760	$S_5 S_1 S_3$
„	„	„	A	CC	136·6	4·4		−20·1 ⎫	Moon		Circle to group
„	„	„	A	CC	135·0	3·7		−20·1 ⎬	or Rigel		Circle to S_1
„	„	„	A	CO	115·9	7·1		−8·2	Sun		Circle to S_6
„	„	„	B	AC	321·2	4·5		+29·7	Castor	1730	$S_5 S_4$ to circle
„	„	„	B	CA	141·2	1·8		−24·4	Sun		Circle to $S_4 S_5$
„	„	„	A	AS	329·6	5·8		+34·0			$S_3 S_2 S_6$
„	„	„	A	SA	149·6	2·0		−27·1			$S_6 S_2 S_3$
A 2/19	Achnabreck		B	SS	159·5	2·1		−29·9	Moon		One fallen
A 2/12	Duncracaig		A	A4	140·7	2·3		−23·7	Sun		Large stones
„	„		A	„	320·7	3·1		+28·2	Moon		„ „
„	„		B	A2	151·9	1·1±		−28·8	Moon		
„	„		B	„	331·9	3·1		+32·2	Capella	1850	
„	„		A	IF	42·3	9·2		+32·5	„	1790	Through holestone
A 2/6	Carnasserie		A	A	169±	2·4±		−30·9±	Moon (?)		
A 2/14	Dunamuck South	A	A2	138·2	3·4		−21·7	Sun		
„	„ „		A	A2	318·2	1·9		+26·4	Pollux	2000	
„	„ „		C	—	339·4	1·3		+32·5	Capella	1790	To A 2/21
A 2/21	Dunamuck North	A	A3	346·1	3·0		+35·6			
A 3/4	Tayvallich		A	CA	32·8	1·9		+29·5	Castor	1800	
A 3/4	„		A	IF	27·7	1·3		+30·4			
A 3/4	„		A	IF	34·1	2·1		+29·3	Castor	1860	
A 4/1	Escart Fm		B	AIF	206·5	0·9		−29·7	Moon		Foresight not checked
A 4/4	Ballochroy		A	IF	315·5	0·9		+24·2	Sun		Ben Cora
„	„		A	AIF	44·2	6·2		+29·4	Castor	1820	
„	„		B	AIF	226	−0·1		−23·6	Sun		Cara fall
A 6/1	Camus an Stacca	C	—	340·6	4·8		+36·6	Deneb		Poor or.
„	„ „ „		C	—	213·7	4·2		−24·2	Sun		No or.
A 6/2	Strone, Jura		B	AIF	298·3?	7·5		+21·6	Sun		One stone fallen
A 6/4	Knockrome		A	SSS	73·7	1·9		+10·4	Spica	1970	
„	„		A	IF	203·4	1·0		−30·4	Moon		Crackaig Hill
A 6/5	Tarbert, Jura		B	SS	106·7	1·5		−8·1	Sun		
A 6/6	Carragh a Chlinne	A	IF	228·0	2·6		−20·0	Moon		Dip
A 8/1	Mid Sannox		A	IF	229·3	6·2		−16·3	Sun		Col
A 9/7	Stravannan Bay		A	AIF	136·0	2·7		−21·7	Sun		Peak
„	„ „		A	A	311·5	0·7		+22·1	Sun		
A 10/2	Lachlan Bay		A	IF	43·0	0·6		+24·2	Sun		
A 10/3	Ballimore		B	PS	228·2	1·8		−20·6	Rigel	1950	
A 10/4	Kilfinnan		B	IF	333·5	6·8		+36·5 ± 0·4	Deneb		

Table 8.1 (*cont.*)

Site			Class	Type	Az	h	h_E	Decl.	Star	Date	Remarks
A 10/6	Stillaig		A	OSIF	325·5	0·8		+27·9	Moon		
A 11/2	Blanefield		A	A4	56·7	+7·2		+24·0±	Sun		
B 1/8	Sheldon of Bourtie		A	CO	119·7	−0·2		−16·0	Sun		
,,	,,	,,	A	CO	55·9	0·0		+17·1±	Sun		
B 1/18	Ardlair		A	CSSS	116·0	+1·1		−13·4	—		
B 1/26	Loanhead		B	CC	41·6	+0·7		+24·0	Sun		
,,	,,		A	CSS	144·0	0		−26·4	—		
,,	,,		A	CSS	139·0	0·2		−24·3	Sun		
B 2/4	Esslie (S)		A	CC	43·1	1·1		+24·1	Sun		To B 2/5
,,	,,		A	CS	306·2	0·2		+18·4±	Moon		
B 2/5	Esslie (N)		A	CC	223·1	2·7		−21·2	Sun		To B 2/4
B 3/3	Raedykes		B	CS	259·2	0·8	1·7	− 4·4	Bellatrix	1670	
,,	,,		B	CC	314·2	2·1		+23·9	Sun		
B 3/5	Kempston Hill		B	SS	231·4	0·6		−19·8	Moon		
B 7/1	Clava		A	PP	216·5	1·7		−24·3	Sun		
B 7/3	Dulnanbridge		A	AS	230·9	0·9		−19·5	Moon		
B 7/10	Easter Delfour		A	CO	219	2·0		−23·6	Sun		
D 1/7	Barbrook		A	CO	284·8	2·3		+10·5	Spica	2000	
,,	,,		B	CO	118·6	2·2		−15·1			Below grass hor.
G 1/4	Ballantrae		A	SSS	11·8	+2·7		+36·5	Deneb		
G 3/3	Laggangarn		B	CS	296	2·1		+16·2			
,,	,,		B	CS	106·2	0·7		− 9·0	Sun		Long stone
,,	,,		B	CS	105·4	0·7		− 8·5	Sun		
,,	,,		B	CS	150·3	0		−30·4	Moon		
,,	,,		B	CS	124·8	0		−19·6	Moon		
,,	,,		B	CC	133·8	0·2		−23·7	Sun		
G 3/12	Drumtroddan		A	A3	43·3	+0·4		+24·8	Sun		Re-erected (?)
G 3/13	Wren's Egg		B	—	227·5	−0·2		−23·6	Sun		To Big Scare
G 3/17	Whithorn		B	SS	254·3	+0·9		− 8·5	Sun		
G 4/1	Carsphairn		B	CO	100·4	+3·2		− 3·5			
G 4/2	The Thieves		C	SS	228	−0·4		−23·4	Sun		Axis of ring
,,	,,		C	SS	48	+6·7		+28·5	Moon		,, ,,
G 4/13	Kirkmabreck		B	SSS	5·9	3·1		+37·7			Meridian (?)
G 4/12	Cambret		A	CCC	296·7	0·2		+14·7			
,,	,,		A	CCC	116·7	5·7		−10·3	Antares	1860	
,,	,,		B	CS	254·3	4·3		− 5·4	Bellatrix	1870	Stone on skyline
G 4/14	Cauldside		A	CSSC	156·8	8·7		−23·9			
,,	,,		A	IF	59·5	0·3		+16·8	Sun		Peak
,,	,,		B	IF	78·2	+0·3		+ 6·6			
,,	,,	,,	B	COIF	281·2	+3·3	0·9	+ 7·2	Altair	1900	
G 6/2	Auldgirth							+ 8·9	Sun		Reported fake
G 7/4	Loupin Stanes		A	CC	306·5±	5·1		+24·1	Sun		
,,	,,	,,	B	CSS	201·2	1·5		−31·0			
G 8/8	Dere Street IV		B	SSC	276·7	2·3		+ 5·4			To Dere St. II
G 8/9	Eleven Shearers		A	A18	94·7	4·1		+ 0·5	Sun		
,,	,,	,,	A	A	109·2	3·1±		− 8·3	Sun		Estimated h
G 9/10	Borrowston Rig		A	CSS	333·3	2·0		+31·8	Capella	1930	
G 9/13	Kell Burn		A	A	129·8	1·8		−19·7	Moon		
,,	,,		A	A	309·8	2·9		+23·5	Sun		
H 1/1	Callanish I		A	CA	9·2	1·5		+32·5	Capella	1790	
,,	,,		A	CA	10·6	1·6		+32·5	,,	,,	
,,	,,		A	AC	190·6	1·3		−30·2	Moon		
,,	,,		A	AC	189·2	1·5		−30·2	,,		
,,	,,		A	CA	270·9	0·5		+ 0·3	Sun		
,,	,,		A	CA	77·8	0·9		+ 6·9	Altair	1760	
,,	,,		B	CC	142	+0·5		−24·5	Sun?		To V
H 1/2	,,	II	B	CC	129·5	+0·3		−19·7	Moon		To VI
H 1/3	,,	III	B	CC	280	0·6		+ 5·4	Sun		To I
,,	,,	III	B	CC	249	+1·7		−10·2	Antares?	1880	To II
H 1/4	,,	IV	B	CC	89	+1·0		+ 1·0	Sun		To VI
,,	,,	IV	B	CC	135	+1·4		−22·8	Sun		To V
H 1/5	,,	V	B	CC	64	+0·7		+13·6	Sun		To VI
,,	,,	V	B	CC	332·8	+0·3		+27·8	Moon		To II
,,	,,	V	B	CC	322	−0·2		+23·8	Sun		To I
H 1/6	,,	VI	B	CC	304·9	−0·2		+16·9	Sun		To I
,,	,,	VI	B	CC	269·0	+1·0		0·0	Sun		To IV
,,	,,	VI	B	CC	244	+0·9		−12·9	Sun		To V

Table 8.1 (*cont.*)

Site		Class	Type	Az	h	h_E	Decl.	Star	Date	Remarks
H 1/7	Gt. Bernera	B	IF	236	1·7		− 16	Sun		Dip
,,	,,	B	IF	83			+6±			Cairn
,,	,,	B	IF	90	0·7		0·3	Sun		Cairn
H 1/10	Steinacleit	B	CO	89·1	0·7±		+0·7±	Sun		Too close
H 1/12	Clach an Trushel	B	AC	77·9	0·9		+6·8	Altair	1700	To H 1/10
H 1/14	Clach Stein	A	CC	24·8	0·4		+28·5	Moon		To H 1/15
,,	,,	A	IF	98·3	0·4		− 4·5	Sun		To Suilven
H 1/15	Dursainean	A	SC	227·9	2·0		−19·3	Moon		H 1/15 on hor.
H 2/1	Clach an Teampuill	B	CC	138	1·9		−21·8	Sun		To Hill
H 2/2	Clach Mhic Leoid	A	IF	271·0	−0·1		0·0	Sun		To Boreray
H 2/3	Borvemore	B	IF	317·2	−0·1		+22·3	Sun		To Gasgier
H 3/1	Cladh Maolrithe	A	IF	296·6	−0·2		+13·2			To Spuir Islet
H 3/2	Clach ant Sagairt	A	IF	287·6	−0·0		+ 8·8	Sun		To Boreray
H 3/3	Clettraval	C	SC	126·5	−0·1		−19·2	Moon		To H 3/11
H 3/5	Fir Bhreige	B		121·8	0±		− 16·0	Sun		To H 3/9
H 3/6	Barpa nan Feannag	C	—	160·7±	0·7		−29·8±	Moon		Az. doubtful; stone on hor.
,,	,, ,,	C	CC	220·0±	0·6		−24·2±	Sun		To Tigh Chloiche
H 3/8	Na Fir Bhreige	B	SSS	288·9	2·3		+11·7	—		Perhaps reverse
,,	,, ,,	A	IF	271·8±	0·4		+ 0·8±	Sun		To H 3/6 and hill
,,	,, ,,	C	IF	253·2	1·3		− 8·2	Sun		To Marrival
H 3/9	Ben a Charra	B	IF	255·7	−0·3		− 8·1	Sun		To Deasgeir
H 3/11	Leacach an Tigh Chloiche	C	IF	304·1	−0·2		+17·0	Sun		To Haskeir
,,	Leacach an Tigh Chloiche	A	CCC	131·8	−0·3		−21·7	Sun		To H 3/20
H 3/12	Clach Mhor à Ché	A	IF	281·9	+0·4	0·9	+ 6·8	Altair	1700	To Craig Hasten
,,	,, ,,	A	IF	281·9	+0·4	0·5	+ 6·4	Procyon	1750	,, ,,
H 3/15	Claddach illeray	C	—	288·3	0·0		+ 9·3	Sun		,, ,,
H 3/18	Sornach Coir Fhinn	A	IF	303·2	+0·6		+21·6	Sun		To Cringraval
,,	,, ,,	A	IF	318·5	+0·8		+24·0	,,		To H 3/11
H 3/20	Craonaval	A	CCC	311·8	+0·6		+20·9	—		To H 3/11
H 4/2	Gramisdale (S)	C	CC	120·7	+0·3		−16·2	Sun		To Hacklet
H 4/4	Rueval Stone	A	IF	303·8	−0·1		+16·9	Sun		To Boreray
H 5/1	An Carra	C	—	315·4	−0·1		+21·9	Sun		,,
H 5/9	Pollachar Inn	C	—	227·6	−0·1		−22·1	Sun		Not visited
H 6/3	Brevig, Barra	A	A	135·0	−0·3		−23·6	Sun		
H 6/5	Berneray	C	CS	342	4·8		+35·9	Deneb		To Hecla
L 1/1	Castle Rigg	A	CO	251·5	3·2		− 8·1	Sun		Good outlier
,,	,,	A	SS	127·0	5·2		−16·0	Sun		Diameter
,,	,,	A	SS	307·0	4·6		+24·3	,,		,,
,,	,,	A	SS	157·1	2·8		−29·8	Moon		Cross axis
L 1/3	Sunkenkirk	B	—	128·8	+0·5		−21·5	Sun		'Entrance'
L 1/6	Burnmoor	A	CC	348·0	+7·5		+42·1	Arcturus	1900	E to A
,,	,,	A	CC	343·5	7·7		+41·5	,,	1800	E to B
,,	,,	B	CC	292·3	6·2		+17·9	Moon		
,	,,	B	CC	311·9	+5·5		+27·6	Pollux (?)	1600	E to D
,,	,,	B	CC	243·6	−0·5		−16·0	Sun		D to C
,,	,,	B	CC	131·9	+1·6		−21·6	Sun		D to E
,,	,,	B	CC	63·6	4·3		+18·5	Moon		C to D
,,	,,	B	CC	112·3	2·6		−10·8	Antares	1700	C to E
,,	,,		CC	358·7			Meridian			C to B
L 1/7	Long Meg, etc.	A	CO	223·4	1·1		−24·2	Sun		To Long Meg
,,	,, ,,	A	CC	65·1	3·4		+16·7	Sun		To Little Meg
,,	,, ,,	B	SS	86·0	3·7		+ 5·2			Cross axis
L 1/10	Seascale	A	CO	354·0	1·0	1·3	+36·3	Deneb		Good outlier
L 1/11	Giants' Graves	A	SSS	30·8	2·1		+31·8	Capella	1920	
,,	,, ,,	B	SSS	210·8	0·5		−30·2	Moon (?)		*h* guessed
L 3/3	Five Kings	B	A4	252·	4·5±		− 6·5	—		Uncertain
,,	,,	A	IF	312·6	21·3		+41·1	Vega	1820	Stone on hor.
L 6/1	Devil's Arrows	B	A3	331·2±	0·7		+31·2	Capella?		Re-erected (?)
,,	,, ,,	B	A3	151·2±	0·4		−30·7	Moon?		Trees?
M 1/4	Dervaig (A)	A	A4	342·0	0·0	0·5	+31·0	Capella	1930	One fallen
M 1/5	Dervaig (B)	B	A7	334·0	0·7±		+29·9	Castor	1700	Poor *h*
,,	,,	B	A7	154·0	1·6±		−28·4	—		,,
M 1/9	Ardnacross	B	A	339±	2·0		+32·7	Capella	1750	Fallen alignment
M 2/6	Ross of Mull	A	IF	59·9	1·5		+17·1	Sun		Peak

Table 8.1 (*cont.*)

Site		Class	Type	Az	h	h_E	Decl.	Star	Date	Remarks
M 2/8	Bunessan	B	IF	330·7	0·2		+28·6	Moon		St. on hor.
M 2/9	Ardlanish	B	CS	282·4	2·6		+ 9·0	Sun		From ring
M 2/10	Uisken	B	IF	229·6	0·3		−21·3	Sun		
M 2/14	Loch Buie	A	CO	123·4	6·8		−12·0			
,,	,, ,,	A	CO	223·6	0·4		−23·7	Sun		
,,	,, ,,	A	CO	237·0	2·1		−16·0	Sun		
,,	,, ,,	B	CO	330·8	14·1		+42·1	Arcturus	1740	
,,	,, ,,	B	CC	297·9	9·0±		+23·2±	Sun (?)		To small circle
,,	,, ,,	A	SSIF	348·5	10·3		+42·9	Arcturus	1980	Stone on hor.
,,	,, ,,	C	SS	65·7	+6·2		+18·2	Moon		
,,	,, ,,	A	OS	245·1	3·5		−10·4	Antares	1850	
,,	,, ,,	B	SCIF	324·7	16·8		+42·4	Arcturus	1900	Peak
,,	,, ,,	C	SC	150·8	5·1		−24·2	Sun		
M 4/2	Tiree S	B	IF	190·2	2·8		−30·4	Moon		Flat hill top
M 8/2	Barcaldine	A	IF	319·5	2·3		+26·6	Pollux	1930	Double stone
N 1/8	Loch of Yarrows	B	SS	343·0	0·0		+29·6	Castor	1800	Reverse?
N 1/13	Latheron Wheel	A	CO	196·1	1·0±		−29·7	Moon		
N 2/1	Learable Hill	A	A	92·8	2·4		+ 0·3	Sun		Multiple rows
,,	,, ,,	A	A	61·6	2·4		+16·6	,,		,, ,,
,,	,, ,,	A	AIF	75·0	2·2		+ 9·5	,,		Single row
P 1/1	Muthill	A	A3	57·3	1·8		+18·7	Moon (?)		
,,		A	A3	237·3	5·6		−12·7	Sun		
P 1/2	Doune	A	A3	13·5±	0·5		+32·7	Capella	1760	
P 1/8	Comrie	A	SS	296·8	5·3		+18·2	Moon		
,,	,,	B	SS	116·8	2·3		−12·3	Sun		
P 1/10	Fowlis Wester	B	CS	30·9	0·6		+29·4			
P 1/13	Monzie	B	CS	305·5	4·8		+22·8			
P 1/14	Tullybeagles	B	CC	264±	3·7		− 0·5±	Sun		
P 1/19	Croftmoraig	B	CO	101·7	8·9±		+ 0·8±	Sun		Close outlier
P 2/8	Shianbank	A	CC	137·5	2·6		−21·9	Sun		
,,	,,	A	CC	317·5	0·6		+24·2	Sun		
P 2/12	Dunkeld	B	A2	310±	3·7		+24±	Sun		
P 2/17	Dowally	B	SS	106·4	6·2		− 3·9	Sun		
P 3/1	Glen Prosen	A	A4	198·1	1·9		−29·9	Moon		
P 7/2	Galabraes	B	SO	86·8	5·6		+ 6·2	Procyon	1840	
S 1/1	The Hurlers	B	A4	76·3	0·8		+ 9·0	Sun		Far uprights
,,	,, ,,	B	A4	256·3	0·5		− 8·6	Sun		,, ,,
,,	,, ,,	B	SCC	16·5	3·4		+40·7	Vega		& Arcturus
,,	,, ,,	B	CC	12·4	3·3		+41·5	Arcturus	1800	Trees (?)
,,	,, ,,	B	CC	10·1	2·4		+41·9	,,	1860	,,
S 1/2	Nine Stones	A	CA	63·5	1·5		+17·5	Moon		
S 1/5	Treswigger	B	CS	317·2	1·9		+29·3	Castor	1840	Poor
S 1/6	Leaze	A	CS	59·1	1·7		+16·3	Sun		
S 1/7	Rough Tor	B	CS	351·5	5·1		+43·7			
S 1/9	Nine Maidens	A	A9	26·1	2·0		+36·5	Deneb		Good line
S 1/11	Nine Maidens	B	CSS	332·7	0·5		+34·4			
S 2/2	Merrivale	A	CO	70·4	3·5		+14·9			
S 3/1	Stanton Drew	B	CC	232·7	1·6±		−21·2±	Sun		Trees
,,	,, ,,	B	CC	52·7	1·3±		+22·9±			,,
,,	,, ,,	B	CC	211·4	1·7±		−30·9±	Moon (?)		*h* unknown
S 5/2	The Sanctuary	A	IF	320·0	0·3		+28·4	Moon		
S 5/3	Avebury	A	CC	339·2	0·5	1·3	+36·5	Deneb		
S 5/4	Woodhenge	A	CS	31·0	0·4	0·5	+32·5	Capella	1790	
S 6/1	Rollright	A	CO	29·0	0·0	0·5	+32·7	Capella	1750	
,,	,,	A	CC	95·0	−0·2		− 3·8	Sun		The Whispering Knights
W 2/1	Penmaen-Mawr	A	CC	60·9	−0·2		+16·4	Sun		Large to small
,,	,, ,,	A	CC	240·9	+3·7		−14·1			Small to large
,,	,, ,,	B	A3	18·6		1·3	+35·5	Deneb		? reverse
W 5/1	Moel ty Ucha	B	IF	256·7	0·1		− 7·6			
,,	,, ,,	A	CS	17·3	−0·2	1·3	+36·1	Deneb		
,,	,, ,,	B	CC	298·6	0·6		+16·9	Sun		To W 5/2
W 5/2	Twyfos	A	CC	118·6	5·0		−12·7	Sun		To W 5/1
W 6/2	Rhos y Beddau	A	CA	79·1	5·0		+10·5	Spica	2000	
,,	,, ,,	B	AC	259·1	3·8±		− 3·7	Sun		
,,	,, ,,	B	CA	72·7	5·5±		+15·0			
W 8/1	Rhosygelynnen	A	A	82·1	0·6		+ 4·9	Sun		
,,	,,	A	A	262·1	2·2		− 3·3			

Table 8.1 (*cont.*)

Site		Class	Type	Az	h	h_E	Decl.	Star	Date	Remarks
W 9/2	Gors Fawr	A	A4	49·6	1·3		+24·3	Sun		
,,	,, ,,	A	A4	229·6	−0·2		−24·2	Sun		
W 9/4	Castell-Garw	A	CCSS	214·3	0·0±		−31·2±	Moon (?)		Trees
W 9/5	St. Nicholas	A	CSS	71·0	0·3		+11·4	—		
W 9/7	Parc-y-meirw	A	A4	301·4	−0·4		+17·8	Moon		
W 11/1	Saeth-maen	B	A8	83·5	3·6		+ 6·6	Procyon	1660	
W 11/2	Y Pigwn	B	CC	53·3	0·4		+21·5	Sun		Stone on horizon
,,	,,	B	CC	233·3	1·0±		−21·0±	,,		
,,	,,	B	CS	131·0	0·9		−23·5	,,		
W 11/3	Maen Mawr	A	CO	335·2	4·3		+38·0			
,,	,, ,,	B	CS	4·5	4·6		+42·4	Arcturus	1950	
W 11/4	Usk River	B	CO	285·0	1·5		+10·1	Spica	1900	
,	,, ,,	B	A3	78±	3·3		+ 9·7±	Sun		
,,	,, ,,	A	CC	295·3	1·2		+16·0	Sun		
,,	,, ,,	A	CC	115·3	2·9		−13·1	Sun		
W 11/5	Ynys Hir	B	IF	126·5	0·2		+21·7	Sun		Vis. unchecked
W 8/3	Four Stones	B	COO	67·5	0·9		+13·9			Distant outliers

the azimuth or horizon altitude was not measured and could not be estimated with sufficient accuracy. A few lines from an outlier to a circle have been included but these have been given a low classification. This may be a wrong decision, but only an entirely new investigation can show if this method of defining a line is admissible.

Bad weather occasionally prevented an astronomical determination of azimuth and once or twice mist and rain prevented complete verification of the intervisibility of sites. Many of the horizon altitudes given in column 5 were measured on the site, but a number were calculated from the O.S. contours and these may be inaccurate where the horizon is near. Trees often prevented a measurement being made and it must be remembered that horizons which are clear today may have carried trees when the stones were erected. This is particularly true of many English circles sited in flat level country. The effect of trees, by raising the horizon, is to increase the calculated declination algebraically whether the declination is positive (N) or negative (S).

The extinction angle (pp. 15 and 160) given in column 6 is that of the star named in column 8, on the assumption that the line belongs to the star. The declination was calculated as shown on p. 17 or taken from a table similar to Table 3.1 but with a closer tabulation interval. For this h or h_E was used, whichever was larger.

It is generally agreed that the date of the erection of standing stones lies between 2100 and 1500 B.C. Accordingly when a star is shown in column 8 it is the star which had the tabulated declination at a date some time in this range. The date given is not necessarily the date of the erection; it is simply the exact time when the star named attained the tabulated declination. Assuming that the intention was really to indicate this particular star, there may still be uncertainty (1) in the survey and (2) in the hill horizon, which may have been affected by scrub or even trees when the line was set out. A

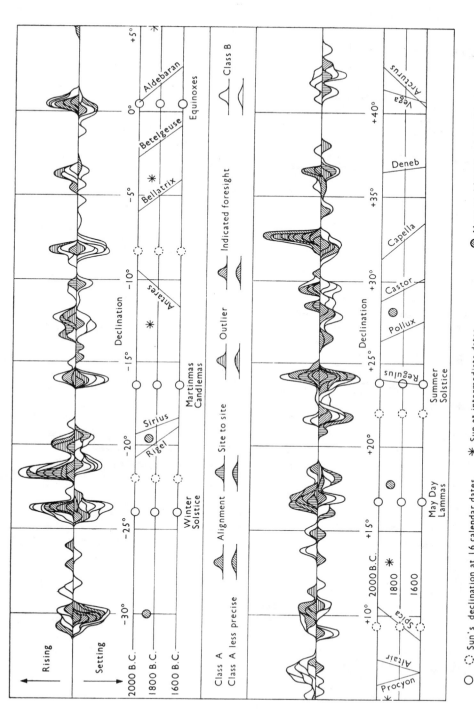

FIG. 8.1. Histogram of observed declinations.

statistical analysis would give a mean date for all the lines brought in and it would give a probability level, but as the author pointed out in 1955 (Thom) these figures would not be reliable unless we are sure that we are taking into account every possible explanation. The date obtained in the paper just mentioned was unreliable because the intermediate calendar dates were not taken into account. As a result declinations in the group around −21° were all assigned to Rigel, whereas, as we shall see, the majority were solar. A second source of error was failure to take account of extinction angle. It so happened that both of these factors tended to make the apparent date earlier than would now be obtained.

The over-all picture of the declinations will be found in Fig. 8.1, which uses the same method of presentation as was used for the circle diameters. Each line is represented by a small gaussian area placed at the corresponding declination. The more precise lines have a higher, narrower area than the less precise. The key to the shapes and shading of the areas used will be found in the middle of the figure. Only Class A lines are shaded, so in forming a first opinion the unshaded areas can be ignored. It will be obvious without statistical analysis that the manner in which the shaded areas tend to form definite groups cannot be explained on the assumption that the observed lines got there by accident. The fact that the lines only group in this way when we plot on declination shows that a large majority of these lines must have an astronomical explanation. The gaussians are arranged to show whether any given declination was obtained from an azimuth between 0° and 180° (rising) or between 180° and 360° (setting). The rising cases are shown above the base line and the setting cases below.

Below the declination distribution will be found plotted: (1) the declinations of all first-magnitude stars in the range, (2) the sun's declination at certain calendar dates, and (3) the declination of the moon in four limiting positions. The sun's declination at the solstices was about ±23°·91. But the declination of the upper limb of the rising sun when it first appeared on a level horizon would be about 0°·22 greater (algebraically) than this and the declination of the lower limb on the horizon 0°·22 smaller. Accordingly, the various positions of the sun are shown by a circle with this radius. If the lines were intended to show, for example, the upper limb on the horizon, then the gaussians ought to pile up to a maximum above the right-hand edge of the circle, as in fact they are seen to do at both solstices. Discussion of these and the other solar and lunar lines will be found in Chapters 9 and 10.

In looking at the histogram it must be remembered that it inevitably carries a number of spurious lines. An arrangement of stones which appears to indicate intentionally an azimuth may be entirely accidental. A line may have been disturbed or we may be looking along it in the wrong direction. An apparently good outlier may have belonged to another circle of which there is now no trace.

But accidental intrusive lines cannot explain the concentration of rising gaussians peaking at $+32°{\cdot}5$. One or two of these lines taken the other way certainly are lunar, but not all, and we conclude that the majority belong to Capella, c. 1800. It will be seen that several of the other first-magnitude stars appear to carry concentrations for a date between 2000 and 1800 B.C., but no group is so outstanding as that ascribed to Capella.

The stars as time-keepers

The times of lower transit of the four first-magnitude stars which were circumpolar as seen from the north of Scotland were as follows for the four seasons of the year.

	Vernal equinox	Midsummer	Autumnal equinox	Midwinter
Capella	1 a.m.	7 p.m.	1 p.m.	7 a.m.
Deneb	6.30 p.m.	12.30 p.m.	6.30 a.m.	12.30 a.m.
Vega	4.30 p.m.	10.30 a.m.	4.30 a.m.	10.30 p.m.
Arcturus	11 a.m.	5 a.m.	11 p.m.	5 p.m.

Unless on an elevated horizon the setting and rising of the last three would not differ by more than an hour or two from the times given for lower transit. From some parts of England, Deneb, with a nearly constant declination of $36\frac{1}{2}°$, would set only in the sense that it would fall below its extinction angle.

Figs. 8.2 and 8.3 have been prepared to give approximate times of rising and setting for first-magnitude stars in latitude 56° at about 2000 B.C. The rising and setting times of the sun are shown on both figures by a full line, while dotted lines show the times when the sun was 5° and 10° below the horizon. It is thus possible to see at a glance the time of year throughout which the star risings or settings would have been visible. The times will be affected by latitude, by the height of the horizon, or by extinction angle, so for any particular site these figures give only a rough idea. The difficulty of seeing fainter stars at all at midsummer in the north is shown by the very short times of darkness at that time of year when twilight lasted nearly all night.

As an example of the use of these figures note that in Scotland Castor was the only star which had a good chance of being seen rising at the summer solstice. It will be seen on the histogram (Fig. 8.1) that Castor has only three Class A lines, all rising, and all three are in the northern part of the country.

Capella's usefulness at setting is seen to begin in the late autumn and thereafter either at setting or rising it was available until just before midsummer.

From the above list it is seen that Deneb transited below the pole about midnight at midwinter and so had about as long a run of usefulness as was possible for any star. Its setting was indicated by the line joining the two large inner circles at Avebury (S 5/3) and by the outlier at Seascale (L 1/10). Its rising is shown by an alignment at Ballantrae (G 1/4) but much more impressively by the very fine alignment the Nine Maidens (Fig. 12.15). Perhaps the explanation of the precise nature of the indications of Deneb's rising and setting is that Deneb is not in itself a very impressive star and other stars in

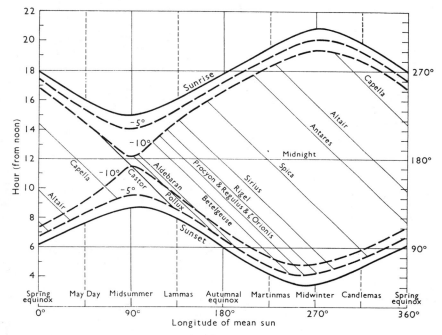

FIG. 8.2. Rising time of stars; sun at alt. 0°, −5°, and −10°. 2000 B.C., lat. 56° N.

the constellation are nearly as bright. This would not, however, explain the necessity for erecting so many stones as there are in the Nine Maidens' alignment.

It is interesting that there is a complete sequence marking the early morning hours at midwinter, when in the long winter night any community wants to have a method of knowing the time. We have then

Sirius setting	2 a.m.
Altair rising	4 a.m.
Capella setting	5½ a.m.
Pollux setting	7 a.m.
Dawn	7–8 a.m.

Sirius has no indicators, but with Orion's belt to show where it would rise or set no other identification would be necessary. The other three stars all

have azimuthal indicators at one site or another. The sequence given gets
earlier by four minutes every day but is soon joined by Capella rising and
Regulus setting. It will be seen that Regulus needs no special indicators. Its
declination throughout the period in which we are interested was that of the
midsummer sun and many sites contain solstitial lines. It will also be seen that

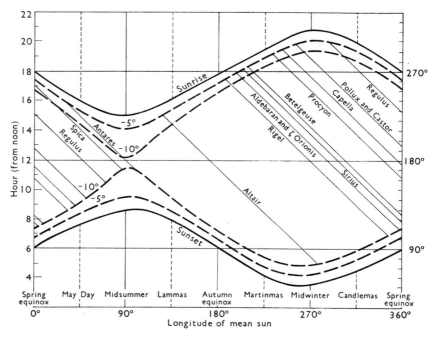

FIG. 8.3. Setting time of stars; sun at alt. 0°, −5°, and −10°. 2000 B.C., lat. 56° N.

at 2000 B.C. the declination of Aldebaran was that of the equinoctial sun.
These two coincidences must have appeared significant to a culture which
about 2000 B.C. was presumably beginning to take a close interest in astronomical phenomena.

9

THE CALENDAR

THE activities of early man were controlled just as ours are by the movements of the sun. So if he used a calendar it had to be related to the sun. As an approach to the subject it is perhaps best to forget for the moment about declinations, etc., observed at the sites and to consider what would be the ideal method of establishing and using a solar calendar assuming that it is to be based on observations of the sun made without instruments as we know them today. The Egyptians seem at one time to have controlled their calendar by observing what are called heliacal risings of certain bright stars, but this method is unsuited to northern countries with their long twilight. Moreover, the movement of the sun along the horizon is much greater in Britain than it is in Egypt and so more suitable as a calendar. It follows that we need have no hesitation in passing over the heliacal rising method and concentrating on a calendar controlled by observing the sun's position on the horizon.

We think naturally of dividing the year into four parts by the solstices and equinoxes. But these four times do not divide the year equally. They would do so only if the Earth's orbit were a circle. The modern definition of the equinox is the instant when the sun's declination is zero. But without instruments we cannot determine this instant. What we can do is to define the equinoxes as those two days which divide the year into two equal parts and on which the sun has the same declination, that is the same rising point. So we set up a mark S to show the position of the rising sun on a day in spring, the day being so chosen (by trial and error) that the mark serves also for a day in autumn half a year later. These two days of the year are thus fixed by the mark S for all future years.

It will be shown that the dates so determined are near the equinoxes but not exactly at the time when the sun's declination is zero. They are the times when the declination is about $+0°·5$. This is, for our investigation, fortunate because if, in the field, we find marks for declinations definitely between 0 and $1°$ we know we are thinking along the right lines.

Now suppose we wish to divide the year into eight and set up a mark showing the rising point one-eighth of a year after our vernal equinox, that is May Day. Will this mark also serve for Lammas if we define Lammas as being the day one-eighth of a year before the autumnal equinox? To give precision to this question it is necessary to define what is meant by one-eighth of a year (in days) and then make the necessary calculations from our knowledge of the Earth's orbit at the time in which we are interested, say 2000 to 1600 B.C.

Let us anticipate and say that in Megalithic remains we do find definite evidence of this kind of division of the year. We saw that when Megalithic man subdivided his units of length he used halves, quarters, and eighths so we need not be surprised to find his year similarly divided. But we also saw that he was capable of measuring long distances counting in tens. He would certainly also count days, otherwise how did he divide the year into two? His obsession with numbers may have led him to produce a calendar which would be numerically correct just as he was led to attempt to produce circles and ellipses which were rational in all their dimensions. Following the method used above we shall try how nearly we can get to an ideal calendar using the methods available to these people, but first we must clear up one or two points.

The reader may have wondered what we meant when we spoke above of half a year, since the tropical year (equinox to equinox) consists of $365\frac{1}{4}$ days, and half a year is $182\frac{5}{8}$ days. Having set up our mark S and seen the sun rise exactly on it on a day in the spring we may have arranged matters so that the sun rises again on the mark after 182 days or after 183 days but certainly not after $182\frac{5}{8}$ days. That would be in the afternoon.

Starting at the declination corresponding to either the 182- or the 183-day arrangement it takes the sun $365\frac{1}{4}$ days to complete a cycle and again come back to that declination. So when it rises after 365 days the declination will not have attained its initial value but will be about $0°\cdot1$ too small. We have seen that if the mark is a good natural foresight it is capable of showing up a very much smaller error than this. In successive years the error will grow until after four years the sun will be late by a whole day and so will be exactly on the mark the following morning.

From the time of Julius Caesar our calendar has inserted that extra day every fourth year. Was the necessity to introduce a leap year known to Megalithic man? We shall see that it is certain that he used a solar method of keeping a calendar and that it depended on horizon marks subdividing the year. But each mark must have been established by counting days from a zero date in the year, and each mark served to define two different epochs, one in the spring half of the year and one in the autumn half. It not only took years of work to establish these marks but many more years to transport and erect the huge permanent backsights. In the interval the marks would have got so badly out as to be useless if an intercalary day were not inserted.

It is true that these people, having set up the mark, might have stopped keeping a tally of days, simply leaving the marks to give the indications. But the Megalithic culture was widespread and communication essentially slow. To transfer the 'date' from one end of the system to the other meant that the messengers must have counted days as they travelled and having arrived at an isolated community the counting had to go on until a year with suitable weather allowed the marks to be set up. The alternative is to assume that each community began independently the arduous task of establishing its own calendar epochs. This is indeed possible, but when we find indications of the same declinations in Cumberland, Lewis, Wales, and Caithness we must consider the possibility that the calendar dates throughout this wide area were in phase.

The sixteen-month calendar

As the author collected more and more reliable lines from the sites certain groups of declinations began gradually to appear in positions on the histogram which were difficult to explain. These were at or near $-22°$, $-8°$, $+9°$, and $+22°$. The group at $+9°$ might be ascribed to Spica at 1700 B.C., but there were no convenient stars to explain the others. If they are solar then we seek the times of year at which the sun had these declinations. Accepting these dates, we find that with the fully established solstices, equinoxes, May/Lammas, and Martinmas/Candlemas days the year is divided into sixteen equal parts. The data in the field on which these subdivisions rest is sufficiently convincing and reliable to make it necessary to go into the matter in detail. We must calculate the sun's declination throughout the year. The necessary formulae are given on p. 24. The constants defining the Earth's orbit will be taken for 1800 B.C. as being representative of the years from say 2000 to 1600 B.C. The values are:

$$\text{Obliquity of the ecliptic} \quad = \epsilon = \quad 23°\!\cdot\!906,$$
$$\text{Longitude of sun at perigee} = \pi = 218°\!\cdot\!067,$$
$$\text{Eccentricity of orbit} \qquad = e = \quad 0\!\cdot\!0181.$$

Having used these to calculate the sun's declinations and plotted these declinations we obtain a curve like that shown in Fig. 9.1. This attains a maximum of $+23°\!\cdot\!91$ at the summer solstice and a minimum of $-23°\!\cdot\!91$ at the winter solstice. As already explained, the two lobes are not of equal length so we take three points S, A, and S' such that $SA = AS'$ and find that the declination at these points is $+0°\!\cdot\!51$. We have seen, however, that we cannot divide the year for our present purpose into two equal parts but must take SA as being either 182 days or 183. In Thom, 1966, 182 was used. Here we shall take 183. Obviously to get 183 days (instead of $182\frac{5}{8}$) the line S_1A_1 must be lowered slightly.

It is now necessary to find the ideal declinations for the other calendar epochs. On Fig. 9.1 we require to find six declinations, represented by three horizontal dotted lines in the positive lobe and three in the negative lobe. Each horizontal line gives a date at each end and the problem is to arrange matters so that these dates with the equinoxes and solstices divide the year as nearly as possible into sixteen equal parts, which we shall call 'months'. The solution referred to above restricted a month to 22 or 23 days. The criterion of a good solution is that the declinations must pair, that is the day in the autumn should have the same declination as the corresponding day in the spring. The solution obtained by the 22/23-day month did not give very good pairing. Accordingly, it was decided to try to find from the *observed* declinations what solution Megalithic man had obtained. Weighted means for

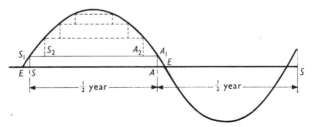

FIG. 9.1. Sun's declination throughout the year. *E, E,* true equinoxes. *A* is mid-way between *S* and *S*. *S* and *A* are Megalithic equinoxes.

the six necessary declinations (seven with the equinoctial value) were formed from the observed values in Table 8.1. Using these the corresponding dates were read off (two for each mean declination) from a large-scale plot of the theoretical declination curve (Fig. 9.1).

It is remarkable that this procedure led to a much better solution than had previously been found. The arrangement of the 'months' is shown in Table 9.1,

Table 9.1. *Calendar declinations*

Epoch Number	Days in 'month'	Epoch Nominal	Days elapsed at sunrise (t)	δ_R decl. at sunrise	δ_S decl. at sunset	Possible decl. range
0	23	0	−0·4	+ 0·37	+ 0·56	±0·19
1	23	23	22·56	+ 9·04	+ 9·24	0·17
2	24	46	45·53	+16·55	+16·72	0·14
3	23	70	69·51	+22·03	+22·13	0·07
4	23	93	92·50	+23·91	..	0·00
5	23	116	115·51	+22·09	+21·99	0·07
6	23	139	138·53	+16·80	+16·62	0·14
7	22	161	160·56	+ 9·31	+ 9·09	0·17
8	22	183	182·60	+ 0·51	+ 0·33	0·19
9	22	205	204·62	− 8·40	− 8·57	0·18
10	22	227	226·67	−16·24	−16·35	0·14
11	23	250	249·69	−21·92	−21·98	0·07
12	23	273	272·70	−23·91	..	..
13	23	296	295·70	−21·82	−21·72	0·08
14	23	319	318·68	−16·30	−16·15	0·14
15	23	342	341·64	− 8·52	− 8·37	0·19
16	..	365	364·60	+ 0·28	+ 0·47	..

Mean values at both sunrise and sunset are identical and are +0°·44, +9°·16, +16°·67 +22°·06, −8°·46, −16°·26, −21°·86.

from which it will be seen that there are 4 months with 22 days, 11 with 23, and 1 with 24. Column 3 shows the number of days from the zero day, the vernal equinox.

The calculation of the exact declination at the various epochs is connected with the question of how the intercalary day was inserted. Let us take it that an extra day was given to the years $T-2$, $T+2$, $T+6$, etc. Ideally the azimuthal lines should be erected to suit the year T. They will then be correct also for the years $T+4$, $T+8$, etc., and they will show the greatest errors in the years $T+2$, $T+6$, etc. So we have to search for the best solution, ascribe this to the year T, and calculate the errors for the years $T+2$, $T+6$, etc.

Having accepted the arrangement of months shown in column 2 there is still a disposable constant, namely, the exact instant of zero time for calculation purposes. This must be chosen to give the best possible 'pairing' of the declinations.

Put

$$\delta_0 = \text{declination at epoch 0,}$$
$$\delta_1 = \text{,,} \qquad \text{,,} \qquad 1,$$

etc.

Then put

$$\epsilon_1 = \delta_0 - \delta_8,$$
$$\epsilon_2 = \delta_1 - \delta_7,$$

and so on up to ϵ_7, forming similar values for setting times.

The ideal value of zero time t_0 is that which makes the root mean square (ϵ_M) value of the fourteen values of ϵ a minimum. Two values of t_0 were tried, namely $t_0 = 0$ and $t_0 = -0.4$ days. It is the solution corresponding to the latter value which is given in Table 9.1, where we accordingly write -0.4 as the time of sunrise on the zero epoch. After 23 days the sun rises about 0.04 days earlier in the morning (and sets 0.04 days later at night). So the interval to the next sunrise is not 23 days but 22.96, and the time of sunrise is 22.96 added to -0.4 or 22.56 days. In this way column 4 is built up.

We now convert these values to 'longitude of dynamic mean sun' (l) by multiplying by $360/365\frac{1}{4}$, and then using the formulae on p. 24 we can calculate the sun's declination at sunrise on the first day of each month. A similar calculation is made for sunset on the same days. The results are given in columns 5 and 6. Finally column 7 contains the changes which take place in two years and so shows the maximum error in the leap-year cycle of four years. We must now make sure that we have used the best possible value for t_0. To do this we calculate the values of ϵ_1, ϵ_2, etc. for rising and setting. Summing the squares of these shows a mean value of about $0°.18$, a highly satisfactory result.

Repeating the calculation for $t_0 = 0$ shows a much higher mean error of about $0°.30$.

There is now enough information to enable us to write each value of ϵ as

$$\epsilon = a + bt_0$$

where the numerical values of a and b are found by comparing the two solutions. It follows that

$$\Sigma\epsilon^2 = \Sigma a^2 + 2t_0\,\Sigma ab + t_0^2\,\Sigma b^2.$$

Differentiating and equating to zero shows that this is a minimum when

$$t_0 = -\Sigma ab/\Sigma b^2.$$

Making the relatively short calculation indicated we find $t_0 = -0.47$. Fortunately this is so near to the value used (-0.40) in Table 9.1 that there is no need to repeat the calculation. We shall accordingly accept the values in that table as the best possible arrangement. Since it is impossible to obtain perfect pairing we form the mean declination for each pair. We find that these mean values are practically identical for the sunrise and sunset declinations. This comes about because for each pair the rate of fall of the declination in the autumn is nearly the same as the rate of rise in the spring. These means, which are the ideal values we must expect if Megalithic man's calendar was identical with that set out in Table 9.1, will be found below the table.

For those who do not want to follow through the above reasoning the results can be stated thus.

If Megalithic man wanted

(1) a calendar of sixteen nearly equal divisions of the year,
(2) marks erected on the horizon to show the rising and setting positions of the sun at the sixteen necessary epochs,
(3) each mark to serve for two of these epochs, one in the spring half of the year and one in the autumn half,

then there was no better method available than to set the marks for the declinations shown below Table 9.1.

Instead of obtaining the necessary declinations by trial calculations we imagine Megalithic man experimenting for years with foresights for the rising and setting sun. We do not know how sophisticated his calendar was, but the interesting thing is that he obtained declinations very close to those we have obtained as the ideal. The comparison can be seen roughly on Fig. 8.1 where the sun's declination at the various epochs is shown by a circle, but the scale is too small to show detail. Accordingly the parts of the histogram near and around the germane declinations have been drawn to a larger scale in Fig. 9.2. The conventions used for showing the observed declinations are generally similar to those of the main histogram, but relative to the declination scale the gaussians are much smaller. Look first at the observed declinations near the solstices. The circle drawn to represent the sun is of such a size as to show the spread of declination produced by the sun's diameter. A majority of the

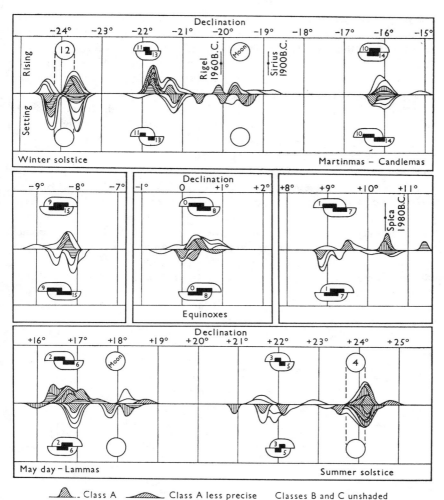

.ᗅᗂᗃ.. Class A   _ᗈᗉᗊ_ Class A less precise   Classes B and C unshaded
For key to shading see Fig. 8·1

FIG. 9.2. Calendar declinations.

observed declinations lie to the right of the disk at both solstices, showing that the upper limb was favoured. That is, the foresight was usually chosen to show the first appearance of the upper edge in the morning or the last at setting. There would appear, however, to be one or two reliable lines showing the sun as it left the horizon in the morning or as it touched it in the evening.

For the other fourteen epochs the declinations calculated for the ideal calendar are shown by little black rectangles, the width of each rectangle showing the unavoidable spread of the declination in the four years of the leap-year cycle. The two rectangles at the top of each section show the rising declinations at the two paired epochs, the displacement of the one relative to the other being the amount by which the solution falls short of perfect pairing, the ϵ of the analysis. All this is for the sun's centre: the limits for the upper and lower limb are shown by the ends of the curve drawn to embrace each rectangle. The calculated setting declinations are shown in the same convention at the bottom of the figures. As already explained, the mean rising and setting declinations are equal, but the spread may be very different.

In comparing with the observed declinations shown by the gaussians it must be remembered that many of these, for one reason or another, may be uncertain by perhaps $\pm 0°\cdot 25$, rather more than is indicated by the gaussians. In spite of this the agreement is good, but when the comparison is restricted to those lines which can be considered to be precise we get excellent confirmation. This is brought out in Table 9.2, which contains all those lines where the declination is considered to be known to $\pm 0°\cdot 1$. The difference between using the upper and the lower limb (on a level horizon) is shown by the two values of the expected declination (δ_E) shown at the head of each column. These values are the means shown below Table 9.1 with $\pm 0\cdot 22$ added. For indicated foresights with a mountain slope nearly parallel to the path of the setting sun the range would be rather greater ($\pm 0\cdot 27$), being in fact the sun's semidiameter.

Table 9.2

Epochs 0 and 8		Epochs 1 and 7		Epochs 2 and 6		Epochs 3 and 5	
$\delta_E \begin{cases} +0°\cdot 22 \\ +0\cdot 66 \end{cases}$		$\delta_E \begin{cases} +8°\cdot 94 \\ +9\cdot 38 \end{cases}$		$\delta_E \begin{cases} +16°\cdot 45 \\ +16\cdot 89 \end{cases}$		$\delta_E \begin{cases} +21°\cdot 84 \\ +22\cdot 28 \end{cases}$	
G 8/8	$+0°\cdot 5$	H 3/2	$+8°\cdot 8$	G 4/14	$+16°\cdot 8$	A 2/5	$+21°\cdot 9$
H 2/2	$+0\cdot 0$	N 2/1	$+9\cdot 1$	H 4/4	$+16\cdot 9$	A 3/18	$+21\cdot 6$
N 2/1	$+0\cdot 3$	G 6/2	$+8\cdot 9$	N 2/1	$+16\cdot 6$	H 5/1	$+21\cdot 9$
				L 1/7	$+16\cdot 7$	W 11/5	$+21\cdot 7$
				W 5/1	$+16\cdot 9$		

Epochs 9 and 15		Epochs 10 and 14		Epochs 11 and 13	
$\delta_E \begin{cases} -8°\cdot 68 \\ -8\cdot 24 \end{cases}$		$\delta_E \begin{cases} -16°\cdot 48 \\ -16\cdot 04 \end{cases}$		$\delta_E \begin{cases} -22°\cdot 08 \\ -21\cdot 64 \end{cases}$	
A 2/8	$-8°\cdot 2$	A 8/1	$-16°\cdot 3$	H 3/11	$-21°\cdot 7$
A 6/5	$-8\cdot 1$	M 4/2	$-16\cdot 2$	N 1/15	$-22\cdot 2$
L 1/1	$-8\cdot 1$			N 1/15	$-21\cdot 7$
N 1/15	$-8\cdot 3$				

It will be seen that we have here conclusive proof that the erectors succeeded to a remarkable degree in getting a reliable calendar of the kind we have developed on theoretical grounds.

Later, brief notes will be given of the reliable calendar sites in Britain, but we may here draw attention to an interesting site near Watten in Caithness (N 1/15). The lines from this site are not included in the histograms or in the main table but they have been included in Table 9.2, above. All that is left at this site is a 6-ft standing stone, a large fallen stone, and an artificial depression, but on looking to the south-west one sees a number of mountain peaks projecting behind an almost level middle distance (Fig. 9.3). Four of

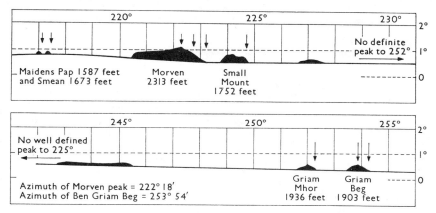

Fig. 9.3. Horizon to south-west from stones near Watten, ND 223516. Arrows indicate measured points.

these are well defined with the right-hand slope giving the necessary conditions for a perfect foresight. The author was so struck by the possibilities that these were carefully measured up and the azimuths of two calculated geodetically from the Ordnance Survey. The particulars for the foot of the slopes are given below.

Peak	Az	h	Decl.	Expected decl.
Morven	222·72	0·87	−22·20	−22·13 or −21·59
Small Mount	224·75	0·53	−21·74	
Ben Griam Beg	254·25	0·38	− 8·28	−8·73 or −8·19

In a position like this with distant peaks seen from relatively level ground it is of course possible to choose a position from which two of the peaks will have the required declinations, but it is very unlikely that a third peak will be in a position to give a third declination. Morven and Small Mount suit the lower and upper limbs of the sun, while Ben Griam Beg is only wrong by 0°·09 for the upper limb. Smean is slightly too far to the left for the solstitial sun and would necessitate an observing position a short distance to the east. Nevertheless it seems likely that this is a genuine calendar site.

A possible further subdivision

The improbability that the year was further subdivided into 32 parts of 11 or 12 days is considerably lessened by the accuracy with which certain otherwise unexplained lines support such a subdivision. As some of the lines are Class A it may be desirable to give the evidence and leave it there for future work to decide the matter. As before, guidance in choosing the epochs was obtained partly from the observed declinations and partly from pairing. Ultimately almost complete pairing was obtained with epochs which, it will be seen (Table 9.3, below), retain the eleven- or twelve-day interval, which would thus very likely apply to the whole year although the evidence at present only exists for twenty-four epochs. The calculated declinations for the four necessary extra pairs are given in the table.

Table 9.3

Nominal day	Decl.	Nominal day	Decl.	Mean of pair
12	+ 4·97	172	+ 5·00	+ 4·98
35	+13·16	150	+13·29	+13·22
194	− 4·00	354	− 3·98	− 3·99
216	−12·54	330	−12·78	−12·66

It will be seen that the pairing is very good. The next table (Table 9.4) contains the observed lines as extracted from the main table. Since these lines all have level horizons the comparisons should be made with the mean values from the above table $\pm 0°·22$.

Table 9.4

Site		Decl.	Expected decl.
L 1/7	Long Meg	+ 5·2	4·76
W 8/1	Rhosygelynnen	+ 4·9	and 5·20
H 3/1	Cladh Maolrithe	+13·2	13·00
W 8/3	Four Stones	+13·9	and 13·44
S 6/1	Rollright	− 3·8	−4·21
W 6/1	Rhos y Beddau	− 3·7	and −3·77
W 8/1	Rhosygelynnen	− 3·3	
P 2/17	Dowally	− 3·9	
B 1/18	Ardlair	−13·4	−12·88
W 5/2	Twyfos	−12·7	and −12·44
P 1/1	Muthill	−12·7	

The agreement shown with the expected declinations is so good that the possibility that the year was divided into periods of eleven and twelve days must be examined further as data become available.

It is proposed here to call the extra dates suggested above 'intermediate calendar dates'.

The exact time of the solstices

Looking at the formulae used for the calculation of the declination we see that the declination was a maximum when $\odot$, the sun's longitude, was $\pi/2$. From the relation between $\odot$ and l we find that l was then $92°\!\cdot\!08$, which is equivalent to $93\!\cdot\!4$ days. From Table 9.1 we see that this was $0\!\cdot\!9$ days after sunrise on the fourth epoch. Similarly the winter solstice was $0\!\cdot\!7$ days after sunrise on the twelfth epoch. Twenty-four hours after the solstice the declination has only fallen by some 12 seconds of arc, which would hardly be detectable. How then does it come about that the solstices were known so accurately? The explanation lies in that the epochs on either side of the solstice were arranged to be the same number of days from the solstice, namely twenty-three days for both summer and winter. This is still one more example of the care with which the calendar was arranged. At a site like Ballochroy (see p. 151) they could satisfy themselves that the declination really was a maximum even though the change was not perceptible for a day or two.

10

INDICATIONS OF LUNAR DECLINATIONS

ONE is inclined to think of the moon as occupying a great range of positions in the sky and so the tendency is to dismiss the moon with the thought that almost any line will show its position on the horizon sooner or later. But we have seen on p. 21 that there are four limiting declinations and it is for these that we must look. We shall see that these positions were considered important and were marked very definitely.

The obliquity of the ecliptic at 1800 B.C. was 23°·91 and the mean value of the inclination of the moon's orbit 5°·15. So at the solstices the four extreme values of the full moon's declination were

$$\pm(23°·91+5°·15), \quad \text{i.e. } \pm29°·06$$

and
$$\pm(23°·91-5°·15), \quad \text{i.e. } \pm18°·76.$$

To compare an observed azimuthal line with one or other of these values the direct method would be to correct the altitude of the horizon for refraction and parallax before it was used to compute the declination. For our present purpose it is, however, easier and sufficiently accurate to reverse the process and to compute the effects of parallax on the declinations. These effects can then be applied to the four above values. The declinations so found might be called the expected declinations (δ_e) and are ready to be compared directly with those given in Table 8.1, which were of course found without any correction for parallax.

Let Δh be the moon's horizontal parallax. Since the altitudes are all small the effect of this on a computed declination is

$$\Delta\delta = \Delta h \times d\delta/dh.$$

Δh is about 0°·95 and in these latitudes $d\delta/dh$ has a value of about 0·94 when δ is 29° and about 0·87 when δ is 19°. So we obtain the following expected declinations:

at the winter solstice
$$\delta_e = 29°·06-0°·95\times0·94, \quad \text{i.e. } +28°·17,$$
$$\text{and } \delta_e = 18°·76-0°·95\times0·87, \quad \text{i.e. } +17°·94;$$

at the summer solstice
$$\delta_e = -29°·06-0°·95\times0·94, \quad \text{i.e. } -29°·95,$$
$$\text{and } \delta_e = -18°·76-0°·95\times0·87, \quad \text{i.e. } -19°·58.$$

Table 10.1. *Observed declinations assumed to be those of the full moon in its extreme positions at the solstices.*

$$\delta = \text{observed declination}, \; \delta_e = \text{expected declination}, \; \beta = \delta - \delta_e$$

Midsummer lowest $\delta_e = -29{\cdot}95$			Midsummer highest $\delta_e = -19{\cdot}58$			Midwinter lowest $\delta_e = +17{\cdot}94$			Midwinter highest $\delta_e = +28{\cdot}17$		
Site	δ	β	Site	δ	β	Site	δ	β	Site	δ	β
A 2/8	−30·3	−0·35	A 2/8	−20·1	−0·52	B 2/4	+18·4	+0·46	A 2/12	+28·2	+0·03
A 2/19	−29·9	+0·05	A 6/6	−20·0	−0·42	L 1/6	+17·8	−0·14	A 10/6	+27·9 P	−0·27
A 4/1	−29·7	+0·25	B 3/5	−19·8	−0·22	L 1/6	+18·3	+0·36	G 4/2	+28·5±	+0·33±
A 6/4	−30·4 P	−0·45	B 7/3	−19·5	+0·08	M 2/14	+18·2	+0·26	H 1/14	+28·5 P	+0·33
G 3/3	−30·4	−0·45	G 9/13	−19·7	−0·12	P 1/1	+18·7	+0·76	L 1/6	+27·5	−0·67
H 1/1	−30·2 P	−0·25	G 3/3	−19·6	−0·02	P 1/8	+18·2 P	+0·26	M 2/8	+28·6	+0·43
H 3/6	−29·8	+0·15	H 1/2	−18·8	+0·78	S 1/2	+17·5	−0·44	S 5/2	+28·4	+0·23
L 1/1	−29·8	+0·15	H 1/15	−19·3	+0·28	W 9/7	+17·8 P	−0·14			
L 1/11	−30·2±	−0·25	H 3/3	−19·2	+0·38						
L 6/1	−30·7	−0·75									
M 4/2	−30·4	−0·45									
N 1/13	−29·7	+0·25									
P 3/1	−29·9	+0·05									

The six Class A lines marked *P* are considered to be reasonably precise.
Any values of β greater than 1°·0 (numerically) are excluded, but for midwinter lowest the limit of 0°·8 was used to avoid confusion with the May Day/Lammas lines.

These are the four declinations which are marked on the main histogram (Fig. 8.1) by four shaded circles. It will be seen that they all carry groups of observed lines, the concentration at −30° being particularly large. Two of these declinations also come into the range covered by the histogram of the

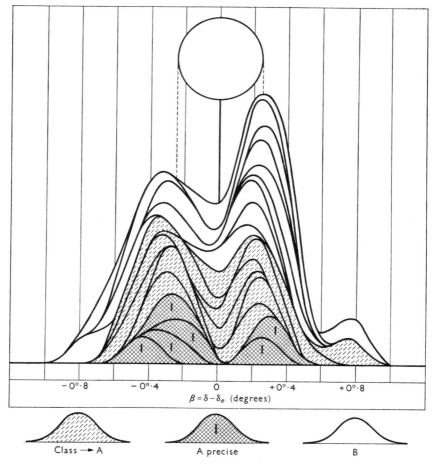

FIG. 10.1. Distribution of suspected lunar lines plotted as observed declination minus expected declination.

calendar lines (Fig. 9.2), where it will be seen how the gaussians tend to pile over the upper or lower limbs. To look into this question of the limbs it was decided to combine all four cases. This can be done conveniently by finding by how much every observed declination differs from the expected and then plotting these as a histogram.

In Table 10.1 will be found all declinations which lie within 1° of the expected values. In Fig. 9.2 it will be seen that one of these expected lunar lines comes near one of the expected solar lines, necessitating here a limit of 0°·8. Otherwise nothing has been excluded and the declinations are just as they were computed from the field material. The deviations from the expected values are tabulated as $\beta = \delta - \delta_e$. A histogram of these values will be found in Fig. 10.1. The remarkable way in which the gaussians form a peak for each limb of the moon will be noticed. The Class A lines are shown shaded and it will be seen that they alone produce the double peak, rather more lines going to the lower limb. There are six lines in the table (marked P) which are considered to give the declination with a precision better than $\pm 0°·1$. The gaussians for these lines are shown hatched in both directions, bringing out clearly how closely these reliable lines cluster about one limb or the other.

There are several obvious ways in which we can make a very rough estimate of the probability that these declinations would accidentally group themselves as they do if they were entirely random. The probability level comes out so very low on any reasonable way of estimating that it can be accepted as certain that these lines were set out intentionally to mark these declinations. As no other explanation can be found for the declinations involved we must accept that they have a lunar significance.

As explained in Chapter 3 there is a periodic term of amplitude 9' or 0°·15 superimposed on the moon's declination and the question arises as to whether the marks were set up for the mean maximum declination or for the absolute maximum. Many of the lines discussed in this chapter are incapable of discriminating, but there are a number of sites where not only can the difference be seen but it can be measured on the mountain tops. Unfortunately, not all of these lines contain unequivocal indicators pointing to the exact spot or spots. Accordingly, to be logical it is necessary to establish that lunar lines were used before going on to consider the evidence showing that Megalithic man actually observed and recorded the 9' oscillation. That has been the object of this chapter.

At the four or five sites where there is a possibility of a precision of $\pm 1'$ it will appear that it was not the mean maximum which was indicated, but that the top and bottom of the little wave shown in Fig. 3.5 (c) were both exactly recorded. But these sites need to be dealt with individually and they will be taken in their own place in the description of sites in Chapters 11 and 12.

In the meantime it may be said that Megalithic man's interest in the 9' oscillation probably arose from the fact that eclipses can happen only when the Moon's declination is near the top of one of these waves.

11

THE OUTER HEBRIDES

MORE space will be devoted to these islands than to any other part of the country because of the relative inaccessibility of many of the sites and because of the very great amount of information which is to be obtained there. There are about a hundred miles of islands with only two passages through, except at the extreme south, and for many months of the year these two channels are rendered impassable by the seas breaking on the shallow water. In a heavy winter gale the courtyard at Barra Head lighthouse is filled with water from the waves dashing on the cliffs and the lighthouse is 680 ft above sea level. Many of the sites can, it is true, be reached by normal transport, but others lie on small islands where the would-be surveyor needs his own boat. Anyone who cares to take the trouble to visit the sites will find himself in country quite different from anything else in the world and will be rewarded by a glimpse of a way of life rapidly passing away.

The east side of the islands is generally rock and heather, but much of the west is flat and supports most of the population. The west coast shows some of the finest stretches of beach in Britain resulting in places in great sand dunes. Naturally practically all the sites are on the west, and are to be found from one end of the archipelago to the other, even at Barra Head itself, which incidentally is not on Barra but on Berneray far to the south. At the north, Lewis and Harris form one island and it is in Lewis that we find Callanish, near which, at the head of Loch Roag, lies the most important group of circles and alignments in Britain. This beautiful loch lies on the north-west coast, its outer bastions of rocks and islands protecting it from the fury of the Western Ocean, here subject to a gale frequency barely surpassed anywhere.

The importance of this group lies not only in Callanish itself with its Type A circle, its small ellipse, and its five alignments, but in the surrounding sites, most of which are intervisible and all of which have some important contribution to make to the present study. Amongst them are four ellipses and one or perhaps two alignments, while collectively they provide by their intervisibility several interesting declinations. There is as yet no complete survey and so the information to be given here must be regarded as tentative pending a complete examination.

The earliest drawing of the main site known to the author is that in Martin's book (1716). The survey by Macculloch (1819) is naïve and crude. He measured in links but called them feet. This survey is, however, valuable in that it seems to be the only record, albeit difficult to interpret, of the stones which were upright before the 'reconstruction' which took place later in the nineteenth century. The only subsequent accurate survey is that by Somerville (1912). Fig. 11.1 shows the central portion of Somerville's plan with the Type A circle and the ellipse superimposed.

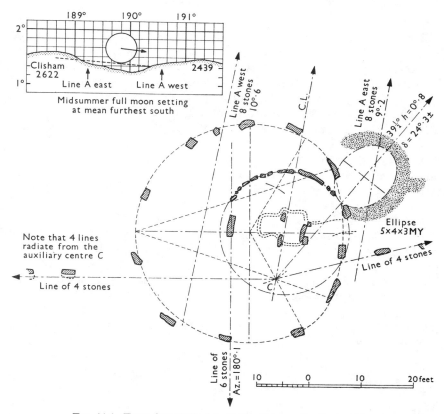

FIG. 11.1. Tursachan Callanish, H 1/1. Stones after Somerville.

Running south from the great menhir is an alignment accurately in the meridian (azimuth = 180°·1). Four other alignments of tall stones run from the ring, the two to the north forming the avenue. It will be noticed that, as pointed out by Somerville, the centre line of the avenue and the east and west lines pass through one point. It now becomes apparent that this point (C) is one of the auxiliary centres for the main ring. We shall see that, except for the meridional line, astronomical requirements decided the exact positioning of the sighting lines and so of the point C. The meridional line was probably moved slightly to the west to allow it to pass through the large natural rock to the south. The author found that at night this rock was the natural place to stand to see the line of menhirs running accurately to the point under the pole, and so from this rock the times of transit of stars to the north could best be judged.

The clearance of the peat from the site which took place last century allowed Somerville to plot the outlines of the beds of small stones. It will be seen that the annular bed on the north-east of the main ring is bounded on its inner edge by an ellipse based on a 3, 4, 5 triangle, the major and minor axes being 5 and 4 MY. The axis of the ellipse also radiates from C at an azimuth of about $39\frac{1}{2}°$ and this, with an estimated horizon altitude of $0°·8$, gives a declination of $+24°·3$, which is within $0°·1$ of the upper limb of the rising midsummer sun. A similar indicator of the solstitial sun will be found at Loanhead, Daviot (Fig. 6.6). Also at the Thieves (Fig. 6.12) the outline of a Type A circle is defined by a bank of small stones. We are at liberty to guess that these stones were originally retained by timber, which may of course have formed something impressive perhaps containing sighting gear. It will also be seen that the axis of symmetry of the main ring is exactly east and west and so parallel to the alignment running to the west which shows the setting point of the equinoctial sun. The alignment running towards the east shows, perhaps intentionally, the rising point of Altair in 1800 B.C.

Somerville accepted the stones he found upright as being in their original positions and found that the sides of the avenue were not parallel but that both lines showed the same declination to the north ($32°·5$). This was possible because of the slight difference of the hill horizon altitude for the two lines. But if we use only the stones which seem to have been upright in Macculloch's time the lines are parallel and 11 MY apart. The identification of the upright stones is, however, a little uncertain (Thom, 1966) and the matter awaits further investigation. This investigation would need to be done by archaeologists excavating the avenue by modern techniques. The importance of this apparently trivial matter lies in a suggestion first made by Professor G. S. Hawkins (1965 (1)) that the avenue was intended to be used looking south, when it gives one of the accurate lunar lines in Table 10.1. We know that some lines were so cleverly sited that they could be used in both directions and so the avenue may have been used for lunar observations to the south and for Capella rising to the north. If this is accepted the date of the erection would be 1800 B.C., which is also the date obtained by assuming the east line is for Altair.

The setting of the moon at its mean lowest declination is shown in Fig. 11.1. If the sides of the avenue diverged as supposed by Somerville we see what may have been intended. The lower limb reappeared on the flank of Clisham on what Somerville called Line A east and again vanished on Line A west. The azimuth of Line A west is not in dispute, so if the two were parallel both would show the disappearance on the slope to the right. As explained on

p. 23, the lowest position attained by the moon at a particular time could be as much as 0°·15, i.e. 9′, lower or higher than the mean lowest. This variation is allowed for by the outline of Clisham. At the absolute lowest the lower limb would touch the bottom of the dip and at the highest would graze the summit of Clisham. This arrangement whereby the limiting positions are shown might be ascribed to chance were it not for the fact that we have

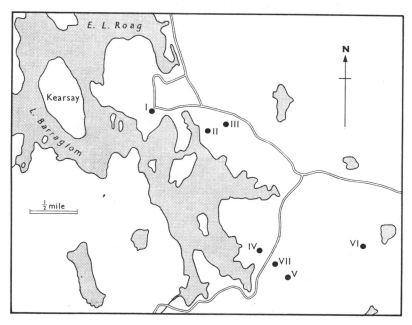

FIG. 11.2. Sites round the head of Loch Roag, Lewis.

reason to think that the same kind of arrangement obtains at several other sites. We shall see that at each of these the declinations 29°·95±0°·15 are shown almost exactly. The importance of getting independent confirmation of the exact conditions at these sites is difficult to overestimate. The discovery of this small variation in the inclination of the moon's orbit was made by Tycho Brahe. Is it possible that its effect was known in the Outer Hebrides in 1800 B.C.? Certainly the necessary observing apparatus for detecting the effect is there.

The positions of the seven known sites round the head of the loch are shown on Fig. 11.2. These sites will now be briefly described. Somewhat rough surveys are given for four, but all ought to be very carefully measured and examined before any of the dimensions and declinations can be accepted as final.

Callanish I, already dealt with, stands on a low peninsula in the loch and so has wide views in all directions.

Callanish II, Cnoc Ceann (Fig. 11.3), is a Megalithic ellipse in that it is based on an approximate Pythagorean triangle and has a calculated peri-

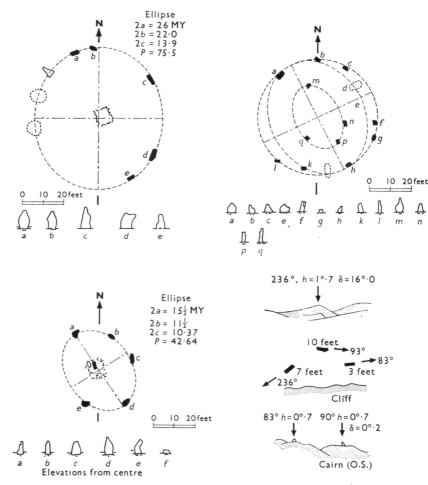

FIG. 11.3. Callanish II, H 1/2; Callanish III, H 1/3; Callanish IV, H 1/4; Great Berneray, H 1/8.

meter just over 75 MY. VI as viewed from II shows a declination estimated to be $-19°·7$. We have seen that one of the expected lunar declinations is $-19°·58$.

Callanish III, Cnoc Fillibhir Bheag (Fig. 11.3). If the author's somewhat hurried survey is substantiated this must be accepted as a most interesting arrangement of two ellipses with the auxiliary circle for the larger clearly indicated. It is the only place where this arrangement has so far been found. One wonders if the erectors realized that the ellipse was a projection of the auxiliary circle. Particulars of the two ellipses show some interesting features:

2a	2b	2c	P
21	17	12·33	59·86 MY
12½	8	9·60	32·59

If 12·33 is accepted for 12½ we see that the foci of the outer ellipse lie at the ends of the major axis of the inner. If the major axis of the inner ellipse is accepted as 12·33 the calculated perimeter is 32·30. With such a small number of stones it is doubtful if a more accurate survey will decide the matter but it makes little difference. The remarkable fact remains that both ellipses satisfy the requirement that the perimeters be multiples of 2½ and yet they are related in the manner above described. Since the diameter of the auxiliary circle is a multiple of 7 its circumference would be assumed to be $3\frac{1}{7} \times 21$ or 66. This reminds us of Moel ty Ucha (chapter 7) where the basic circle was a multiple of 7 and the modified ring a multiple of 2½.

Callanish IV, Ceann Thulabeg (Fig. 11.3). Here, again, we have an obvious Megalithic ellipse with a perimeter of 42·6 MY. The line to the north stone at V, and only the north stone is visible, passes through VII and on to a hill top, South Cleitshall. The declination (−22°·8) is difficult to explain unless we accept it as belonging to one of the intermediate calendar dates discussed at the end of chapter 6.

Callanish V, Airidh nam Bidearn (Fig. 11.4). The sketch plan was made by Dr. A. S. Thom in 1957 and the other information is taken from the Ordnance Survey. Unless something very close locally obstructs the view to the south-south-east the mountains at the head of Loch Seaforth are visible from the site and the moon in its mean furthest south position would have risen as shown at the top of the figure. It will be seen that the moon could be 9 or 10 minutes lower before the lower limb grazed Sithean an Airgid and 9 or 10 minutes higher before the upper limb cleared Mor Mhonadh. It will be seen that the azimuth of the alignment suggests that these mountains are the foresight. The outline to the north was also constructed from the Ordnance Survey but the two little hills shown over Callanish II are too near to permit of any great accuracy. It would appear that the setting moon at its mean furthest north just cleared these hills. Callanish I is also visible and shows the setting point of the midsummer sun. VI perhaps by accident shows the declination (+13°·6) of an intermediate calendar date.

Callanish VI is situated on a low eminence at about 125 ft O.D. with I, II, IV, and V visible. There are here two slabs 5½ ft and 3 ft high with orientations of about 323° and 270°. The latter indicates IV, which shows a declination of about 0°·0. Callanish I is indicated by the other stone and shows a declination of $+16°·9$. So from this site we obtain two calendar declinations, with perhaps an intermediate date from the line to V, which shows a declination of about $-12°·9$.

Callanish VII seems to be a ring of stones, 10 MY diameter, situated on the line between IV and V some 50 ft south-south-east of a ruin.

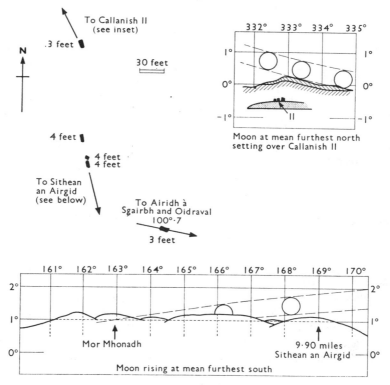

FIG. 11.4. Callanish V, H 1/5, sketch plan of site.

Great Berneray. On this island there is a site overlooking the narrows of Loch Barraglom which connect East and West Loch Roag. The arrangement of the three large slabs here is sketched in Fig. 11.3. It is seen that each slab indicates a hill top, but the cairns shown on two of these have not been visited and may be modern structures. Across the narrows on the Lewis side there is (or was) a single stone. These two sites so far as is known are not intervisible with any of the Callanish sites.

At Carloway near the mouth of Loch Roag stands *Clach an Tursa*. This 8-ft high stone has two fallen neighbours each about 16 ft long. The group appears to have formed an impressive alignment with an azimuth of perhaps about 153°.

Steinacleit. This site lies some fifteen miles further north. The outline is a Megalithic ellipse but the stones are small and may have retained some kind of cairn or tumulus. The polygonal ridge round the main site is not the only enclosure of this kind in Scotland, and has something in common with the structure high up above Macrihanish in Kintyre. There are other remains near Steinacleit, amongst them a small outlier to the east.

Clach an Trushel (H 1/12). This is perhaps the tallest if not the largest stone in Scotland. It is about 20 ft high and may have been part of an alignment. It is not flat enough to define an azimuth accurately but it might be said to indicate Steinacleit, which is visible on the horizon about 1·4 miles distant. If this was intentional perhaps the declination belongs to Altair, but one would expect a stone of this size to have a more important duty.

On the other side of Lewis in the Eye Peninsula stands, in a commanding position, a somewhat amorphous group of stones called *Dursainean* (H 1/13). This site is intervisible with *Clach Stein* (H 1/14) and a 6-ft slab in the valley some 600 yds to the north-east (H 1/15), not mentioned but perhaps marked on the 6-in O.S. This slab stands on a long mound and is orientated about 304° giving a declination of 16°$\pm$. The higher stones in Dursainean are just visible on the horizon giving a declination of $-19°·3$, one of the lunar lines. Dursainean is also the foresight from Clach Stein for another lunar declination, but the small stone beside Clach Stein is orientated on Suilven, that most spectacular of British peaks, on the other side of the North Minch 40·4 miles distant. If the corresponding declination ($-4°·5$) is accepted it can only belong to one of the intermediate calendar dates.

Coming south from Loch Roag there are no sites known to the author in the mountainous Forest of Harris. But they begin again on Taransay, where there is a large stone (Clach an Teampuill) on the low neck of land in the island. The horizon to the north is obscured, but from the slab, which stands roughly north and south, it ought to be possible to see *Clach Mhic Leoid* on the Harris shore. Unfortunately this was not checked. The line leads to a col and shows a declination of $-21°·8$ on the shoulder of Heilisval More, obviously one of the primary calendar declinations. Clach Mhic Leoid itself is an impressive stone orientated 280° and so pointing slightly to the north of Boreray, the most northerly island of the St. Kilda or Hirta archipelago. This precipitous island is 1245 ft high and so its peak (fifty-five miles away) projects above the sea horizon otherwise unbroken except by Hirta itself. In Fig. 11.5 Boreray's appearance is shown from Clach Mhic Leoid and from three stones in North Uist, Benbecula, and South Uist. It is seen that in every case the island is hull-down. These sites will be discussed in their proper place, but meanwhile it may be noted that all give primary calendar declinations. The setting sun has been shown on all in what seems the most obvious position, but it will be understood that in any given year it might never be seen in the position shown because on one night it might be to the left and the next have moved to the right past the peak. The movement per day along the horizon for three of these sites would be greater than the diameter of the disk.

There is a stone on Ensay in the Sound of Harris, perhaps giving the mid-winter sun rising on the Skye mountains, but there is a much more important site on Berneray, another island in this rock-strewn sound. The stone here, *Cladh Maolrithe*, stands inside a large grass (and stone) ring and is orientated

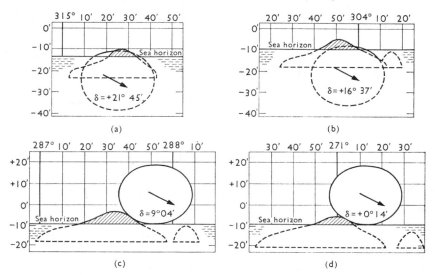

(a)   (b)

(c)   (d)

FIG. 11.5. Boreray as seen from menhirs at (*a*) An Carra, South Uist, H 5/1, 59·4 miles; (*b*) from orientated stone in Benbecula, H 4/4, 52·3 miles; (*c*) from Clach ant Sagairt (orientated), North Uist, H 3/2, 48·5 miles; (*d*) from Clach Mhic Leoid (orientated), Harris, H 2/2, 55·2 miles. The declinations in Table 8.1 are those of the island summit.

on a boulder some distance outside the ring. The line so defined indicates the small islet of Spuir in the offing. The corresponding declination (+13°·2) gives another of the reliable intermediate calendar lines.

North Uist. The positions of the sites in the west of the island are shown in Fig. 11.6. *Clach Mhor à Chè* is an impressive menhir accurately orientated on Craig Hasten and so showing the declination of Altair about 1700 B.C. (see p. 162). This may or may not have been the intention but Craig Hasten was examined and proved to be a huge rectangular natural rock standing on an eminence and so forming a natural landmark. Close to it, to the south-east, there is in the field what seems to be a small erected stone which is perhaps the backsight for the rising equinoctial sun. The site at Claddach illeray (H 3/15) was noticed just north of the shore road. It seems to have been a small stone circle, but the only stone now upright is a slab standing near the centre in the meridian. The stone which gives its name to Ben a Charra is a large upright slab orientated about 250°.

Leacach an Tigh Chloiche is, as the name implies, a house of stone on the ridge. It is the most important site in the island and consists of a mixture of open kists and upright stones. The latter seem to form an ellipse 20 × 13 MY, which gives a calculated perimeter of 52·42. From the south these stones stand out on the skyline so clearly that they were noticed from the circle *Sornach Coir Fhinn*, nearly three miles away but much lower. There are two

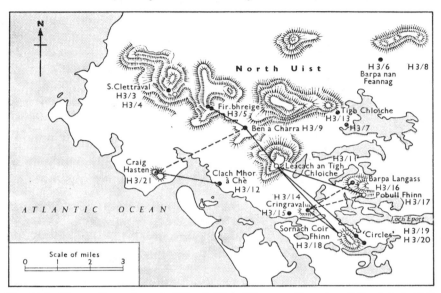

FIG. 11.6. Sites on the west coast of North Uist. (The seventh series of the 1-inch O.S. map interchanges the names of H 3/17 and H 3/18.)

large slabs projecting through the deep peat inside the latter circle. Both are orientated on Leacach an Tigh Chloiche, but as one is wedge-shaped one of its faces may be intended to indicate the site on Cringraval, where the stones stand out again on the horizon. Both lines give primary calendar declinations. The view to Leacach an Tigh Cloiche is shown on Fig. 11.7, where we see from the *centre* of Sornach Coir Fhinn the solstitial sun setting behind the stones. A few nights before and after the solstice the observer could, by moving to the right, get the edge of the disk on the stones, and the slabs at Sornach Coir Fhinn are to the right of the centre. So this circle may show us the same kind of adjustment as will be discussed in connexion with Ballochroy (pp. 151–3).

The sketch plan also shows how the large menhir at Leacach an Tigh Chloiche points roughly in the direction of Wiay, which lies close to the south-eastern corner of Benbecula. The moon in its mean most southerly position is shown rising behind Ben Tuath, the hill on Wiay. It will be seen that here again the position of the sighting point is such that the two extreme positions are marked at $\pm 10'$, almost exactly Tycho Brahe's range. The points on the profile as calculated from the Ordnance Survey contours are shown by black dots. The distance to Wiay is large enough to permit of these points being correct to $\pm 1'$ in altitude and $\pm 7'$ in azimuth, and so we can be reasonably sure of the particulars given, but it is desirable to have a profile accurately made on the spot. We have now seen that there are three sites in the Hebrides

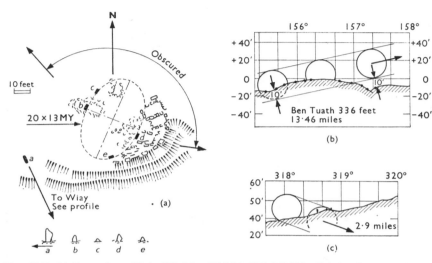

FIG. 11.7. (a) Leacach an Tigh Chloiche, H 3/11 (57° 34′ 38″, 7° 21′ 17″), scale sketch; site is at 260 ft O.D. on a ridge running down towards south-west. (b) Moon rising over Wiay (island) at mean furthest south as seen from Leacach an Tigh Chloiche. (c) Midsummer sun setting over the stones of Leacach an Tigh Chloiche as seen from the centre of the circle at Sornach Coir Fhinn (H 3/18), which has two orientated stones inside. Azimuths and altitudes $\pm 2'$.

showing not only the lunar declination but the declination limits correct to a minute or so. While the distance as the crow flies from Leacach an Tigh Chloiche to Callanish is only fifty miles, the journey today by public transport would probably involve crossing to the mainland and at best would mean chartering a ferry to cross ten miles over the Sound of Harris in addition to seventy miles of road travel. We see that the group of sites we are looking at belonged to a different community to that on Loch Roag.

Looking towards Leacach an Tigh Chloiche from the stones on South Clettraval (H 3/3) gives a declination of $-19°·2$, which is again one of the 'expected' lunar values, but this site has not been visited. Looking from Leacach an Tigh Chloiche to the south-east, Scurr nan Gillean in Skye nearly sixty miles away stands 2503 ft and gives the declination of the upper limb of the mid-winter rising sun, but the exact values on the slope of the mountain are not known. Curiously, the two ruined sites called 'Circles' on the O.S., but more like kisted tumuli, are exactly in line with this site and give one of the primary calendar declinations.

Thus it appears that The House on the Ridge is one of the most important sites in Britain, placed in such a position that it yields at least four declinations and possibly several more. Its position, dictated by the lunar line to Wiay, fixed the position of Sornach Coir Fhinn and so of Cringraval and almost certainly of several more of the sites shown in Fig. 11.6. Particulars of some of these and of other North Uist lines will be found tabulated. One of these ought to be mentioned. It is reported that the huge stone, Clach ant Sagairt, has been artificially erected, the claim being based on the packing seen below the base. It is orientated to point to Boreray, but bad weather prevented full verification of the calendar declination given from here by this universal foresight.

Benbecula has two or perhaps three circles, one of these at the North Ford being in a ruinous condition, but much more interesting is the stone just west of Ben Rueval. This stone is not shown on any O.S. map, but lies just south of the old cart-track round Ben Rueval to Loch Uskavagh and a little to the west of Loch na Ba Una. It is a small upright slab so accurately orientated on Boreray that it first drew the author's attention to the importance of this foresight by giving accurately the declination for one of the important calendar dates.

The largest stone in South Uist is An Carra, and like the great stone in North Uist it gives the name to another, Ben a Charra, and perhaps to the pass behind. It is 16 ft high and 5 ft wide at the base. It is orientated at about 53°, probably to indicate the sun rising on the shoulder of Hecla with a primary calendar declination of about $21\frac{1}{2}°$. But its main use was to give the same date in the evening with Boreray as an accurate foresight. This is the fourth and last of the stones in the islands using Boreray to give a primary calendar date. There is only one other position from which Boreray could be so used and that would be in the mountainous region in the Long Island, where, as already mentioned, we find no sites.

Almost buried in the sand dunes behind Ru Ardvule there are several stones, only one now upright. From here Maoil Daimh, one of the foothills of Hecla, appears behind An Carra to give the lower limb of the rising midsummer sun. Less than a mile away, near the west end of the causeway over Loch Kildonan, there is a rough ring of stones which may be the remains of a circle. With the sand dunes removed this might be visible from the Ru Ardvule site and if so would indicate a line to the shallow col between Ben Shuravat and Layaval and so would give 129°·4, $h = 1·0$, declination $= -19°·6$. This belongs to the lunar group, but is too uncertain to be used without considerable investigation.

In Barra, in addition to the stones on the west coast shown on the Ordnance Survey, there are at least two other sites. At the top of the pass through the island there is a stone $16 \times 4\frac{1}{2} \times 2$ ft reported by Dr. A. S. Thom to be almost fallen flat. On the east coast near Brevig there is a site believed to be called *An D'Ord* consisting of two alignments and a large upright. One is a solstitial line and the other is nearly in the meridian. The barps or tumuli in the hills are well known to archaeologists.

On Vatersay there are two stones forming part of an oval, and on the most southerly of the islands, Berneray, we find remains which may well have been a circle and an outlier.

12

A VARIETY OF SITES

TABLE 12.1 contains all the sites surveyed by the author which contribute to the material of this book. The position of each site is shown by the map reference with sufficient accuracy to enable it to be located on the 1-in O.S. maps. The table also contains in code a brief description of what is to be found at each site and a reference to the figure which contains a reproduction of the survey or a reference to a publication where a reproduction can be found.

This chapter will give particulars of a few of the more interesting sites chosen to illustrate the different kinds of structures found.

In the Dartmoor district there are several circles similar to those found elsewhere but there are also numerous avenues consisting of double rows of not very large stones. The avenues often lead from (or to?) small circles. These avenues have been described by various writers but there is no comprehensive study to enable a decision to be made regarding their possible astronomical significance. It seems best to ignore them all until they can be studied as a whole.

The so-called Recumbent Stone Circles are found only in the Aberdeenshire district and perhaps in the west of Ireland. The author has surveys of twenty-four sites showing either complete or ruinous examples. But there are many more judging by the list given by Keiller (1934) and the photographs and descriptions given by Browne (1921). A good example easy of access is to be found in Midmar churchyard (Fig. 12.6). Here we see the two flankers standing at each end of the recumbent stone. The flankers may be the tallest stones in the ring and the recumbent stone is always large, often impressively so. At Sunhoney (Fig. 12.5) it is 17 ft long. These two examples show a feature which is almost, but not completely, universal. In both, the left-hand flanker is nearer the centre than the right. In fourteen examples which were sufficiently complete to make a comparison possible twelve showed this peculiarity. The average distance by which the right flanker is further from the centre in the fourteen examples is 1·5 ft. At Midmar it will be seen that there are traces of a structure inside the flankers and recumbent stone. This feature is found in many of these circles and takes various forms, as can be seen by looking at the examples shown (see also Fig. 6.6). If originally the inner ring, traces of which are seen in many of these structures,

Table 12.1. *List of Sites*

Code in which descriptions are given:

C	Circle	3C	3 circles
CC	Concentric circles	3M	3 menhirs
CA	Flattened Circle Type A	CR	Recumbent Stone Circle
CB	Flattened Circle Type B	M	Menhir
CD	Flattened Circle Type D	S	Stone
CE	Ellipse	T	Tumulus, cairn
CI	Egg shape Type I	Al	Alignment
CII	Egg shape Type II	K	Kist

Site		Map ref.	Description	References	Remarks
A 1/2	Loch Nell	NM 906291	C, CB, M		*Clach na Carra*
A 1/4	Loch Seil	NM 801206	Al+M	Thom, 1966, Fig. 10	
A 2/1	Inveraray	NN 095090	M		
A 2/5	Kintraw	NM 830050	T, M, C	Fig. 12.1	
A 2/6	Carnasserie	NM 834009	Al		
A 2/8	Temple Wood	NR 827979	C, 3Al, etc.	Thom, 1966, Fig. 5	
A 2/12	Duncracaig	NR 833964	C, 2Al, M, etc.	Thom, 1966, Fig. 6	
A 2/14	Dunamuck S	NR 845925	Al		
A 2/19	Achnabreck	NR 856899	2M		
A 2/21	Dunamuck N	NR 847929	Al		
A 3/4	Tayvallich	NR 728861		Thom, 1966, Fig. 7	
A 3/6	Loch Stornoway	NR 742616	Al, M		
A 4/1	Escart	NR 847668	Al		Large menhirs
A 4/4	Ballochroy	NR 730524	Al, K	Fig. 12.2	
A 5/8	Colonsay	NM 387938			Solstitial
A 6/1	Camus an Stacca	NR 455647	M		
A 6/2	Strone	NR 508638	Al	Thom, 1966, Fig. 8	One standing
A 6/4	Knockrome	NR 548715	3M	Thom, 1966, Fig. 10	
A 6/5	Tarbert	NR 609822	2M		
A 6/6	Carragh a Chlinne	NR 513665	Al	Thom, 1966, Fig. 8	One fallen
A 8/1	Mid Sannox	NS 014456	M		Orientated
A 9/7	Stravannan Bay	NS 085553	Al	Thom, 1966, Fig. 7	
A 10/2	Lachlan Bay	NS 004943	M		Orientated
A 10/3	Ballimore	NR 933818	K, M		Passage
A 10/4	Kilfinnan	NR 926793	M		
A 10/6	Stillaig	NR 935678	Al, M	Thom, 1966, Fig. 8	
A 11/2	Blanefield	NS 533807	Al		
B 1/1	Strichen	NJ 937545	CR		Re-erected?
B 1/5	Upper Auchnagorth	NJ 839563	C		Perhaps CC
B 1/6	Easter Aquorthies	NJ 733207	CR	Fig. 12.3	
B 1/7	Kirktown of Bourtie	NJ 801249	CR		Ruinous
B 1/8	Sheldon of Bourtie	NJ 823249	CC	Fig. 6.4	
B 1/9	South Ythsie	NJ 884305	CB		
B 1/10	Fountain Hill	NJ 880328	C		
B 1/11	Balquhain	NT 736242	CR, M		Perhaps CC
B 1/12	Wantonwells	NJ 620272	CR		Remains only
B 1/13	Old Rayne	NJ 680280	CR		Remains only
B 1/14	Inchfield	NJ 624293	CR		„ „
B 1/16	Westerton	NJ 706190	C		Stones small
B 1/18	Ardlair	NJ 553280	CR	Fig. 12.4	Part only
B 1/21	Mains of Druminnor	NJ 510271	CR		Ruinous
B 1/23	Yonder Bognie	NJ 600458	CCR		Outlier removed
B 1/24	Blackhill of Drachlaw	NJ 672465	CR		
B 1/25	Charlesfield	NJ 700426	C		Ruinous
B 1/26	Loanhead, Daviot	NJ 748289	CR, CE, etc.	Fig. 6.6	
B 1/27	Sands of Forvie	NK 010260	CR, C, CC, etc.	Fig. 6.20	Stones small
B 2/1	Tyrebagger	NJ 859132	CR		
B 2/2	Sunhoney	NJ 716057	CR	Fig. 12.5	
B 2/3	Castle Fraser	NJ 715124	CR		
B 2/4	Esslie, South	NO 717916	CCE	Thom, 1961(2), Fig. 5	
B 2/5	Esslie, North	NO 722921	CCR		
B 2/6	Garrol Wood	NO 725912	CR, etc.		Perhaps Type B
B 2/7	Cullerlie	NJ 785043	C		Inner eells
B 2/8	Tarland	NJ 471052	C		Stones small
B 2/9	Tomnaverie	NJ 487034	CCR		

Table 12.1 (*cont.*)

Site		Map ref.	Description	References	Remarks
B 2/14	Leylodge	NJ 767132	CCR		Remains only
B 2/16	Tannagorn	NJ 651077	CCR		
B 2/17	Midmar Church	NJ 699064	CR	Fig. 12.6	
B 2/18	Tillyfourie Hill	NJ 643134	CR, T		Remains
B 3/1	Aquorthies, N	NO 902963	CCR, etc.	Fig. 12.7	
B 3/2	Old Bourtree Bush	NO 903961	CR?		Ruinous
B 3/3	Raedykes S	NO 832907	CC		Ruinous
B 3/4	Raedykes N	NO 832907	CC		
B 3/5	Kempston Hill	NO 876894	2M		
B 3/6	Glassel, Torpins	NO 649997	Oval		Pointed oval
B 3/7	Clune Wood	NO 795950	CR, etc.		Complex site
B 4/1	Carnousie Ho.	NJ 678505	2C, S		
B 4/2	Burreldales	NJ 676550	C		
B 4/4	Millton	NJ 550487	C		Part only
B 5/1	Urquhart	NJ 290640	C		
B 6/1	Little Urchany	NH 866482	CC		
B 6/2	Moyness	NH 951536	CC		Stones close
B 7/1	Clava	NH 757444	C, C, CE, 3T, etc.	Thom, 1966, Fig. 11 and Thom, 1961(2), Fig. 3	
B 7/2	Miltown of Clava	NH 751438	CC, T?		
B 7/3	Dulnabridge	NJ 011246	Al, etc.		
B 7/4	Boat of Garten	NH 967210	CE	Fig. 6.19	
B 7/5	Daviot	NH 727412	CE	Fig. 6.17	
B 7/6	Dalcross Castle	NH 780484	C, 2S		
B 7/9	Cantraybruich	NH 778459	C		Part only
B 7/10	Easter Delfour	NH 845086	CC, T, M	Fig. 7.4	Compound
B 7/11	Clava Lodge	NH 760446	C		Very crude
B 7/12	Aviemore	NH 897134	CCA	Fig. 6.22	
B 7/13	L. nan Carraigean	NH 905154	CC, T		Outer ring?
B 7/14	Belladrum	NH 516416	C		Small
B 7/15	Mains of Gask	NH 680359	CC	Fig. 12.8	
B 7/16	Farr, West	NH 680335	CCA		
B 7/17	Farr, P.O.	NH 682332	C		Inner passage
B 7/18	Druid Temple	NH 685420	CCI	Fig. 6.13	
B 7/19	River Ness	NH 621380	CC		Inner passage
D 1/2	Wet Withers	SK 226790	C+		
D 1/3	Nine Ladies	SK 249634	C, M		
D 1/4	Ninestone Close	SK 226624	C		Re-erected
D 1/7	Barbrook	SK 279755	CB, S	Fig. 6.11	
D 1/8	Owler Bar	SK 284773	CB		
D 1/9	Moscar Moor	SK 215869	CA		
D 2/1	Mitchell's Fold	SO 305983	CA, M		
D 2/2	Black Marsh	SO 324999	CA	Fig. 6.10	
G 1/4	Ballantrae	NX 087818	Al, 3M		
G 2/4	Port Logan	NX 160425	8 or 9S		Widespread
G 3/3	Laggangarn	NX 222718	Al, 4M		Also ring
G 3/7	Torhouse	NX 383565	CA, Al, 2S		Second C?
G 3/12	Drumtroddan	NX 364443	Al		
G 3/13	Wren's Egg	NX 362415	S, 2S, 2S		Large stone
G 3/17	Whithorn	—	S, S		
G 4/1	Carsphairn	NX 553942	CE		Probably ellipse
G 4/2	The Thieves	NX 404716	2M, CB	Fig. 6.12	
G 4/3	Drannandow	NX 400710	C		
G 4/9	Loch Mannoch	NX 661614	C		
G 4/12	Cambret	NX 510582	CA, 2C, S	Fig. 6.9	2C destroyed
G 4/13	Kirkmabreck	NX 498562	Al, etc.		
G 4/14	Cauldside	NX 530571	C, 2S, T	Fig. 6.3	Also ring
G 5/1	Dalarran	NX 639791	M		Slab
G 5/9	Maxwellton	NX 920740	CE?		Ruinous
G 5/10	Communion Sts.	NX 860790	4Al		
G 6/1	Twelve Apostles	NX 947794	CB		Large
G 6/2	Auldgirth	NX 918852	C, 2S, etc.		Fake
G 7/2	Seven Brethren	NY 217827	CA, S		
G 7/3	Wamphray	NY 140960	C		Ruinous
G 7/4	Loupin Stanes	NY 257966	CA, C, Al		
G 7/5	Girdle Stanes	NY 254961	C		Part only

Table 12.1 (*cont.*)

Site		Map ref.	Description	References	Remarks
G 7/6	Whitcastles	NY 225881	CB, M, Al		Special
G 8/2	Ninestone Rig	NY 518974	C		
G 8/5	Dere Street I	NT 750155	2Al, etc.	Thom, 1966, Fig. 20	
G 8/6	,, ,, II	NT 751161	C		Ruinous
G 8/7	,, ,, III	NT 752169	C		
G 8/8	,, ,, IV	NT 759159	2S		
G 8/9	Eleven Shearers	NT 790194	2Al	Fig. 12.9	Also ring
G 9/6	East Linton W	NT 581769	M		
G 9/10	Borrowston Rig	NT 560521	CII, 3S	Fig. 6.15	
G 9/11	Nine Stone Rig	NT 626650	C		Type?
G 9/13	Kell Burn	NT 643642	Al, etc.	Thom, 1966, Fig. 10	Not on O.S.
G 9/15	Allan Water	NT 470063	CI	Fig. 6.14	
H 1/1	Callanish I	NB 213330	CA, 5Al	Fig. 11.1	
H 1/2	,, II	NB 221326	CE	Fig. 11.3	
H 1/3	,, III	NB 226326	C, 2CE	Fig. 11.3	
H 1/4	,, IV	NB 230304	CE	Fig. 11.3	
H 1/5	,, V	NB 234299	Al, S	Fig. 11.4	
H 1/6	,. VI	NB 247304	2S		Slabs
H 1/7	Gt. Bernera	NB 163343	3M	Fig. 11.3	Slabs
H 1/8	Clach an Tursa	NB 204430	Al		2 fallen
H 1/10	Steinacleit	NB 306540	CE, 3S, etc.		
H 1/12	Clach an Trushel	NB 375538	M		+One fallen?
H 1/13	Dursainean	NB 524330	C?		Scatter
H 1/14	Clach Stein	NB 516318	2M		One fallen
H 1/15	Near H 1/13	NB 529334	M+		Not on O.S.
H 2/1	Clach an Teampuill	NB 010009	M		
H 2/2	Clach Mhic Leoid	NG 040973	M	Fig. 11.5	Slab
H 3/1	Cladh Maolrithe	NF 912807	M, S		In ring
H 3/2	Clach ant Sagairt	NF 880760	S	Thom, 1966, Fig. 8	Large
H 3/5	Fir Bhreige	NF 770703	2S		
H 3/6	Barpa nan Feannag	NF 857720	T		50×10 yds.
H 3/7	L. Scadavay	NF 837688	T, 2S		Great kist
H 3/8	Na Fir Bhreige	NF 888718	3S		
H 3/9	Ben a Charra	NF 787691	M		
H 3/11	Leacach an Tigh Chloiche	NF 800669	M, 4S, etc.	Fig. 11.7	
H 3/12	Clach Mhor à Chè	NF 770661	M		
H 3/13	Tigh Chloiche (E)	NF 833696	T		30 yds. diam.
H 3/14	Cringraval	NF 816645	2S		
H 3/15	Claddach illeray	NF 795646	C, 2S		Not on O.S.
H 3/16	Barpa Langass	NF 840658	T	St. Ac. 137	Type A?
H 3/17	Pobull Fhinn	NF 844650	C		Flattened
H 3/18	Sornach Coir Fhinn	NF 829630	C 2S	Thom, 1966, Fig. 14	
H 3/19	Craonaval N	NF 839629	T		
H 3/20	,, S	NF 842625	T		
H 3/21	Craig Hasten	NF 742667	Rock, S		
H 4/1	Gramisdale	NF 826562	C		Ruinous
H 4/2	Gramisdale (S)	NF 825552	C, S		
H 4/4	Rueval Stone	NF 814533	Slab	Fig. 11.5	Not on O.S.
H 4/6	Hacklet	NF 852528	T		
H 5/1	An Carra	NF 770321	M	Fig. 11.5	16 ft
H 5/3	Ru Ardvule	NF 727286	S, etc.		3 fallen
H 5/4	C. Ard an Ongain	NF 747269	4 kists		Perhaps circles
H 5/6	Loch Kildonan	NF 736277			
H 5/9	Pollachar	NF 748144	M		
H 6/3	Brevig	NL 688988	2Al		
H 6/4	Vatersay	NL 633942	M, S, ring		
H 6/5	Berneray	NL 564803	C, S		Ring, etc.
H 7/1	Uig Bay	NG 394628	S		Other traces
H 7/9	Strathaird	NG 5418			
H 8/4	Garrisdale	NG 209053			
L 1/1	Castle Rigg	NY 292236	CA, M	Fig. 12.10	
L 1/2	Elva Plain	NY 177318	C		
L 1/3	Sunkenkirk	SD 171882	C		
L 1/6	Burnmoor	NY 174024	CA, 4C	Fig. 6.5; Thom, 1966, Fig. 23	

Table 12.1 (*cont.*)

Site		Map ref.	Description	References	Remarks
L 1/7	Long Meg, etc.	NY 570372	CB, M	Fig. 12.11	
L 1/9	Glassonby	NY 572394	C		
L 1/10	Seascale	NY 034024	CD, M		
L 1/11	Giants' Graves	SD 136803	3M		
L 1/12	Lacra E	SD 147812	2C		
L 1/14	Dean Moor	NY 040223	C		
L 2/10	Gunnerkeld	NY 569178	CC		Ruinous
L 2/11	Castlehowe Scar	NY 587155	C		Rough
L 2/12	Harberwain	NY 597148	CD or E, C		Ruinous
L 2/13	Oddendale	NY 592129	CC		
L 2/14	Orton	NY 641080	CA		All fallen
L 3/1	Duddo	NT 931438	C		
L 3/3	The Five Kings	NT 955000	Al		
L 3/4	Lilburn	NT 971205	CB		
L 5/1	Birkrigg Common	SD 292740	CC		
L 5/2	Three Brothers	SD 495735	3S		Very large
L 6/1	Devil's Arrows	SE 389663	Al		Re-erected?
L 6/2	Fylingdales	NZ 920039	3M		
L 6/3	Stainton Dale	SE 984970	C		Cairn circle
M 1/3	Quinish	NM 413552	Al		
M 1/4	Dervaig A	NM 435531	Al		
M 1/5	,, B	NM 440520	Al	Thom, 1966, Fig. 8	
M 1/6	,, C	NM 440519	3S	Thom, 1966, Fig. 7	
M 1/7	Glengorm	NM 436571			
M 1/8	Tobermory	NM 500541	Al		
M 1/9	Ardnacross	NM 542491	2S, Al		
M 2/2	Duart	NM 725343	M. C		
M 2/6	Ross of Mull	NM 354224	M	Thom, 1966, Fig.8(*f*)	
M 2/7	Dail na Carraigh	NM 371218	T, Al, 2S		
M 2/9	Ardlanish	NM 378189	2S		2 ft ring cut on flat stone
M 2/10	Uisken	NM 391197	M, T, etc.		T small heap
M 2/14	Loch Buie	NM 618251	2C, 4S		C perhaps T
M 4/1	Tiree N	NM 077484	M, T		
M 4/2	Tiree S	NM 974426	M, C		Poor C
M 6/1	Killundine	NM 586497	4S		Small rings
M 8/1	Loch Creran	NM 944408	C, 2M		
M 8/2	Barcaldine	NM 9441	2S	Thom, 1966, Fig. 8	
M 8/3	Benderloch	NM 903382	C, 2S		C on bluff
M 9/1	Lismore	NM 862435	M		
N 1/1	Mid Clyth	ND 295384	Rows	Fig. 12.12	
N 1/2	Achavanich	ND 190416	Oval		Unique
N 1/3	Upper Dunreay	ND 011661	Stone rows	Thom, 1964, Fig. 3	Parallel
N 1/5	,, ,,	ND 008661	M		
	Forse	ND 208363	C		Part only
N 1/8	Loch of Yarrows	ND 316430	2S		
N 1/9	Wattenan	ND 315413	Stone rows	Thom, 1964, Fig. 2	Radiating
N 1/13	Latheron Wheel	ND 180350	C		
N 1/14	Camster	ND 261439	Stone rows		Radiating
N 1/14	Watten	ND 223517	2M, etc.	Fig. 9.3	One fallen
N 2/1	Learable Hill	ND 892234	7Al, 3T, M	Fig. 12.13	
N 2/2	The Mound	ND 770991	C		
N 2/3	Shin River	NC 582049	2C		Small
P 1/1	Muthill	NN 824159	Al		
P 1/2	Doune	NN 755004	Al		
P 1/3	Killin	NN 577327	CE		
P 1/4	Weem	NN 802488	C		Small
P 1/5	,,	NN 830494	C		
P 1/6	Fortingal	NN 746470	9S		3 triangles
P 1/7	Aberfeldy	NN 880505	S		Small
P 1/8	Comrie	NN 755225	2S		
P 1/9	Clach na Trom-pan	NN 830330	M, T		Also ring
P 1/10	Fowlis Wester	NN 924250	C, M		
P 1/13	Monzie	NN 881241	C, M S		
P 1/14	Tullybeagles	NO 010361	2S		

Table 12.1 (*cont.*)

Site		Map ref.	Description	References	Remarks
P 1/16	Meikle Findowie	NN 960385	CE		
P 1/18	Clachan an Diridh	NN 925558	3M	Fig. 12.14	Al
P 1/19	Croftmoraig	NN 797473	2C, CE, 2M		
P 2/1	Leys of Marlee	NO 160439	C		
P 2/2	Ballinluig	NN 977534	CE		
P 2/3	Blindwells	NO 125314	C		
P 2/4	Courthill	NO 184481	C		
P 2/5	Hill of Drimmie	NO 185500	C		Poor
P 2/6	Colen	NO 110311	C		Ruinous
P 2/7	East Cult	NO 072420	3M		Cups
P 2/8	Shianbank	NO 156272	2C	Thom, 1966, Fig. 26	
P 2/9	Guildtown	NO 143317	CE		Ruinous
P 2/11	Scone	NO 133264	CE		Ruinous
P 2/12	Dunkeld	NO 047410	Al		
P 2/14	Glenshee	NO 117701	C		Small
P 2/17	Dowally	NO 0048	Al		
P 3/1	Glen Prosen	NO 349601	Al, etc.	Thom, 1966, Fig. 20	
P 3/2	Blackgate	NO 485529	C		
P 7/1	Cairnpapple	NS 988718	CI, CE, etc.	H.M.S.O.	Complex
P 7/2	Galabraes	NS 988701	M, S		
S 1/1	The Hurlers	SX 258714	2C, CII, etc.	Thom, 1966, Figs. 27 and 28	
S 1/2	Nine Stones	SX 236781	C, Al		
S 1/3	Duloo	SX 236583	CA		
S 1/4	Stripple Stones	SX 144751	C		
S 1/5	Treswigger	SX 1375	C		
S 1/6	Leaze	SX 137773	C, S		
S 1/7	Rough Tor	SX 145800	CD, S	Fig. 6.1	
S 1/8	Dinnever Hill	SX 126800	CA	Fig. 6.2	
S 1/9	Nine Maidens	SW 936675	Al	Fig. 12.15	Good
S 1/10	Nine Maidens	SW 683365	C		Part only
S 1/11	Nine Maidens	SW 436351	C, 2S		
S 1/12	Porthmeor	SW 446367	CB, S		
S 1/13	Boscawen-un	SW 412274	CB, M	Thom, 1961(1), Fig. 4	
S 1/14	Merry Maidens	SW 433245	C, S, M		
S 1/16	Botallack	SW 387324	CA		
S 2/1	Grey Wethers	SX 639831	2C	Thom, 1966, Fig. 30	Re-erected
S 2/2	Merrivale	SX 553746	CB, M	Thom, 1955, Fig. 3	
S 2/3	Brisworthy	SX 565655	C		
S 2/4	Ringmoor Down	SX 562662	2C, rows		
S 2/5	Trowlesworthy	SX 576640	C, rows, etc.		
S 2/7	Lee Moor	SX 584622	C, rows		
S 2/8	Postbridge	SX 676787	CE	Fig. 6.21	
S 3/1	Stanton Drew	ST 601631	3C		
S 4/1	Winterbourne Abbas	SY 611904	CE	Thom, 1955, Fig. 3	
S 4/2	Kingston Russell	SY 578879	CB	Thom, 1955, Fig. 3	
S 4/3	Hampton Down	SY 596865	C		
S 5/2	The Sanctuary	SU 118680	Concentric		8C
S 5/3	Avebury	SU 102700	See text		
S 5/4	Woodhenge	SU 151432	6CI	Fig. 6.16	Outliers
S 5/5	Winterbourne Bassett	SU 094755	C, S		All fallen
S 5/6	Day House Lane	SU 182824	C		Part only
S 6/1	Rollright	SP 296309	C, S, etc.	Fig. 6.8	
W 2/1	Penmaen-Mawr	SH 723746	CE, C, etc.	Fig. 6.18	
W 4/1	Penbedw Hall	SJ 170680	C		Arc only
W 5/1	Moel ty Ucha	SJ 057371		See text, Chapter 7	
W 5/2	Tyfos	SJ 028388	Cairn C		
W 5/3	Meini Hirion	SH 583270	2M		
W 6/1	Kerry Pole	SO 157860		See text, Chapter 7	
W 6/2	Rhos y Beddau	SJ 058302	C, 3Al	Fig. 12.9	
W 8/1	Rhosygelynnen	SN 906630	Al	Thom, 1966, Fig. 33	
W 8/2	Rhos Maen	SO 143580	C (ruin)	*Arch. Camb.* 1861	The Fedw Circle
W 8/3	Four Stones	SO 245607	C, 2M		
W 9/2	Gors Fawr	SN 134294	C, 2M		Long Al
W 9/3	Cwm-Garw	SN 119310	2M		
W 9/4	Castell-Garw	SN 145270	2C, 2M		Ruinous

Table 12.1 (*cont.*)

Site		Map ref.	Description	References	Remarks
W 9/5	St. Nicholas	SM 913354	C, M, 2S		Ruinous
W 9/7	Parc-y-Meirw	SM 999359	Al	Thom, 1966, Fig. 33	
W 11/1	Saeth-maen	SN 9560	Al	Thom, 1966, Fig. 33	
W 11/2	Y Pigwn	SN 833310	C, CC, S, Al		
W 11/3	Maen Mawr	SN 851206	CI, M, 3S	Thom, 1966, Fig. 34	
W 11/4	Usk River	SN 820258	CE, C, Al	Fig. 6.23	
W 11/5	Ynys Hir	SN 921383	C, etc.		
W 13/1	Gray Hill	ST 438935	C, M, Al, etc.		

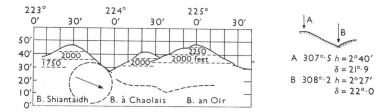

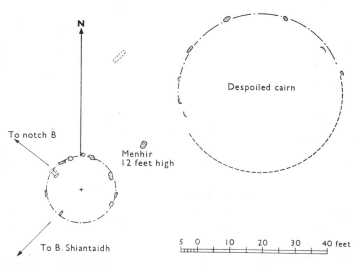

FIG. 12.1. Kintraw, A 2/5 (56° 11′ 17″·4, 5° 29′ 48·″4). Inset, view to south-west over near ridge from top of cairn; with cairn at full height the slope of Ben Shiantaidh would be visible.

contained a cairn or a tumulus, then presumably the tumulus had a spur reaching to the inside of the recumbent stone. Unfortunately tumuli were often in such a position as to form a too-convenient quarry from which local houses and churches could be built. An example where there was no such temptation is that on Tillyfourie Hill (B 2/18), but the whole site would need extensive excavation to discover what lies below. At Ardlair or Holywell (Fig. 12.4) there are three outliers roughly in line, and the line seems to lead more nearly from the recumbent stone than from the centre. From the stone

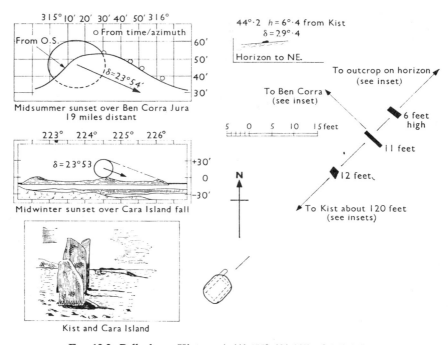

Kist and Cara Island

FIG. 12.2. Ballochroy, Kintyre, A 4/4 (55° 42′ 44″, 5° 36′ 45″).

the declination is −13°·0, a value which exactly suits an intermediate calendar date, but this is insufficient evidence on which to base a claim that the recumbent stone was always the backsight. The recumbent stone is sometimes slightly inside the main ring as at Midmar. It is nearly always in the south quadrant, with a preference for the south-west end of this arc. In four or five examples it is near the south point. One example was found with the stone on the north side. This circle near Strichen has been otherwise ignored; it is reported to have been rebuilt, but whoever rebuilt it seems to have known to place the left-hand flanker nearer the centre than the right.

Where a site contains two or more apparently concentric rings these are not always set out to the same centre. Systematic excavation by archaeologists such as that recently applied by Professor Stuart Piggott to Croftmoraig may show that the rings belong to different periods, but it may be that the separa-

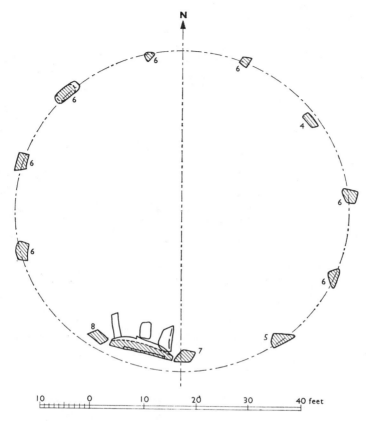

FIG. 12.3. Aquorthies, Manar, B 1/6 (57° 16′·6, 2° 40′ ·7).

tion of the centres at the Mains of Gask (Fig. 12.8) was intentional. The centre of the inner ring is two Megalithic yards north of that of the outer. The huge slab in the south-west quadrant of this circle should be noted. As elsewhere in this volume the elevation of the stone is roughly to the same scale as the plan. In the northern part of the country it is common to find the largest stone, whether it be in the ring or outside it, in this quadrant. Long Meg is an example, but Long Meg is not wide and is so dwarfed in plan by the scale of the site that it shows accurately the midwinter setting sun. Other examples are seen at Druid Temple (Fig. 6.13), Daviot (Fig. 6.17), and Easter Delfour (Fig. 7.4). At the latter site the narrow top of the stone again shows the setting solstitial sun, but in most sites the stone is so large that we cannot now deduce any declination. If we knew the reason for placing the largest stone in this quadrant we might understand why the recumbent stones are so often placed there.

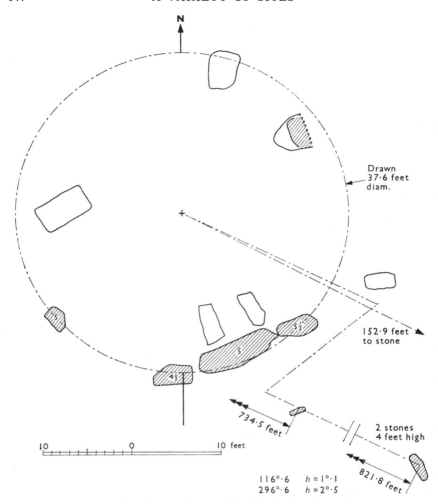

N

Drawn
37·6 feet
diam.

152·9 feet
to stone

5

5½

4½

734·5 feet

2 stones
4 feet high

10   0   10 feet

116°·6   h = 1°·1
296°·6   h = 2°·5

821·8 feet

FIG. 12.4. Ardlair, B 1/18 (57° 20′, 2° 44′).

The biggest Type B flattened circle is Long Meg and her Daughters (Fig. 12.11). This circle had a neighbour apparently in the next field but no trace remains. It is to be hoped that crop markings will eventually reveal its position and so allow details to be obtained by excavation. The so-called Little Meg is a ruinous small circle which, were the ground cleared, would from the main circle be on the line to Fiends Fell and so gives one of the calendar declinations. One of the stones carries spiral markings and reminds us of the large number of places where cup-and-ring markings are found in association with standing stones.

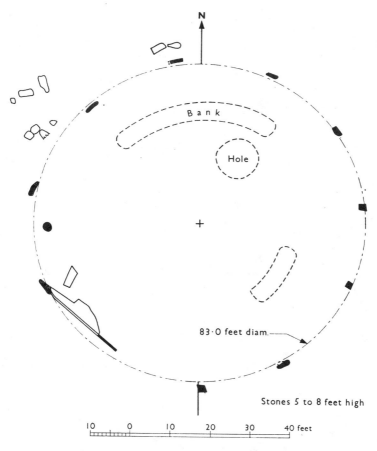

N

B a n k

Hole

83·0 feet diam.

Stones 5 to 8 feet high

10   0   10   20   30   40 feet

FIG. 12.5. Sunhoney, B 2/2 (57° 8'·5, 2° 28'·2).

The other well-known circle in the north of England is Castle Rigg near Keswick. In this circle we see in what a remarkable way the geometry of a Type A construction has been made to serve the astronomical requirements. The stones of the ring show seven solar or lunar declinations. One would draw attention to this and pass on were it not for the fact that four of the azimuths giving these declinations are defined by the Type A geometry. In Fig. 12.10 the Type A construction has been superimposed on the survey with the axis of symmetry at an azimuth of 67°·0, and from what follows this must be within a few minutes of the orientation used by the builders. The azimuths of all the lines in the construction can now be calculated. The diameter ACB passing through the right-hand auxiliary centre C is at an azimuth of 67°+60° or 127°, which, with the known hill horizon altitude,

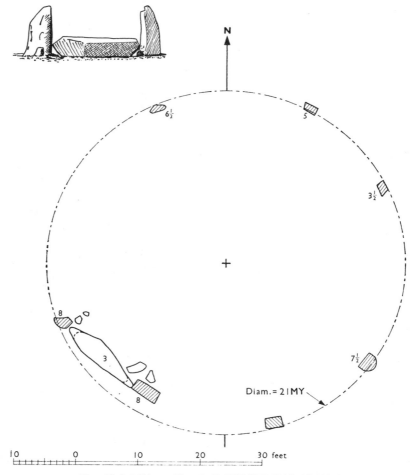

FIG. 12.6. Midmar Church, B 2/17 (57° 08′·9, 2° 29′·8).

yields a declination of −16°·0 or exactly the upper limb of the sun at the
ideal calendar declination of −16°·27. Looking along the same line in the
opposite direction shows a declination very close to that of the upper limb
of the midsummer sun. The azimuth of the transverse axis or of the parallel
line through C is 67°+90° or 157°, giving a declination of −29°·9±0°·2. The
exact altitude is uncertain but there is no uncertainty about this being the
moon rising in its most southerly position. The calculated angle between E
and F is 14°·48 making the exact azimuth of F 142°·52, which yields with
$h = 4°·4$ a declination of −23°·5 differing by only 0°·1 from the upper limb
of the midwinter sun. Apart from small uncertainties in the horizon altitudes,

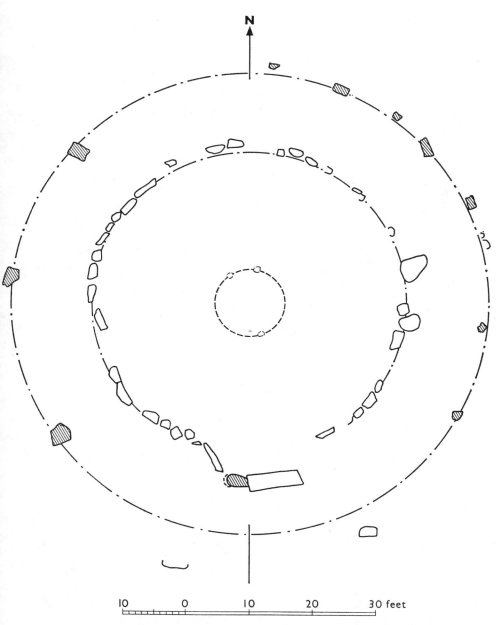

FIG. 12.7. Aquorthies, Kingausie, B 3/1 (57° 03′·4, 2° 04′·8).

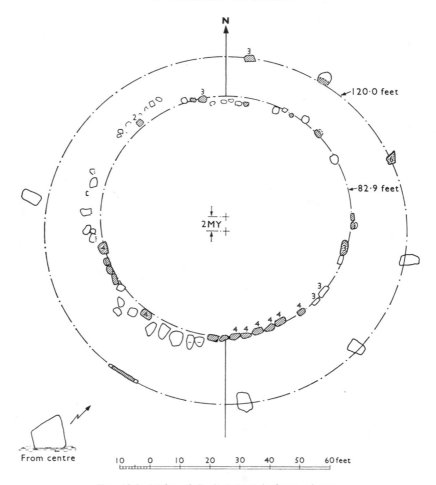

FIG. 12.8. Mains of Gask, B 7/15 (57° 24', 4° 12').

most of which were photographically determined, there can be no doubt
about the above values. But how was a position found which would permit
a Type A circle to be orientated to give so accurately these four declinations?
Ask any engineer with experience of field-work to locate a site with similar
properties and he will want a large group of surveyors working for an
indefinite time fully equipped with modern instruments and calculating
facilities. Add that the ring must occupy a level piece of ground and he will
ask for equipment to level the ground when he has located the exact spot.
It will be realized that it is only the mountainous nature of the country which
makes it possible to find a site with the necessary properties, and yet Castle

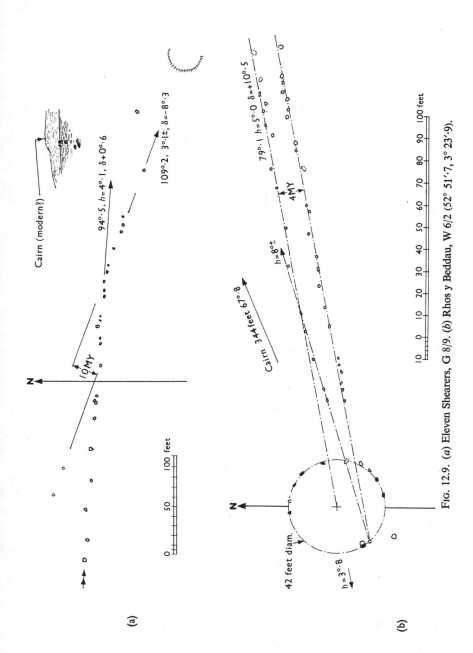

Fig. 12.9. (a) Eleven Shearers, G 8/9. (b) Rhos y Beddau, W 6/2 (52° 51′·7, 3° 23′·9).

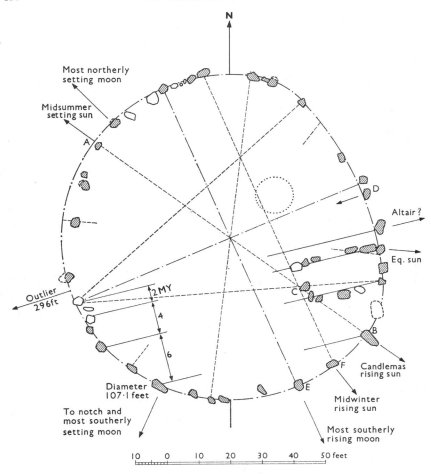

FIG: 12.10. Castle Rigg, L 1/1 (54° 36′·1, 3° 05′·5). Survey at base of stones.

Rigg, as tens of thousands of visitors know, is beautifully situated on a flat level part of the field.

The other declinations shown by this circle have no connexion with the geometry. The setting points of the moon at its most northerly and southerly positions are shown by two large stones. The equinoctial rising sun (declination = +0°·6) is shown by two stones, one being in the ring, and this point in the ring is also on one of the four parallel lines spaced 2, 4, and 6 MY apart which are indicated on the figure. All four pick up points marked by stones at each end and two of them define the inside of the stones in the cove or cell. The use of this structure, or of the lines if they were intentional, is quite unknown. It will be seen that the stone at C conforms to the universal

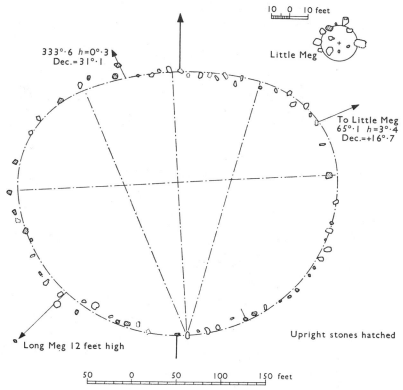

333°·6 *h*=0°·3
Dec.=31°·1

10   0   10 feet

Little Meg

To Little Meg
65°·1 *h*=3°·4
Dec.=+16°·7

Upright stones hatched

Long Meg 12 feet high

50   0   50   100   150 feet

FIG. 12.11. Long Meg and her Daughters, L 1/7 (54° 44′, 2° 40′).

rule of being, not on the centre, but beside it. This centre being on the right is the same as that which occupies such an important position at Callanish.

Looking from the stone *D* across the ring the large outlier some 300 ft away is seen exactly over the main centre. On this evidence the outlier must be important and in fact this was one of the lines which convinced the author of the necessity to examine the calendar hypothesis in detail.

The most interesting and instructive solstitial site is that at Ballochroy on the west coast of Kintyre (Fig. 12.2). The line of the stones and the kist shows the midwinter sun setting on the fall of Cara, but equally if not more important is the orientation of the stones indicating unambiguously Ben Corra in Jura. The outline of the mountain shown was calculated from the Ordnance Survey. Since the distance is nearly twenty miles this can be done accurately, but as a check four points on the slope were measured by theodolite, the azimuth being obtained astronomically. These points are shown by little rings and are seen to agree as closely as can be expected considering that the instrument was a small theodolite reading to minutes. Note that the slope of the

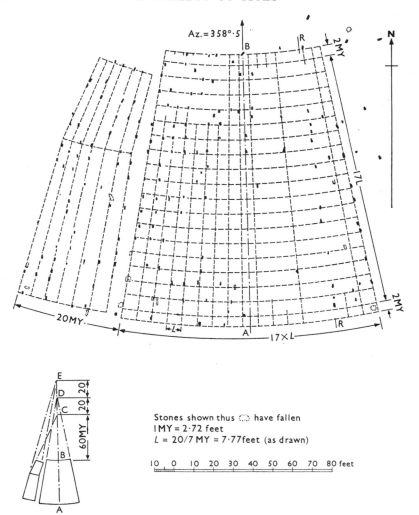

Stones shown thus ⟨⟩ have fallen
1 MY = 2·72 feet
L = 20/7 MY = 7·77 feet (as drawn)

10 0 10 20 30 40 50 60 70 80 feet

FIG. 12.12. Mid Clyth, N 1/1 (58° 20′, 3° 12′).

outline is slightly steeper than the slope of the sun's path. The distances on the site are such that the declination of the sun grazing the top of the slope as viewed from the north-east stone is almost the same as that of the sun grazing the bottom of the slope as seen from the kist. Both are about 23° 54′ as calculated with a temperature of 50° F or a minute greater if the temperature is assumed to be 65°. Unfortunately refraction at low altitudes is a very uncertain quantity and is liable to be affected by local conditions and of course by temperature and pressure.

The observing technique on a day near the solstice would be for the observer to stand on the line of the stones in such a position that the sun just vanished at the top of the slope. When the edge reappeared lower down he would move to the left keeping it grazing until it finally vanished. He would then mark the extreme position he had reached. A repetition of the experiment made on the next evening would reveal if the sun's declination had

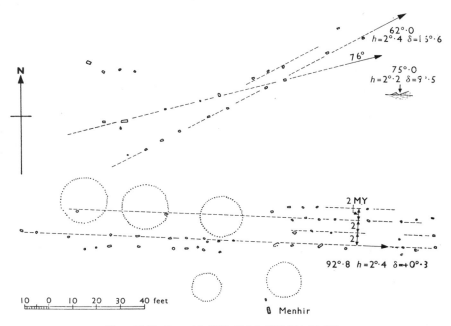

FIG. 12.13. Learable Hill, N 2/1 (58° 11′, 3° 53′).

decreased or increased and so would show whether or not the solstice had been passed. The conditions are such that it would take the sun about three minutes of time to run down the slope and so there would be time for the observer to adjust his position. But there must have been difficulties, because twenty-four hours before or after the exact time of the solstice the sun's declination is only about 0′·2 less than the maximum, and we have seen that a few degrees change in the temperature or indeed a change in the meteorological conditions over the sea could affect the refraction by much more than this. These difficulties are almost certainly reflected in the arrangement of the stones at Ballochroy. Just as these people had almost certainly detected changes in the extreme positions of the moon they would certainly have detected what they must have thought were anomalous movements in the sun's extreme position. Perhaps at Ballochroy they were attempting to investigate the irregularities. The apparatus there is of ample sensitivity. One minute

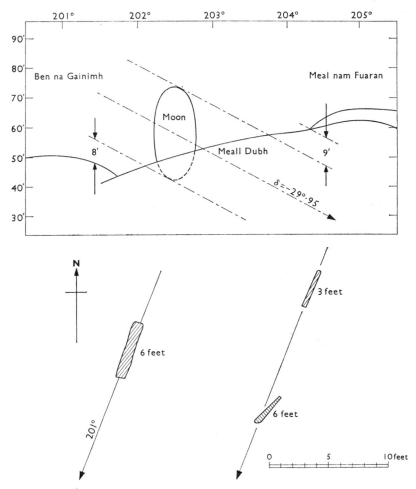

FIG. 12.14. Clachan an Diridh, P 1/18.

of arc in the declination or in the refraction would produce roughly a 30-ft change in the observer's final position if he were using the technique described above.

Some thirty-five miles to the north there is a site (Fig. 12.1) which may be another solstitial observatory capable of giving a very accurate value of the obliquity of the ecliptic. It stands on a small level piece of ground on an otherwise steep hillside. It seems to be the only suitable place for a circle from which the midwinter sun would graze the bottom of the col at the foot of the Ben Shiantaidh slope. Ben Shiantaidh is one of the Paps of Jura near Ben Corra and so this site may be the counterpart for the other solstice to that at

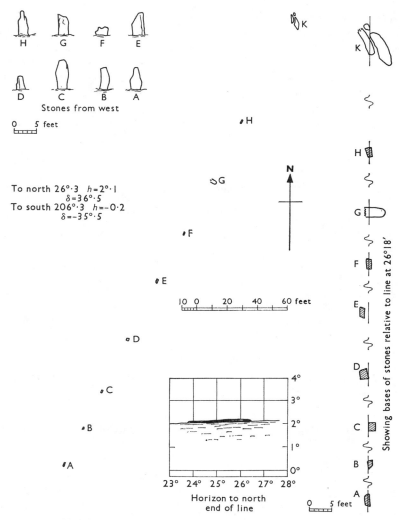

FIG. 12.15. Nine Maidens, S 1/9 (50° 28'·3, 4° 54'·4).

Ballochroy. Because of an intervening ridge now tree-covered the phenomenon is not visible from ground level and it has not so far been possible to find how far the eye would need to be raised to see the col. It looks as if a few feet would be sufficient and the suggestion is made that the top of the original cairn would have been high enough. There is a very large collection of sheep fanks with thick walls on the same plateau and if these were built with material from the cairn it must have been very large. On the evidence available it would seem that the cairn was built first with a level top from which the observer could decide on the exact line. This line may then have been marked by the top of the 12-ft menhir. The declination of the sun in the position shown on the profile is 23° 54′ S. The value of the obliquity of the ecliptic at 1800 B.C. was 23° 54′·3 but it was changing by less than a minute in a century. The close agreement makes it desirable to investigate the conditions at this site more fully. Ballochroy teaches us the technique of the moving

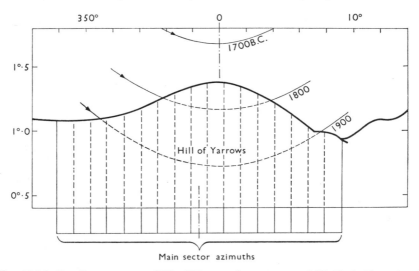

FIG. 12.16. Capella as seen over Hill of Yarrows from stones at Mid Clyth. The azimuths shown by the lines in the main sector are indicated.

observer but we do not know his exact final position. At this site the observer's position is very restricted and the greater distance to the mountains also makes for greater accuracy.

We find examples of parallel alignments in several parts of the country, but it is only in or near Caithness that the author has seen the fan-shaped constructions of which the outstanding example is that at Mid Clyth (Fig. 12.12). Here we find a main sector with an annex to the west. A few stones still in place suggest that there may have been a similar annex to the east. This would make the whole design symmetrical about a north–south line. It is possible that the missing stones were used in the foundation of the road which passes close to the site. An accurate large-scale plan was made of the 200 stones which were still there in 1959 and its orientation determined and checked. On the site one is immediately struck by the way in which each slab lies along the line in which it lies. An attempt was made to determine as accurately as possible the three centres from which these lines radiate. Referring to the key plan the dimensions are probably $BC = 60$, $BD = 80$, and $BE = 100$ MY. An analysis of the site is given in Thom, 1964, from which it appears that the

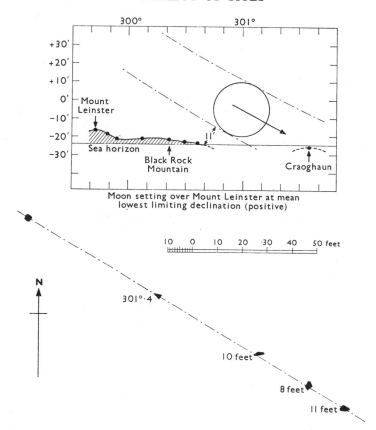

FIG. 12.17. Parc-y-Meirw, W 9/7 (51° 59′·1, 4° 54′·9). Inset, moon setting over Mount Leinster at mean lowest limiting declination (positive).

seventeen radial intervals in the main sector show a definite quantum of 7·70 ft. The top and bottom arcs have been added independently as shown. It will be seen that along the bottom arc it has been assumed that there are seventeen intervals each being the same as the radial intervals.

The site stands about 350 ft above sea level and is open to the sea horizon in the south. The ground on which the stones stand rises at some 4° from south to north, rather more steeply on one side than the other. After the last stones it falls, with the result that the positions of the centres cannot be seen except from the top of the sector. The consequent difficulties encountered by the erectors in setting out the site are obvious and show that there must have been reasons for choosing such an awkward position. We do not know these reasons and can only make suggestions. The horizon to the north, as seen from the upper end of the site, is sketched roughly with a much exaggerated vertical scale in Fig. 12.16. Capella's apparent path for three different dates is indicated and from these it appears that about 1760 B.C. the star became circumpolar. Prior to that date it set on the west side of the hill and rose on the east. The azimuths given by the lines on the main sector are shown and it will be seen that these bracket the phenomena for over 150 years. If the main sector was intended to study the changes in Capella's position work on the site must have started about 1900 B.C. Subsequent to 1760 the only use would have been for observing transits. And this may have been the real use of the structure.

At the same definite time of night a star on or near the northern horizon would appear each night about 0°·85 further to the right. But the lines are spaced at 1°·26. This spacing suits much better stars transiting to the south. Provided the star's declination was not greatly different from zero, the daily movement in azimuth at the same time of night would be about 1°·2, and so by using a different line of the sector every night the arrangement would act as a kind of star dial which would show the identical hour for eighteen nights. A criticism of this use of the site is that the slope of the ground is down slightly towards the south.

Perhaps it ought to be mentioned that the lines in the northern end of the annex bracket the setting points of the upper and lower limbs of the moon in its lowest position, when it is setting on foresights formed by the Monadhliath Mountains.

If the stone rows of Caithness have so far defied explanation, we are encouraged to believe that for at least some of them an astronomical use existed when we look at the stone rows on the Sutherland side of the Helmsdale river. Those on Learable Hill above Suisgil Lodge are easy of interpretation. To the west the ground rises gently, but to the east across the valley there is a perfect clean-cut horizon. It is seen in Fig. 12.13 that there are three definite azimuths and each of these gives a calendar declination. The Statistical Account carries a survey of a good ellipse (see Table 4.4) but this was not found. It may be added that the survey of the main site in the Account is so wildly different from the author's in orientation that a second visit was thought necessary to make sure of the azimuths, which, in the end, were checked astronomically and geodetically. This site is in some ways very similar to the Eleven Shearers (Fig. 12.9 (a)) at the other end of Scotland. The latter is simpler but it also shows calendar declinations.

Sites at any great altitude are uncommon, but there is an interesting group of stones, Clachan an Diridh, at about 1170 ft O.D. These stones (Fig. 12.14) are in one of the new forests not many miles from Pitlochry. Perhaps this is a lunar site. The exact orientation of the stones intended by the erectors cannot be determined any closer than ±2°, unless indeed more stones are revealed by excavation, but it cannot be far from 201°. The outline of the mountains far to the south, to an exaggerated vertical scale, is shown on this azimuth. It will be seen that the path of the setting moon at its mean furthest south is enclosed by two points on the hill tops, and that these points allow for the variation of 9′ on either side. This outline ought to be checked before the site is completely hidden by the growing trees.

Three or four miles from Fishguard there is another interesting lunar site. This is Parc-y-Meirw, a row of large menhirs in the bank by the roadside. The row is long enough to give a good azimuth and this is one of the good lunar lines discussed in Chapter 10. The alignment at the top end is not far short of 650 ft above sea-level, making it possible, at least in theory, to see the Irish hills. The outline of these hills was carefully constructed from the third edition of our 1-in O.S. by using the methods given on p. 25. It will be seen (Fig. 12.17) that Mount Leinster shows about 8′ above the sea horizon just to the left of the alignment azimuth. The spur to the east consisting of the Black Rock Mountain runs into the sea about 11′ from the track of the lower limb of the moon setting at its mean lowest limiting positive declination. The moon would then set exactly on the line of the stones. The mountains slightly to the north are below the sea horizon so there is no 9′ upper limit such as we saw at other sites. Nevertheless, this is an important site as it shows that the 9′-oscillation was known to apply to the minima of the limiting declination curves as well as to the maxima. It would be interesting if someone could, on a clear day, pick out the outline from the alignment.

Much can be learned from those sites where the upper and lower limits of the 9′-oscillation are shown. There are, at the time of writing, four of these known and from each it is possible to find the amplitude of the oscillation. It is also possible to estimate the mean declination and by deducting the inclination of the moon's orbit to get a value for ϵ, the obliquity of the ecliptic. Assuming that all four are real we get for the amplitude of the oscillation a mean value of 9′·2. Tycho Brahe's value was $9\frac{1}{2}$′ and astronomers today tell us the actual value is 9.

The mean deduced value of ϵ from the four sites is 23° 53′·9 with an unknown uncertainty which might be put at ±0′·7. The corresponding date is 1700 B.C. ±100 years. To improve the accuracy of this estimate requires not only precise measurements of the profiles made under conditions approximating to those obtaining in summer at the time of night when the erectors operated, we must also measure the actual refraction sustained by a heavenly body on the marks.

It may be remarked that most of the sites arranged for making these precise measurements made use of the southerly positions of the moon. Perhaps people of Megalithic times, like people of today, objected to spending time in these exposed sites at midwinter.

13

THE EXTINCTION ANGLE

THE lowest apparent altitude at which we can see a particular star on a perfectly clear night is called its extinction angle. This angle depends primarily on the magnitude of the star and to a lesser extent on the observer. The atmospheric conditions are of secondary importance because the definition excludes anything but the clearest conditions. We must not think of the man-made conditions which exist in Britain today in any inland position where no matter what the direction of the wind the atmosphere carries sufficient smoke to reduce visibility on the horizon to a few miles. Think rather of clear conditions on the north-west coast, where we can see mountains perhaps a hundred miles away.

Table 8.1 shows the collected azimuths of observed lines and the consequent declinations. A star, with a date attached, is named in column 8 if between 2000 and 1600 B.C. its declination was near the deduced value. In a number of cases the horizon altitude was below the probable extinction angle and so Neugebauer's value for the latter was used instead of the observed altitude. These lines are collected in Table 13.1 and the reverse process applied. That is, we assume a date and calculate the altitude which, with the latitude and the observed azimuth, will give the declination of the star at that date. This altitude is assumed to be the extinction angle for the star, but it will only be the true extinction angle if we have assumed the correct date or if the star's declination did not change seriously with time. On plotting all the values so obtained on the magnitudes of the stars, we ought to obtain the relation between extinction angle and magnitude. What we in fact find is a rather scattered picture which nevertheless helps us to form an opinion on the legitimacy of associating these lines with stars. We could only expect to find a nice tidy line if we were in a position to assign the correct date to each site. All we can do is to use a mean date for the whole country and by trying two or three such dates we may be able to see which suits best. It will be realized that this procedure makes use only of the small number of lines which have a low enough horizon altitude.

The method of calculation can be arranged to make use of Table 3.1, relating declination with azimuth, altitude, and latitude.

Let h_E be the extinction angle. Correcting this for refraction gives the corresponding true altitude h_T.

Put $\delta_0 =$ declination as calculated from the observed azimuth and the

Table 13.1. *Extinction angles deduced by assuming a date*

Site	Az.	δ_0	a	Star	Mag.	1800 B.C. δ	$(\delta-\delta_0)/a$	h_E	1900 B.C. h_E	Remarks
B 3/3	259.2	−5.84	0.84	Bellatrix	1.7	−5.07	+0.92	+1.16	+0.84	Uncertain outlier
G 4/14	78.2	+6.76	0.82	Altair	0.9	6.98	0.27	0.72	0.90	
H 1/1	77.8	6.40	0.86	"			0.67	1.07	1.27	
H 1/3	280	5.25	0.83	Procyon	0.5	6.28	1.24	1.58	1.34	Azimuth uncertain
H 3/12	281.9	6.36	0.85	Altair	0.9	6.98	+0.73	1.12	1.24	Azimuth definite
"				Procyon	0.5	6.28	−0.09	0.41	0.80	"
L 1/10	354.0	35.36	1.00	Deneb	1.3	36.64	+1.28	1.62	1.54	Good outlier
M 1/4	342	31.58	0.98	Capella	0.2	32.47	0.91	1.28	0.75	Azimuth uncertain
P 1/2	13.5	32.77	0.99	Capella	0.2	32.47	−0.30	0.24	−0.22	Azimuth uncertain
S 5/3	340.2	35.91	0.96	Deneb	1.3	36.64	+0.76	1.26	+1.25	
S 5/4	31.0	32.48	0.92	Capella	0.2	32.47	−0.01	0.48	−0.01	
S 6/1	28.7	32.71	0.93	"	"	"	−0.26	0.26	−0.20	
W 2/1	18.6	34.56	0.98	Deneb	1.3	36.64	+2.12	2.40	+2.30	Peculiar site
W 5/1	17.3	35.15	0.98	"	"	"	1.52	1.83	1.76	
"	349.8	36.41	0.99	"	"	"	0.23	0.68	0.62	Azimuth uncertain

M

known latitude with *zero* true altitude. Then we can with sufficient accuracy write the actual declination as

$$\text{declination} = \delta_0 + ah_T,$$

where δ_0 and a are both found from Table 3.1, a being $d\delta/dh$ or the change in declination produced by unit change in h_T.

Let δ be the star's known declination at the assumed date. Then if we are correct in associating the observed azimuth with the star,

$$\delta = \delta_0 + ah_T,$$

from which $$h_T = (\delta - \delta_0)/a.$$

Applying the appropriate refraction difference we obtain the extinction angle h_E.

The above method of reduction is applied in Table 13.1 to all germane lines in Table 8.1. Although the existence of the intermediate calendar dates may not yet be fully accepted it seemed better to omit lines which would belong to these instead of trying to associate them with stars. These lines were not omitted in the calculation made in Thom, 1966, because when that paper was written the existence of intermediate dates dividing the year into thirty-two parts was only beginning to be suspected. It will be noticed that the accurate line at H 3/12 has been associated with two different stars, Altair and Procyon. Since both assumptions yield reasonable extinction angles we may assume that this line was an indicator for both these stars. The different magnitudes, by producing different extinction angles, allowed the line to be used with two different declinations. While the foresight (Craig Hasten, see p. 130) makes such a definite mark it might not be visible in starlight, but this is no real objection to this line. The backsight Clach Mor à Chè is so accurately orientated that the identification of the stars would have been quite possible even if no fire was lit at the foresight. There would of course be no danger of confusing these two stars one with another.

The calculation is shown in some detail assuming a mean date of 1800 B.C., and the results only for 1900 B.C. The extinction angles so found are plotted in Fig. 13.1 (*a*) and (*b*). On the whole it will be seen that 1800 B.C. gives a more reasonable set of points than 1900, and certainly shows better agreement with Neugebauer's values, which are indicated by a dotted line.

Amongst the points are two or three ascribed to Deneb. For finding extinction angle this is the most useful star because its declination is practically independent of the date.

Apparently no improvement would be obtained by trying 1700 B.C. and so it appears that if we are right in associating these lines with the stars shown the resulting date is not far from 1800 B.C. A totally different approach is possible and that is to assume the *true* extinction angle h_T to be linear with

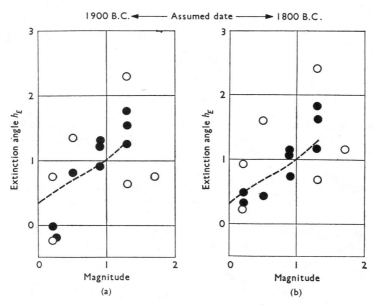

FIG. 13.1. Extinction angles deduced from observed azimuths assuming (a) 1900 B.C. and (b) 1800 B.C. Unreliable values are shown by open rings. Neugebauer's values are shown by a dotted line.

magnitude and the stars' declinations to be linear with time. Every line then gives an equation with three unknowns. Solving these by the usual least-squares method yields the date and extinction angle. This method was tried at an earlier stage of the investigation and gave reasonable results, but it is felt that there are objections, even if an extension was made to include lines with horizon altitudes above the extinction angle. There is not enough material for a fully fledged statistical calculation of this kind and an over-all mean date is all that could be obtained.

14

CONCLUSIONS

WE have in foregoing chapters tried to assess Megalithic man's knowledge of metrology, geometry, and astronomy. An attempt has been made to present the evidence in such a way that the reader can form his own opinions. Perhaps in this summary the author may be allowed to give his own conclusions. The reader of necessity sees the subject from a different standpoint and the earlier chapters on statistics, mathematics, and astronomy were inserted to make it easier for him to understand the author's viewpoint and methods of working.

Once we had discovered how the flattened circles were designed it became obvious that we were dealing with a people who had mastered elementary geometrical construction. When the egg-shaped rings were studied they revealed the remarkable interest shown by the builders in units of measurement and the concomitant attempt to discover Pythagorean triangles. This led to the discovery that the obsession with integral lengths extended also to perimeters; witness the manner in which integral diameters were so often slightly adjusted to make the circumference more nearly a multiple of the larger unit. The ellipse may have been extensively used because of the greater freedom it presented in choosing sizes which would satisfy the desire to use integers in the perimeter as well as in the straight dimensions. Symmetrical figures were the rule and yet the greatest circle of all, at Avebury, shows no symmetry. The other great site at Callanish shows symmetry only in the Type A ring at the centre. There is only one obvious explanation of the skew construction used at Callanish and that is that the alignments were for astronomical purposes. The fact that these alignments and the axis of the small ellipse lead from one of the auxiliary centres of the main ring shows that peculiar attempt to combine geometrical construction with astronomical azimuths which achieves its most spectacular success at Castle Rigg. In this connexion the circles at Burnmoor are not far behind, although there we need to dig a little deeper to appreciate fully what was achieved. The greatest and most remarkable circle in Britain, if not in the world, is at Avebury. Its greatness does not lie in its size alone but in the remarkable manner in which its arcs are built up from a basic Pythagorean triangle so that each retains an integral character, and in the exceedingly high precision of the setting out, a precision only surpassed today in high-class surveying. Avebury provides the final proof of the exact size of the Megalithic yard and demonstrates the use of the larger linear units, $2\frac{1}{2}$ and 10 yds.

It is strange that the beauty of design achieved at Moel ty Ucha or Easter

Delfour is not and cannot ever have been apparent on the site. Nor can it ever have been obvious that these designs incorporated those peculiar integral ratios which form the main theme of all the constructions. These features cannot have meant much to the majority of the people any more than they would to the man in the street today. Yet to invent designs with these properties probably took years of many men's time. Perhaps the proportions were worked out on the sands of the seashore, only to be expounded to the chosen few.

So much for metrology and geometry. What about astronomy? The evidence mutely presented by Ballochroy shows unequivocally the intense interest in the solstices. The division of the year into eight parts will hardly be denied by anyone. The evidence for the division into sixteen parts has been growing for many years and is of such a nature that it only falls into place when the idea is worked out in detail. Whether we are prepared to accept it or not a similar, albeit smaller, body of evidence is accumulating for the division into thirty-two parts. The idea that these parts were always either eleven or twelve days fits better than any other arrangement. The great body of the information on the calendar has come from the north as far down as Wales. The paucity of the south country in this respect may be due to destruction of sites or to the difficulties associated with tree-covered horizons. But until more evidence comes along we cannot exclude the possibility of a different form of calendar.

To a people so interested in the sun much thought must have been given to the possibility of predicting eclipses. Soon it would be apparent that this involved a study of the moon. As far back as 1912 Somerville suggested that there was a lunar line in the Callanish layout. The author, through a fear of building evidence subjectively, resisted accepting lunar lines until the final evidence came objectively. When the first histogram of the possible lunar lines was plotted it showed a double peak corresponding to the two limbs of the moon. This result was unexpected and it was so unlikely to have happened by accident that it seemed desirable to look more closely into a number of sites where the indication of the necessary azimuth at the site itself was weak. This study showed up that Megalithic man was well acquainted with the small amplitude ripple on the moon's declination and has left such definite indicators that we can, with their help alone, determine its magnitude. We do not know of any technique which could have been used to examine this oscillation with the moon at the nodes, but they could have made a measurement of its period and may have connected it with the eclipse year.

Attempts to date the sites by stellar declinations depend on being able to associate an observed azimuth with a particular first-magnitude star. If the evidence put forward in the chapter on extinction angle is accepted then one is entitled to go one step further and construct a histogram, on a date basis, of all the associations in Table 8.1. Three such histograms are shown in Fig. 14.1. The interval is fifty years and when a date is at the boundary between two intervals half has been allotted to each of the intervals. Fig. 14.1 (*a*) shows all lines in England, Wales, and Scotland south of the Clyde. Fig. 14.1 (*b*) shows all lines north of the Clyde, and Fig. 14.1 (*c*) is for all Britain. It is difficult to think of a reason for the clumping together

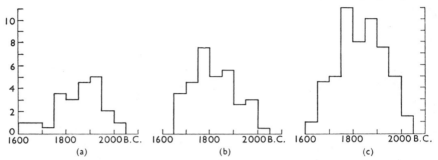

FIG. 14.1. Histograms of dates from star declinations (see Table 8.1), (*a*) south of Clyde, (*b*) north of Clyde, (*c*) all Britain. Dates like 1800 B.C. have been put half each way.

of the dates in both (*a*) and (*b*) other than that many of the observed azimuths really were set out for first-magnitude stars. It may be noted that the centre of the concentration is about 1860 B.C. for the southern lines and about 1810 for the northern, and that most of the *stellar* lines were erected between say 2000 and 1700 B.C.

Because of the slow rate of change in the obliquity of the ecliptic it is difficult to get an accurate date from a solstitial site, but in Thom, 1954, a value close to 1800 B.C. was obtained by an elaboration of this method. There is a possibility that the lunar lines which showed up the small oscillation mentioned above will give a more accurate measure of the obliquity than the solar lines. Already in Chapter 12 it appears that they show a mean date for the north of 1800 B.C. ± 100 and there seems to be hope of improving the accuracy. But the whole position will be much more satisfactory when archaeologists date the sites by entirely different means and the kind of data used in this book can be used to make a detailed study of the astronomical work of Megalithic man.

When we think of the conditions under which these people worked and the limited material aids which they could employ we begin to appreciate what they did achieve. There are hundreds of sites throughout Britain which can surely teach us a great deal more if they are examined in an unbiased manner. Whatever we do we must avoid approaching the study with the idea that Megalithic man was our inferior in ability to think.

Archaeology is today advancing so rapidly that its findings may link up with the major findings of the present study and may give a meaning to much that is obscure.

LIST OF DISTRICTS

H 1	Lewis	N 1	Caithness	B 1	Aberdeen N
H 2	Harris	N 2	Sutherland	B 2	,, S
H 3	N. Uist	N 3	Ross & Cromarty	B 3	Kincardine
H 4	Benbecula			B 4	Banff
H 5	S. Uist	P 1	Perth W of Tay	B 5	Elgin
H 6	Barra	P 2	,, E ,,	B 6	Nairn
H 7	Skye	P 3	Forfar	B 7	Inverness (mainland)
H 8	The Small Isles	P 4	Fife		
		P 5	Kinross	W 1	Anglesey
M 1	Mull N	P 6	Clackmannan	W 2	Caernarvon
M 2	,, S	P 7	Stirling	W 3	Denbigh
M 3	Coll			W 4	Flint
M 4	Tiree	G 1	Ayrshire	W 5	Merioneth
M 5	Ardnamurchan	G 2	Wigtownshire W	W 6	Montgomery
M 6	Morven	G 3	,, E	W 7	Cardigan
M 7	Appin	G 4	Kirkcudbright W	W 8	Radnor
M 8	Benderloch	G 5	,, E	W 9	Pembroke
M 9	Lismore	G 6	Dumfriesshire W	W 10	Carmarthen
		G 7	Dumfriesshire	W 11	Brecknock
A 1	Lorne	G 8	Roxburgh	W 12	Glamorgan
A 2	Argyll	G 9	Midlothian	W 13	Monmouth
A 3	Knapdale	,,	East Lothian		
A 4	Kintyre	,,	Berwick	D 1	Derbyshire
A 5	Colonsay	,,	Peebles	D 2	Shropshire
A 6	Jura				
A 7	Islay	L 1	Cumberland		
A 8	Arran	L 2	Westmorland		
A 9	Bute	L 3	Northumberland		
A 10	Kerry and L. Fyne E	L 4	Durham		
A 11	Loch Lomond	L 5	Lancashire		
		L 6	Yorkshire		
S 1	Cornwall				
S 2	Devon				
S 3	Somerset				
S 4	Dorset				
S 5	Wiltshire				
S 6	Oxfordshire				

APPENDIX

On calculating the azimuth of a line from the coordinates of the two ends

TODAY, as more and more of the country is covered by large-scale Ordnance Survey maps plotted on the National Grid, it is seldom necessary to use geographical coordinates (latitude and longitude) for the calculation of an azimuth.

The National Grid is a transverse Mercator projection. In the sense that the axis of the usual Mercator projection is the equator, the axis of the National Grid is a north–south line at longitude 2° W. This does not mean that the origin of coordinates is at 2° W. The origin is displaced to the south-west so that both coordinates are always positive for the land areas of Britain.

No error greater than $\frac{1}{4}$ minute of arc will be introduced by the following simple procedure. If great accuracy is required the special tables published for the Ordnance Survey must be used.

Read the coordinates of the two points from the largest-scale Ordnance Survey map available and to the greatest accuracy possible. Treat these coordinates as simple Cartesian coordinates and so calculate the azimuth from its tangent. Then *for the end of the line at which the azimuth is wanted* find the difference between grid north and true north. This is stated on the maps but interpolation may be awkward, especially with the 1-inch maps. So it is often easier to calculate the correction from the relation

$$\text{correction} = \Delta\lambda \sin \varphi,$$

where $\Delta\lambda$ is the amount by which the longitude differs from 2° W. and φ is the latitude. The sign of the correction will be apparent from the values given in the map margin. The latitude and longitude can easily be obtained with sufficient accuracy from the 1-inch Ordnance map.

If one end of the line lies in an area not yet covered by the maps then it is perhaps best to convert the geographical coordinates of the point to grid coordinates by the tables referred to above. It should be mentioned that the explanation of the use of the tables is contained in another small publication also issued by H.M. Stationery Office.

BIBLIOGRAPHY

BROADBENT, S. R., Quantum hypotheses, *Biometrika*, **42**, 45–57 (1955).
—— Examination of a quantum hypothesis based on a single set of data, *Biometrika*, **43**, 32–44 (1956).
BROOKS, C. E. P., The climate of prehistoric Britain, *Antiquity*, **1**, 412 (1927).
BROWNE, G. F., *On Some Antiquities in the Neighbourhood of Dunecht House, Aberdeenshire*. Cambridge University Press (1921).
CALLENDER, H., Notice of the stone circle at Callernish in the island of Lewis, *Proc. Soc. Ant. Scotl.* **2**, 380 (1854–7).
DANIEL, GLYN, *The Megalith Builders of Western Europe*. Hutchinson (1958); Penguin Books (1963).
HAWKINS, G. S., Stonehenge decoded, *Nature, Lond.* **200**, 306 (1963).
—— Stonehenge: a neolithic computer, *Nature, Lond.* **202**, 1258 (1964).
—— Callanish, a Scottish Stonehenge, *Science*, **147**, 127 (1965).
—— and ROSENTHAL, S., A 5000 year star catalog, *Smithson. Contr. Astrophys.* (in press).
—— in collaboration with J. B. WHITE, *Stonehenge Decoded*. Doubleday (1965).
HEATH, T., *A History of Greek Mathematics*. Clarendon Press, Oxford (1921).
KEILLER, A., *Megalithic monuments of north-east Scotland*, British Association, 1934. Reprint for Morven Institute of Archaeological Research by Vecher, London (1934).
—— *Windmill Hill and Avebury*. Oxford University Press (1965).
KILBRIDE-JONES, H. E., An account of the excavations of the stone circle at Loanhead of Daviot, etc., *Proc. Soc. Ant. Scotl.* **69**, 6th series, **9**, 168 (1934–5).
LOCKYER, N., *Stonehenge and other British Stone Monuments*. Macmillan (1909).
MACCULLOCH, J., *A Description of the Western Islands of Scotland*, vol. 3, p. 49 (1819).
MARTIN, M., *A Description of the Western Islands of Scotland*, M. Martin, Gent. (1716).
NEUGEBAUER, P. V., *Tafeln zur astronomischen Chronologie*. Leipzig (1929).
ORR, J., Standing stones and other relics in Mull, *Trans. Glasg. Arch. Soc.* **9** (2), 128–34 (1937).
PIGGOTT, S., Architecture and ritual in Megalithic monuments, *Jl R. Inst. Br. Archit.* (Ser. 3) **63**, 175 (1956).
ROY, A. E., McGRAIL, N., and CARMICHAEL, R., A new survey of the Tormore circles, *Trans. Glasg. Arch. Soc.* **15**, 56–67 (1963).
SITTER, W. DE, On the system of astronomical constants, *Bull. astr. Insts Neth.* **8**, 213 (1938).
SMITH, J., *Prehistoric man in Ayrshire*. Elliot Stock (1895).
SOMERVILLE, B., Astronomical indications in the Megalithic monument at Callanish, *J. Br. astr. Ass.* **23**, 83 (1912).
SZYMAŃSKI, H., *Jednostki Miar*. Państwowe Wydawnictwa Techniczne, Warsaw (1956).
THOM, A., The solar observatories of Megalithic man, *J. Br. astr. Ass.* **64**, 397 (1954).
—— A statistical examination of the Megalithic sites in Britain, *Jl R. statist. Soc.* A. **118**, 275 (1955).
—— The geometry of Megalithic man, *Mathl Gaz.* **45**, 83–93 (1961) (2).

THOM, A., The egg-shaped standing stone rings of Britain. *Archs int. Hist. Sci.* **14,** 291 (1961) (2).

—— The Megalithic unit of length, *Jl R. statist. Soc.* A. **125,** 243 (1962).

—— The larger units of length of Megalithic man, *Jl R. statist. Soc.* A. **127,** 527 (1964).

—— Megalithic astronomy: indications in standing stones, *Vistas in Astronomy,* **7,** 1 (1966).

—— *Megalithic lunar observatories.* Clarendon Press, Oxford (1971).

WORTH, R. H., *Dartmoor.* Devonshire Association for the Advancement of Science (1953).

Many plans will be found in the journals of archaeological societies in various parts of Britain, in the County Inventories of the Royal Commission on Ancient Monuments, and in the Old and New Statistical Account (Scotland).

AUTHOR INDEX

SUBJECT INDEX

A list of sites according to locality will be found at p. 136. A list of some sites from other sources will be found at p. 44.